CONTRACT AS ASSUMPTION II

This second collection of Brian Coote's previously published writings is for the most part a follow-up to his *Contract as Assumption* (Hart Publishing, 2010). Part of the theme of that collection was that in a bilateral contract the obligations of the parties, both primary and secondary, are those which at formation they have each assumed, that is, have taken upon themselves. Being exchanged at the point of formation, these assumptions constitute the consideration. The institution of contract provides a facility the purpose of which is to enable the parties thereby to bind themselves to legal (contractual) obligation.

This emphasis on what happens at formation has prompted the inclusion of several of the papers in this collection. These focus on intention, offer and acceptance, the qualification of primary and secondary obligations whether express or implied, agency, and the effect of illegality on pre-existing rights. Falling outside this group are two pieces respectively on chance and the burden of proof and on impecuniosity, in each case in tort as well as in contract.

The collection ends with the author's valedictory lecture, 'Contract: An Underview'. In this paper, delivered on his retirement from the University of Auckland, he summed up his thinking on Contract. It is now for the first time given general currency.

Contract as Assumption II

Formation, Performance, and Enforcement

Brian Coote, Emeritus Professor of Law,
The University of Auckland

Edited and with a Preface by JW Carter, Emeritus
Professor of Law, The University of Sydney, Consultant,
Herbert Smith Freehills

•HART•

OXFORD • LONDON • NEW YORK • NEW DELHI • SYDNEY

HART PUBLISHING
Bloomsbury Publishing Plc
Kemp House, Chawley Park, Cumnor Hill, Oxford, OX2 9PH, UK

HART PUBLISHING, the Hart/Stag logo, BLOOMSBURY and the Diana logo are trademarks of Bloomsbury Publishing Plc
First published in Great Britain 2016

First published in hardback, 2016
Paperback edition, 2018

A catalogue record for this book is available from the British Library.

Library of Congress Cataloging-in-Publication Data

Names: Conference on the Law of Obligations (7th : 2014 : Hong Kong, China) | Robertson, Andrew, 1966– editor. | Tilbury, M. J. (Michael J.), editor.

Title: Divergences in private law / Edited by Andrew Robertson and Michael Tilbury.

Description: Hart Publishing, Oxford : 2016. | "Originally presented at the Seventh Biennial Conference on the Law of Obligations held in Hong Kong in July 2014"—ECIP galley. | Includes bibliographical references and index.

Identifiers: LCCN 2015038968 | ISBN 9781782256601 (hardback : alk. paper)

Subjects: LCSH: Obligations (Law)—Congresses. | Civil law—Congresses. | Common law—Congresses.

Classification: LCC K830.A6 D58 2016 | DDC 346—dc23 LC record available at http://lccn.loc.gov/2015038968

ISBN: PB: 978-1-50992-446-2
HB: 978-1-78225-668-7

Typeset by Compuscript Ltd, Shannon

PREFACE

This is the second collection of the published work of Emeritus Professor Brian Coote CBE. The first—*Assumption*—appeared in 2010 under the editorship of my *Journal of Contract Law* colleague, Rick Bigwood. The origin of this collection is a conversation with Brian during a visit to Auckland in 2014. Given the success of *Assumption*, and the amount of other material available for publication in the same format, I suggested a second work and was delighted when Brian accepted my offer to assist in an editorial capacity.

We first met in 1980, when Brian undertook supervision responsibility for one term of my PhD dissertation at Cambridge during his sabbatical leave at Queens'. It was certainly a propitious time to become a pupil of Brian. On Valentine's Day of that year the judgments in *Photo Production Ltd v Securicor Transport Ltd* [1980] AC 827 were delivered by the House of Lords. In his argument in reply (see [1980] AC 827 at 839) in that case, Richard Yorke QC, leading the successful appellants, rightly found support for his argument in Brian Coote, 'Discharge for Breach and Exception Clauses Since *Harbutt's "Plasticine"*' (1977) 40 *MLR* 31, 41–46. The influence of that article can also be seen in the judgments. It is reprinted as one of the two components of Chapter 8 of this book. We next met up in Oxford in 1987, when we were both on sabbatical leave. At the time, I was searching for copy for the first volume of the *Journal of Contract Law*, and also for members of an editorial board. Brian obliged on both counts. He agreed to become a foundation member of the Board, and very generously offered me a paper that was subsequently published, in two issues of volume 1, as 'The Essence of Contract' (1988) 1 *JCL* 91 and (1989) 1 *JCL* 183. Twenty-odd years later, the article was reprinted as Chapter 2 of *Assumption*. Given that the Journal's longevity was by no means assured, it was a very generous decision by Brian. It was also one which helped to establish the international standing of the Journal.

In the years that followed, Brian gave freely of his time in refereeing articles, contributing book reviews, participating in each of the Journal's several Auckland conferences, and contributing more penetrating articles. Brian's considerable contribution to the Journal was one motivation for a series of essays published in 1995 (following his retirement from teaching at the University of Auckland) as a Special Issue in volume 9. More generally, it honoured Brian's very substantial contribution to contract scholarship. Included in the Special Issue were essays by contract scholars from Australia, Canada, England, New Zealand, and the United States, as well as an introduction by Sir Robin Cooke. A bound volume of the issue was presented to Brian (much to his surprise) at a dinner following the

Journal's 1995 conference in Auckland. Professor Francis Reynolds contributed an essay and was also joint editor of the issue. (As proof that all things are interconnected, Francis was the external examiner of my PhD.) In his Introduction to this book (Chapter 1), Brian records that the essay reprinted as Chapter 7 of this book ('Deviation and the Ordinary Law') first appeared in a *festschrift* for Francis.

It is a worthy goal for any academic to write one or two articles which make a genuine contribution to learning. Brian's published work includes many. (See the review essay on *Assumption*: 'Contract as Assumption—The Scholarship and Influence of Professor Brian Coote' (2011) 27 *JCL* 247, by Justice Andrew Phang of the Singapore Court of Appeal (and also a member of the *Journal of Contract Law* editorial board).) It is a boon to the academy that many of Brian's important contributions are now collected in two handsome volumes. The articles have been reprinted with only minor amendments. However, because the chosen articles focus mainly on issues of general (common law) importance, they by no means tell the whole story. In particular, they leave out the fruits of 20 years on the Contracts and Commercial Law Reform Committee that led to New Zealand's distinctive contribution to contract law, namely, statutory reform. I well remember Brian pulling out a copy of the Contractual Remedies Act 1979 during one of our meetings at Queens' in 1980. It was somewhat disturbing to see the topic of my dissertation elegantly summarised in 16 sections occupying little more than half a dozen pages! Judging by some of his commentary on application of that Act in the courts (see, for example, 'Remedy and Relief under the Contractual Remedies Act 1979' (1993) 6 *JCL* 141), others would also have profited from Brian's supervision skills.

I was extremely pleased when Brian selected three of his contributions to the *Journal of Contract Law* for publication in *Assumption*. Two more are reprinted as Chapters 4 and 12 of this volume (respectively, '*Dunlop v Lambert*: The Search for a Rationale' and 'Contract as Assumption and Remoteness of Damage'). The latter was Brian's final publication in the *Journal of Contract Law*. He has, however, continued to give me the benefit of his advice on submissions to the Journal touching on New Zealand law.

The forgoing is, undoubtedly, an overly long introduction for the Preface to a book reprinting articles representative of the work of one of the most highly regarded scholars of contract law in the common law world. For a fellow retiree, one thing this book has in common with *Assumption* is that it includes several 'old friends'. I have mentioned Brian's 'Exception Clauses Since *Harbutt's "Plasticine"*'. Its companion piece ('The Effect of Discharge by Breach on Exception Clauses') is the other component of Chapter 8. Both are as invaluable to students, academics, and practitioners today as they were to me in my PhD research over 35 years ago. Unsurprisingly, they continue to be cited in discussions of discharge for breach. Material in one or two other chapters may perhaps be less well known to contemporary scholars than articles such as those, or at least not as readily accessible. Their inclusion in this book will bring them into prominence again. More importantly, inclusion ensures their ready availability to the current generation of contract lawyers. I have in mind 'Reflections on Intention in the Law of Contract'

(Chapter 2) and 'The Instantaneous Transmission of Acceptances' (Chapter 3). Age has by no means withered these articles. For example, for those still struggling to decide whether an analogy with the postal acceptance rule should be drawn for the purpose of deciding when an acceptance sent by email is effective, the latter (although published in 1971) provides a ready answer.

The articles reprinted in this book do indeed span a considerable period of time—nearly 40 years. Yet, as with the older material included in *Assumption*, the arguments presented are as thought provoking now as when they were first published. In 1972, Brian said in 'Another Look at *Bowmakers v Barnet Instruments*' (Chapter 9) that difficult though the legal analysis in that case undoubtedly is, no better solution to the issues debated had emerged in the period between 1945 and 1972. The same is true today. Thus, the so-called 'conscience test' came and went. See *Tinsley v Milligan* [1994] 1 AC 340. (See also *Nelson v Nelson* (1995) 184 CLR 538 where, incidentally, Brian's article is cited by McHugh J.) This volume also includes several articles that may appear to be more specialised than most of those in *Assumption*. One example is 'Deviation and the Ordinary Law' (Chapter 7). Even so, as Brian explains in his Introduction (Chapter 1), the 'assumption of obligation' theme—very much at the heart of the first book—also runs through this collection as well. That is only to be expected.

It is clearly correct to say that understanding the 'essence' of any legal concept is vitally important to its coherent development and application. Brian's article on 'Contract as Assumption and Remoteness of Damage' (Chapter 12) discusses the speeches of Lord Hoffmann and Lord Hope in *Transfield Shipping Inc v Mercator Shipping Inc (The Achilleas)* [2009] AC 61; [2008] UKHL 48. (The case was mentioned only briefly in Chapter 8 of *Assumption*.) They illustrate the continued relevance and importance of Brian's assumption theme. The arguments in '*Dunlop v Lambert*: The Search for a Rationale' (Chapter 4) and 'Sale of Goods at Auction without Reserve' (Chapter 5), are also reasoned from an assumption perspective. The latter has a link with Chapter 3 of *Assumption* (which debunked *Williams v Roffey Bros & Nicholls (Contractors) Ltd* [1991] 1 QB 1), in denying that a subsequent conferral of benefit can count as consideration for a promise in (what is alleged to be) a bilateral contract.

In his Preface to *Assumption*, Rick Bigwood aptly described Brian's writing style as 'elegant, coherent and precise without fuss'. It does indeed set a standard to which any academic would be wise to aspire. The description can equally be applied to Brian's scholarship. Many of the contributions in this book also illustrate Brian's keen sense of the history of contract. A good example is 'Correspondence with Description in the Law of Sale of Goods' (Chapter 6). But Brian's scholarship has never denied that contract law is a process of constant development. Of course, any tension between the position under general principles and resolutions of particular contract issues in specific contexts calls for some explanation. Opinions may differ on what the explanation should be, but orderly and coherent development of the law requires that an answer be found. There is no better example than Chapter 7, the title of which tells us much ('Deviation and the Ordinary Law').

This collection of essays includes three chapters on damages. As well as Chapter 12 (mentioned above), are 'Chance and the Burden of Proof in Contract and Tort' and 'Damages, *The Liesbosch*, and Impecuniosity' (Chapters 10 and 11 respectively). From the perspective of subject matter, these serve to give this volume a broader scope than 'contract'. They therefore illustrate the breadth of Brian's scholarship. So too does 'Reflections on Intention in the Law of Contract' (Chapter 2), which includes consideration not only of contract and tort, but also a comparison between the sense of 'intention' in contract and the criminal law. The final chapter (Chapter 13) of the book is 'Contract: An Underview'. This was Brian's Valedictory Lecture on retirement from the University of Auckland. It draws together many strands of Brian's scholarship, as they stood in 1994. However, as several chapters in both collections indicate, there was a good deal more to come. Like *Assumption*, this book will I am sure leave readers wishing for more. Of course, there remains a great deal of material which has not been reprinted in the two volumes. But for every serious contract scholar, Brian's retirement from the pastime of article writing leaves a distinct gap.

I am pleased to join with Brian in thanking Sandra Shaw and the publishers. In particular I am grateful to Bill Asquith for his patience, commitment, and assistance with the project. This book reprints material from diverse sources, each having its own editorial requirements. Because of that diversity, the publishers very kindly agreed to depart from their usual practice of bringing the material into common form.

JW Carter
Sydney
September 2015

ACKNOWLEDGEMENTS

Except for Chapter 1, the chapters in this book have been published elsewhere either in article or in book-chapter form. Each piece, however, has been edited and lightly modified for the purpose of their inclusion in this book. The author and editor wish to thank the publishers mentioned below for their permission to reproduce works in this book. Copyright in all of the reproduced works was retained by the author.

Chapter 2: First published as Brian Coote, 'Reflections on Intention in the Law of Contract' [2006] *New Zealand Law Review* 183–208. Reprinted with the permission of the Legal Research Foundation.

Chapter 3: First published as Brian Coote, 'The Instantaneous Transmission of Acceptances' (1971) 4 *New Zealand Universities Law Review* 331–42. Reprinted with the permission of Thomson Reuters and the *New Zealand Law Review.*

Chapter 4: First published as Brian Coote, '*Dunlop v Lambert*: The Search for a Rationale' (1998) 13 *Journal of Contract Law* 91–102. Reprinted with the permission of LexisNexis Butterworths.

Chapter 5: First published as Brian Coote, 'Sale of Goods at Auction without Reserve' [2001] *New Zealand Law Review* 277–92. Reprinted with the permission of the Legal Research Foundation.

Chapter 6: First published as Brian Coote, 'Correspondence with Description in the Law of Sale of Goods' (1976) 50 *Australian Law Journal* 17–25. Reprinted with the permission of Thomson Reuters.

Chapter 7: First published as Brian Coote, 'Deviation and the Ordinary Law' *Lex Mercartoria, Essays on International Commercial Law in Honour of Francis Reynolds* (ed Francis D Rose) LLP Professional Publishing (London, 2000) 13–37. Reprinted with the permission of Taylor & Francis Group LLC.

Chapter 8: Part I first published as Brian Coote 'The Effect of Discharge by Breach on "Exception Clauses"' [1970] *Cambridge Law Journal* 221–40. Reprinted with the permission of the *Cambridge Law Journal.* Part II first published as Brian Coote, 'Discharge for Breach and Exception Clauses Since *Harbutt's "Plasticine"*' (1977) 40 *Modern Law Review* 31–46. Reprinted with the permission of John Wiley & Sons Ltd.

Chapter 9: First published as Brian Coote, 'Another Look at *Bowmakers v Barnet Instruments*' (1972) 35 *Modern Law Review* 38–51. Reprinted with the permission of John Wiley & Sons Ltd.

Chapter 10: First published as Brian Coote, 'Chance and the Burden of Proof in Contract and Tort' (1988) 62 *Australian Law Journal* 761–73. Reprinted with the permission of Thomson Reuters.

Chapter 11: First published as Brian Coote, 'Damages, *The Liesbosch*, and Impecuniosity' [2001] *Cambridge Law Journal* 511–36. Reprinted with the permission of the *Cambridge Law Journal.* Note on *Lagden v O'Connor* first published as Brian Coote, 'Impecuniosity Pays Off' (2004) 120 *Law Quarterly Review* 382–87. Reprinted with the permission of Sweet & Maxwell Ltd.

Chapter 12: First published as Brian Coote, 'Contract as Assumption and Remoteness of Damage' (2010) 26 *Journal of Contract Law* 211–20. Reprinted with the permission of LexisNexis Butterworths.

Chapter 13: First published as Brian Coote, 'Contract—an Underview' in *Contract—an Underview. A Souvenir of a Valedictory Lecture* (compiled by BJ Brown) Legal Research Foundation (Auckland, 1995) 13–36. Reprinted with the permission of the Legal Research Foundation.

CONTENTS

ABBREVIATIONS

Assumption: Brian Coote, *Contract as Assumption: Essays on a Theme*, ed Rick Bigwood (Hart Publishing, Oxford, 2010).

Exception Clauses: Brian Coote, *Exception Clauses: Some Aspects of the Law Relating to Exception Clauses in Contracts for the Carriage, Bailment and Sale of Goods* (Sweet & Maxwell Ltd, London, 1964).

TABLE OF CASES

TABLE OF LEGISLATION

International

New Zealand

United Kingdom

1

Introduction

This is the second collection of my shorter pieces to be published by Hart Publishing of Oxford, the helpfulness of whose staff throughout has been very much appreciated. Each collection owes its existence to the generosity of a colleague who volunteered, inter alia, to act as editor and to provide a Preface. For the earlier collection, it was Professor Rick Bigwood, then of Auckland and now at Bond University in Queensland. This time, it is Emeritus Professor John Carter of the University of Sydney. In his case, the relationship goes back to his time at Cambridge reading for a PhD. Being there myself on leave I was invited for a term to act as his temporary supervisor. For that slight service he has repaid me many times over, not least by publishing quite a number of my articles and notes in his *Journal of Contract Law*.

The title of the first collection, *Contract as Assumption*[1] reflected the fact that all the writings in it were in some way related to a theory of contract, the main aspects of which include:

- Contractual obligations are not imposed by the law *ab extra* but are those which at formation the parties have assumed, that is, have taken upon themselves. Whether there has been such an assumption falls to be determined objectively.
- Bilateral contracts are formed by an exchange of assumptions at formation, it being the assumptions themselves which constitute the consideration.[2] Performance can be consideration only when the contract is unilateral.
- Contractual obligations and liabilities, otherwise known as primary and secondary obligations, are two sides of the one coin. An assumption of the one is an assumption of the other.
- In the institution of contract, the law provides a facility the purpose of which is to enable parties to bind themselves to contractual obligations so far as the law allows. The motives for so providing may, of course, be various.

More extended statements of the theory appear in Chapters 2, 12, and 13 of this present collection. The arguments for it, and its main implications, were set

[1] Hereinafter *Assumption*.

[2] Accordingly, in a bilateral contract, there are not one but two considerations. These are not the parties' promises, as such, nor their respective subject matters, let alone their actual performance. The considerations each party provides for the other are the assumptions of legal contractual obligation *expressed* in their promises.

out in 'The Essence of Contract' which now forms Chapter 2 of *Assumption.*[3] It emphasises the prime importance of both the formation of the contract and the objectively determined intention of the parties to contract. Predictably, therefore, the first paper in this collection attempts, inter alia, to distinguish an intention to assume from other meanings of the word ascribed by law.

Also concerned with formation is the second paper, on the instantaneous transmission of acceptances. While the paper was written more than 40 years ago, means of instantaneous communication have been available much longer. The suggested conclusions all derive from common law principles and, unless and to the extent that they have been, or are, overtaken by legislation, ought still to remain relevant. It is significant that in the subsequent *Brinkibon* case,[4] Lord Wilberforce summarised the law in terms not so very different from those expressed in the article.

The next piece, on *Dunlop v Lambert*,[5] more closely reflects the assumption theory. Its thesis is that the particular answer to the perceived problem of privity in that case lay not with a very problematic rule of law applied *ab extra*, but in the obligations assumed by the parties at formation. Similarly, the answer to a perceived 'black hole' is found in the notion that obligation and liability are two sides of the one coin, each determining the content of the other.

The article on the sale of goods at auction without reserve turns largely on the distinction between consideration where the contract is bilateral, and consideration if it is unilateral. It is argued, as the assumption theory requires, that performance as such can be the consideration only when the contract is unilateral.

The next three chapters deal with exception clauses, the discussion of which involves direct application of aspects of assumption. Such clauses are seen to function not as taking effect just as defences at adjudication, but as going instead to the definition of the obligations assumed at formation. Another aspect particularly relevant to exception and limitation clauses is its emphasis on the interrelationship of obligation and liability (otherwise the primary and secondary obligations), an exception or limitation that affects the one having a corresponding effect on the other.

Chapter 6, on correspondence with description, was prompted by the flat contradiction in *Ashington Piggeries Ltd v Christopher Hill Ltd*[6] of the earlier case of *Arcos Ltd v EA Ronaasen & Son*,[7] both decisions of the House of Lords. The contradiction was brought about by a failure in the later case to distinguish the description of goods from their identification. The wording of the contract was clear enough but, instead of interpreting those words, their Lordships under the continuing influence of fundamental breach chose to apply, *ab extra*, criteria inconsistent with the apparent intention of the parties and imposed something quite different.

[3] It appeared originally as Brian Coote, 'The Essence of Contract (Parts I and II)' (1988–89) 1 *JCL* 91–112 and 183–204.

[4] *Brinkibon Ltd v Stahag Stahl* [1983] 2 AC 34, 40–42.

[5] (1839) 6 Cl & F 600; 7 ER 824.

[6] [1972] AC 441.

[7] [1933] AC 470.

Chapter 7 was originally a contribution to a festschrift honouring Professor FMB Reynolds.[8] One of the best known features of deviation from the contract route in contracts for the carriage of goods by sea is that on such a departure, unless it is justified, the carrier loses the protection not only of any contractual exception or limitation clauses, but of the common law exceptions as well. He becomes liable for any loss or damage to the goods carried unless he can show that it would have been suffered anyway. This might be taken to be evidence that, far from forming part of the definition of the obligations and liabilities assumed by the parties at formation, such clauses have independent existence as mere defences. The chapter shows why that is not the case. It also explains why, notwithstanding the deviation, freight can still be recovered if the goods are delivered safely. Exceptionally, a short passage in this chapter had to be substituted because of a 'not', the unsuspected existence of which was drawn to my attention by Professor Carter.[9]

The two papers reproduced here as Chapter 8 were, in effect, the second and third instalments of a three-stage attack on the then highly regarded and warmly welcomed doctrine of fundamental breach developed by the courts since 1953. 'Fundamental breaches' and 'fundamental terms' were seen as so fundamental that no exception or limitation clause, however clearly worded, could exclude or limit any aspect of a promisor's liability in the event of breach. It owed its existence largely to the belief that such clauses function as mere defences to claims based on obligations defined without reference to them, and that they took effect, if at all, only at adjudication.

All this directly contradicted the central premise of my *Exception Clauses* (1964),[10] that such clauses helped define the obligations and liabilities, there called primary and secondary obligations, assumed by the parties at formation. Fundamental breach was the subject of that book's chapter 8 but, because of its central premise, it might be possible to see the entire book as an attack on the new doctrine!

As it happened, less than two years later, the House of Lords in the *Suisse Atlantique* case[11] had an opportunity to review this new development. For the most part, their Lordships dismissed the notion that 'fundamental breach' was a rule of law and were agreed that, at least in general, the effect of such clauses depended on their interpretation. But some of their Lordships, and Lord Reid in particular,[12] were inclined to the view that those clauses would automatically cease to have

[8] *Lex Mercatoria: Essays on International Commercial Law in Honour of Francis* Reynolds (FD Rose ed, LLP Professional Publishing, London, 2000).

[9] The original had cited, in support, the following passage from the judgment of Lord Diplock in *Photo Production Ltd v Securior Transport Ltd* [1980] AC 827, 850, as reported in Appeal Cases: 'The bringing to an end of all primary obligations under the contract may also leave the parties in a relationship, typically that of bailor and bailee, in which they owe to one another by operation of law fresh primary obligations of which the contract is the source'. John Carter had discovered that the Appeal Cases account was later corrected to read 'is *not* the source' (italics supplied).

[10] It was based largely on my PhD dissertation.

[11] *Suisse Atlantique Société d' Armement Maritime SA v NV Rotterdamsche Kolen Centrale* [1967] 1 AC 361.

[12] Ibid at 398.

effect on a discharge of the contract for breach. (That was a view derived from *Hain v Tate & Lyle*[13] where the House of Lords appeared to have ascribed the special effects of deviation to an automatic termination of the contract on a discharge for breach unless the breach were waived.) To reduce the impact of their expressed views on fundamental breach, by suggesting that such clauses would cease to have any application upon discharge for breach, was predictably to tempt fate (or at least, Lord Denning MR). As it also happened, in 1966[14] Lord Justice Diplock, as he then was, was reported as beginning a series of judgments in which he expanded upon the view that the obligation to pay damages for breach (or as he called it the secondary obligation) is consensual and becomes binding at formation. On that reasoning, the restrictive clauses would have the effect of defining liabilities *ab initio* rather than operating as mere defences.[15]

It also happened that on the day the result in *Suisse Atlantique* was reported in the press, Lord Denning was in New Zealand and, at a dinner in Auckland soon afterwards, told the audience that while he had been away their Lordships had been 'up to no good'. But he assured those present that when he returned to England he would see that things were 'put right'. *Harbutt's Plasticine*[16] was his opportunity to do just that, and the means he employed were basically those foreshadowed in the already mentioned dicta of Lord Reid.

Of the two articles reproduced in Chapter 8 the first half of the earlier one was, therefore, devoted to a detailed argument that, on a discharge for breach, termination was not of the contract but of the injured party's obligation to perform. Any analogy with deviation was false. Reliance was placed on dicta in *Heyman v Darwins Ltd.*[17] The balance of that article and the whole of the second one are given over to a range of other arguments against fundamental breach and in support of the view that the effect of exception and limitation clauses should depend on their interpretation.

The outcome of all this was that, in *Photo Production Ltd v Securicor Transport Ltd*,[18] the House of Lords for a second and, as it has turned out, the last time, affirmed that at common law the effect of exception and limitation clauses depends on their interpretation. Referring to dicta in *Heyman v Darwins*, their Lordships confirmed that on a discharge for breach, what terminated was not the contract but the injured party's obligation to perform. The analogy with deviation was false. For his part, Lord Diplock based his concurring judgment mainly on a further, much more extended, exposition of the theme that secondary obligations were consensual and, hence, related back to formation.

[13] *Hain Steamship Co Ltd v Tate & Lyle Ltd* [1936] 2 All ER 597.

[14] *The Heron II* [1966] 2 QB 695, 730–31.

[15] To rather similar effect was a passage in the judgment of Lord Wilberforce in *Suisse Atlantique*, above note 11 at 431F. By another coincidence, one of the counsel for the appellant in *Suisse Atlantique*, RA MacCrindle QC had, I understand, been one of the examiners in 1959 of my Cambridge PhD dissertation, an experience which, if that were true, somehow failed to inhibit their defence of fundamental breach!

[16] *Harbutt's 'Plasticine' Ltd v Wayne Tank & Pump Co Ltd* [1970] 1 QB 447.

[17] [1942] AC 356.

[18] [1980] AC 827.

The paper on *Bowmakers* (Chapter 9) analyses a case in which the answer to what had been perceived by commentators to be an illegality problem is, the paper submits, to be found instead in the agreement made between the parties at formation.

The inclusion in this collection of the three pieces making up Chapters 10 and 11 is admittedly a departure not just because they deal with tort as well as contract, but also because they are concerned primarily with enforcement rather than formation. Even so, it is hoped that the analyses they contain may be of some continuing interest. Certainly, in the case of Chapter 10, chance and the burden of proof can still present problems of application of the kind there identified. As to Chapter 11, it has generally been taken much for granted that *The Leisbosch*[19] and impecuniosity have no relevance to actions in contract. The article suggests that was a misunderstanding of the authorities. After analysing the relevant cases in both contract and tort, it concludes by expressing regret that in *Alcoa Minerals of Jamaica Inc v Herbert Broderick*,[20] the Privy Council missed an opportunity to lend its weight to the view that *The Liesbosch* ought no longer to form part of the law. More recently, a second opportunity presented itself in *Lagden v O'Connor*,[21] this time before the House of Lords and this time it was taken, the *Leisbosch* article being cited in the judgments of Lord Hope of Craighead and Lord Walker.

The twelfth chapter returns to the theme of the assumption, at formation, of obligations and liabilities, this time referred to as primary and secondary obligations. It draws at least a measure of support from the judgment of Lord Hoffmann in *Banque Bruxelles Lambert SA v Eagle Star Insurance Co Ltd*[22] and especially those of Lord Hoffmann and Lord Hope in *The Achilleas*.[23] For the former it seemed 'logical to found liability for damages upon the intention of the parties objectively ascertained because all contractual liability is voluntarily undertaken'. Both he and Lord Hope spoke of an 'assumption of responsibility for loss'. The paper explores the extent to which the two judgments support, or are at least not inconsistent with, the assumption theory of which a summary is also given. It finds the two judgments at least 'encouraging'.

The final chapter reproduces its author's valedictory lecture given in December 1994 to mark his then imminent retirement. That was 20 years ago but, even so, it has been thought a not inappropriate way to end the present collection, not least because it summarises much of what is still the author's thinking about Contract. In 1994, it was included in a small 'souvenir' booklet for circulation locally. This is the first time it has been given wider currency.

It remains to express my most grateful thanks to the publisher, to the University of Auckland Law School, and especially to John Carter and Sandra Shaw, for their support in their several ways which, together, have brought this project to fruition.

19 *Owners of Dredger Liesbosch v Owners of Steamship Edison* [1933] AC 449.
20 [2000] 3 WLR 23.
21 [2004] 1 AC 1067.
22 [1997] AC 191.
23 *Transfield Shipping Inc v Mercator Shipping Inc (The Achilleas)* [2009] 1 AC 61.

2

Reflections on Intention in the Law of Contract

The common law purports to treat contracts as expressions of intention, which in turn has implications for their formation, interpretation, and construction, and in some circumstances their termination, and the consequences of breach. In practice, however, because of its emphasis on objective intention and its recourse to certain types of implied term, the law seems to pay relatively little regard to what individual contracting parties actually intend. The view taken in this article is that, rather than being a matter for criticism, this disjunction is simply a rational and necessary response to practical constraints, by which a balance of convenience has been struck. On the other hand, the extent of the disjunction ought not to be exaggerated. What the law chooses to treat as intention may in many cases come closer to the real intentions of the parties than some might suppose.

What do We Mean by Intention?

A Common Definition

The traditional definition of intention in the law is one that appeared in such nineteenth-century works as Austin on *Jurisprudence*, Kenny on *Criminal Law*, and Holmes on *The Common Law*. Intention, it is said, combines desire with knowledge and foresight or prevision.[1]

[*] Author's Note: The text of this piece was written in the early 1990s but had to be set aside before any footnoting could be done. The annotations now supplied are less full than they would then have been.

[1] For a detailed discussion, see White, 'Intentions, Purpose, Foresight and Desire' (1976) 92 *LQR* 569. See also Simister & Brookbanks, *Principles of Criminal Law* (2nd edn, 2002) 100 ff; Collins, *The Law of Contract* (1986) 92. A well-known series of articles on objectivity in contract includes: Spencer, 'Signature, Consent, and the Rule in *L'Estrange v Graucob*' [1973] *CLJ* 104; Howarth, 'The Meaning of Objectivity in Contract' (1987) 103 *LQR* 274; Vorster, 'A Comment on the Meaning of Objectivity in Contract' (1987) 103 *LQR* 527; and Goddard, 'The Myth of Subjectivity' [1987] *Current Legal Problems* 263.

Some Problems with the Definition

It would be wrong, though, to conclude from this that intention must have a single, universal meaning in law, any more than it has in life. The definition itself raises immediate problems. One lies with the word 'desire'. At least in common parlance, actors can intend things that they do not desire, an obvious example being the person who kills another under threats from a third party to his own life if he does not. It can, of course, be argued that the reluctant killer must 'want' to kill because he wishes to save his own life or, in other words, that something can be both desired and abhorred, simultaneously. The alternative is to accept that one can will an end without desiring the means required to achieve it.

A second problem arises from the circumstance that knowledge, foresight, and prevision involve matters of degree. How fully and exactly do I have to foresee the consequences of my act before I can be said to have intended them? Must I be taken to have intended every consequence that I did foresee? A person who shoots another may in law be taken to have intended to kill even if he foresaw only a serious wounding. On the other hand, an organisation that holds a legitimate meeting on private premises does not intend to produce breaches of the peace merely because it foresees as inevitable that its antagonists will commit them. A more marginal case would be someone who broadcasts for the enemy in time of war in order to preserve the lives of members of her family who are being held as hostages. It might well be said that the broadcaster in such a case should not be held to have intended to assist the enemy. Almost certainly, though, a different view would be taken if what moved the broadcaster were merely a desire to earn a fee.

A third problem is that the intention itself can be a matter of degree. In the case of many crimes, recklessness is equated with intention although that is not the case with murder or with criminal attempts. And, depending on the context, a guilty intention might be careless, reckless, deliberate, dishonest, fraudulent, or malicious.

Intention in the Criminal Law

These examples illustrate that intention is a variable concept, the meaning and application of which may depend very much on the context in which it is used. More importantly, they reflect the fact that in the criminal law the meaning of intention depends on the role that intention plays in the determination of criminal liability. To be guilty, an accused must not only have committed the act complained of (the actus reus) but also in most cases have done so with the requisite intent (mens rea). In other words, in the criminal law intention goes to culpability, to the ascription of guilt. The degree and kind of intent required for a particular crime is prescribed by the law itself and depends on how the crime is defined. Accordingly, 'intention' in the criminal law is a term of art, the meaning of which can vary from one crime to another. Just as importantly, for reasons related to the purposes of the criminal law such as deterrence and punishment as well as guilt, the emphasis is characteristically on states of mind that are actually or subjectively held to the extent that these can be deduced from the evidence (which can include the *ipse dixit* of the accused) rather than objectively ascribed, imputed, or implied.

Criminal Law as a Special Case

By contrast, in the law of torts, where the concern is primarily with compensation for injury or loss rather than with the punishment of guilt, intention in the full sense is as much a matter of identification of the tort as of a prescription of its incidents. In torts that turn on the presence of fraud or malice the concern will, as in the criminal law, be with states of mind. But, for the greater part, the concern of the law of torts is with carelessness, in which context, rather than seeking to discover subjective states of mind, the law judges an actor by reference to objective standards of conduct. The law of contract is necessarily different again. There, it is not sufficient that a party merely hold an intention or act upon it. Almost invariably, contractual intention, if it is to be at all relevant, must at some point be communicated, whether to another contracting party, to a third person, or to a court. After all, one of the most common purposes of a contract is to enable, or even to induce, reliance on it. Reliance, in turn, argues for a degree of certainty and security, which requires that like is treated as like. Communication and its requirements must, therefore, be central concerns of contract law, as is achieving a balance between the competing concerns of the parties.

Not surprisingly, much of the detailed analysis of the nature of intention in the law has been concerned either primarily or wholly with the criminal law. Not only is a guilty intent integral to most crimes, the very purposes of the criminal law also mean that the focus has usually to be on intention subjectively held, so far as that is capable of deduction. The consequences of a finding of liability to the physical person of the actor tend also to be more immediate than are findings of liability in tort or contract. The criminal law has therefore to be sensitive to nuances of intention in a way that has invited close academic and judicial analysis. The resulting analyses not unnaturally reflect the preoccupations of the criminal law.

Intention in Contract

It has to be asked, then, how far perceptions of intention as it applies in the criminal law should be applicable in the very different context of the law of contract. Must an intending party 'desire' to enter a contract or even 'purpose' to do so? How fully and exactly must a party have knowledge, foresight, or prevision of the consequences of entering a contract before she can be said to intend to be bound by its terms? And how far ought the law of contract be concerned with subjective states of mind as distinct from their outward manifestations?

As everyone familiar with the common law of contract knows, parties can in fact be bound by contracts without in any active sense so desiring, as well as by terms of which they had no very clear knowledge, foresight, or prevision at the time of formation, common-form contracts being the leading and long-standing example. The central role of communication between the parties or with third persons requires that the law of contract be more concerned with the outward appearance of intention than with its subjective reality. Any other approach would place unrealistic burdens on those called upon to understand and respond. The result is not that the common law of contract pays no real regard to intention as such, but that a body of law concerned with communication has come to reflect a use of the concept of intention different from that thought appropriate to the rather different bodies of law concerned with the ascription of guilt and the prescription of compensation for injury caused by fault. One might argue that, say, for the sake of consumer protection, the law of contract ought to move closer than it has to popular or philosophical notions of intention, or to mens rea in the law of crimes. But because of their quite different preoccupations, it would seem idle to suggest that those who have developed the common law of contract have been wrong merely because they have chosen not to treat intention in the same way as does the criminal law or the law of torts.

Why Intention?

Contract Theories

Perceptions of the role of intention in contract, and hence of the sort of intention the law requires, no doubt go back to basic premises concerning the nature of contract and its purposes as an institution. Several theories have been influential. One is that contracts are promises that the law will enforce, and that the law does so in order to encourage and support the practice of promising. Promises create expectations, which in turn induce reliance. Accordingly, two other theories, respectively, maintain that the purpose of the law is to protect the reasonable expectations of the parties, or their reliance. Then there is a theory, which says that contracts are to be upheld by law if and because they are bargains.

None of those theories is inconsistent with a central role for intention, but the only one that might be said necessarily to require it is the promissory theory. A promisor must have intended to promise or at least appear to have so intended. But the theory that places most emphasis on intention, and the one which has most influenced perception of its role in contract, is the will theory—that contracts are to be enforced because they are expressions of the human will, and particularly so in the case of agreements, which are the conjunction of two or more wills in union, one with another.

The various theories were surveyed in an earlier article[2] which sought to show, inter alia, that while each contains some element of truth, all are deficient in one way or another, and none sufficiently shows what a contract is, or what the justifications are for contract as an institution. It is not proposed to repeat that exercise here. But because of its importance for present purposes, something more does have to be said about the will theory.

The Will Theory[3]

It is a theory that seems to have been most strongly held in systems that derive from Roman law. So far as the common law is concerned, the seeds of the idea that consent is necessary to a contract are to be found recorded as early as the sixteenth century. In the nineteenth century it had a strong, if only temporary, influence on the development of offer and acceptance and mistake, and of the notion that consent must be full, free, and true. It also melded nicely with libertarian views of the freedom of contract and with the laissez-faire economic theories of the period. However, with the gradual evolution of the welfare state, the idea of the supremacy of the individual will lost its ideological underpinning. It also became rather too metaphysical for modern tastes. Notions of freedom of contract and that consent must subjectively be full, free, and true seemed inconsistent with the development and enforcement of standard-form contracts and implied-by-law terms and, for that matter, with the fact that parties frequently disagree about meaning. They were inconsistent, too, with the security of transactions and, to a degree, with equity, which is based on conscience rather than on will or intention.

These inconsistencies with the will theory and its consequent eclipse meant that the enforcement of the parties' will could no longer be taken to explain or justify the existence of contract as an institution. The new-right politics and economics of more recent times have not reversed that conclusion.

So long as the sanctity of the human will was thought to justify contract, it could be deduced that the concern of the law ought primarily to be with the actual, or subjective (as distinct from objective), intentions of the parties, analogous to intention in the law of crimes. The demise of the will theory does not mean that intention in contract is unimportant, or that the law can no longer in any circumstances be concerned with intentions subjectively held. What it does mean is that if subjective rather than objective intention is to be relevant, it must be for some justification other than the will theory.

[2] Coote, 'The Essence of Contract' (1988) 1 *JCL* 91 (Part I) and 183 (Part II) 97–107 reprinted as Chapter 2 of *Assumption*.

[3] Ibid at 99–101.

Contract as Assumption

In the already mentioned earlier article,[4] it was argued that although it may take many forms, a legally binding contract is in essence a promise or undertaking (or set of promises or undertakings) in respect of which legal contractual obligation has been assumed by means that the law recognises as effective for that purpose, the intention so to assume obligation being an incident of intention to contract. On that view, a bilateral contract at common law is, in effect, an exchange of contracts and the considerations provided by the parties are (and can logically only be) their respective assumptions of contractual obligation. What, it was claimed, validates this view is that it solves the problem of the so-called 'secret paradox', which has engaged contract scholars since the nineteenth century, of finding considerations that neither precede nor result from the formation of a contract but are exchanged at the very moment of formation.

What has tended to obscure the availability of this solution is the widespread perception that contractual obligations are imposed by law, *ab extra*, upon contracting parties to agreements so that any assumption by them must be of obligations which at that point are necessarily less than contractual. The truth, it is submitted, is that while the law of contract defines and prescribes the legal consequences of entering into a contract, the parties must first appear to have taken those consequences upon themselves by the act of assuming specifically contractual obligations. This they are able to do at common law by promising for consideration with an intention to contract.

On this view, rather than being (other than consequentially) an instrument for the regulation of conduct, contract is first and foremost a facility to enable the effective assumption of contractual obligation. Although other purposes might be grafted onto it, its incidents for the most part flow from that initial function. And while its existence could have any number of justifications, which might vary from time to time and as between one legal system and another, it seems likely that the principal reason for the institution in all societies is its usefulness, and that it is made available for the classic reasons of peace, order, and good government. If that is accepted, an approach to intention that differed from that of the criminal law, in the regard it paid to such utilitarian concerns as communication, reliance, certainty, and the needs of third parties, would be not only appropriate but also required. It would also mean that, at common law, the emphasis should primarily be on what obligations the parties assumed, and only then on what additional obligations the law itself imposed on them.

[4] Ibid at 191–95.

Intention to Contract

If the traditional contract theories are suspect, what are the real reasons why intention should be so important in contract? Almost certainly the answers lie in the nature of the institution itself. A party can enter a contract reluctantly or unwillingly, but she must always intend to do so or at least give that appearance. If it were otherwise, contract would just be another means, like torts and restitution, by which obligations were imposed *ab extra*.

Historically, most societies seem to have denoted a contract by the use of distinctive signs or symbols. These have taken many forms, ranging from the affixing of a seal or the use of writing, to the exchange of hostages, the giving of a token, shaking hands, taking a meal or a drink together, or just touching the ground. Where contracts are marked off in distinctive ways, there can be little doubt both that an intention to contract is needed and that it is present in a particular case. On the other hand, with contracts made at a distance, the use of signs in this way would usually be impracticable. It is not surprising, therefore, that as the common law has evolved it should have come to deduce intention to contract in a much more abstract manner.

Although entry into a contract may in many circumstances still be regarded as a question of fact, in practice recourse is often made to the meaning of the words used or to inferences from them. Whether, for example, 'I guarantee' are words of contract seems more a matter of interpretation (and hence of law) than of the establishment of a fact.[5] Such recourse to the meaning of words or to inference makes it rather more likely that an intention to contract will be ascribed to someone who, actually or subjectively, does not hold it, and that possibility may have helped to persuade some commentators that intention to contract is an unnecessary fiction,[6] or even merely a late-nineteenth-century invention.[7] In truth, intention to contract is inherent in the nature of contract and vital to its existence as a distinct institution. But whether that always means it must be an intention subjectively held is quite another matter to which we will need to return at a later point. If it is accepted that intention to contract is an independent requirement for formation, it would follow that the presence of offer, acceptance, or a quid pro quo for an agreement would not by themselves determine whether a contract had been formed.

Intention as to Terms

An intention to enter into a contract must also include an intention to be bound by all its terms. That much seems axiomatic. The real question is whether for the parties to be bound it is necessary that they have in mind, or advert to, every

[5] Eg, *Heilbut Symons & Co v Buckleton* [1913] AC 30, 51.

[6] Cf *Williston on Contracts* (4th edn, 1990) § 3.5; Hepple, 'Intention to Create Legal Relations' [1970] *CLJ* 122; Collins, above note 1 at 35–36.

[7] Eg, in *Carllil v Carbolic Smoke Ball Co* [1893] 1 QB 256.

word of every term individually. The answer, clearly, is that in practice they do not. Thus, for example, it is quite possible for many of the terms in a contract to be prescribed by law rather than by the parties. That has happened, for example, in France without stopping French lawyers embracing the will theory,[8] and it can happen in common law countries too. In such cases, it must be irrelevant to the binding force of the prescribed terms that the parties were unfamiliar with the relevant law or legislation. They would intend to be bound, but in the sense that acceptance of contractual obligation includes acceptance of whatever that obligation might turn out to be. In the same way, one may intend to be bound by the terms of a document one has not read and to signal that intention by signing it,[9] or to be bound by the potential legal consequences of a marriage without knowing quite what those are.

Common law drafters of contracts characteristically try to cover every eventuality.[10] But there tend to be gaps, and when they occur the law may well fill them by implying additional terms. In so doing, the courts may in some cases be prescribing obligation just as surely as a legislature might in a different legal system. What makes the common law's implied term approach different is, at least nominally, that it takes the parties' intentions as its yardstick. It does not necessarily ensure that the terms implied will correspond with the actual or subjective intention of the parties. They may have formed none on the point, anyway. What it does mean is that the relevant terms can frequently be tailored to the particular contract to an extent that would not be possible if they were prescribed by legislation.

Another aspect of intention as to terms is that the parties must intend what the terms should be that will form part of their contract. A generic intention would sufficiently cover the terms contained in a contract document, and implied-by-law terms would be included in a generic intention to accept legal contractual obligation. But in situations where the question is whether a particular representation has become a term, the intention must be more specific and that would also be true of some implied-in-fact terms. Again, whether that means the particular intention must actually or subjectively be held is another matter.

Intention and Interpretation

The third major area where intention is central to the law is that of interpretation and construction. The common law purports to see the words of the contract as expressions of the parties' intentions, however obliquely those intentions may

[8] Nicholas, *The French Law of Contract* (1982) 49; de Moor, 'Contract and Agreement in English and French Law' (1986) 6 *OJLS* 275, 279.

[9] *L'Estrange v Graucob* [1934] 2 KB 394; *McCutcheon v David Macbrayne Ltd* [1964] 1 WLR 125, 133–34, where Lord Devlin rejects the nineteenth-century notion that this depends on an estoppel.

[10] Cf Nicholas, above note 8 at 59.

actually have been held. Here again, it must, as a general principle, be possible for parties to intend to be bound by words despite having formed no subjective intention as to their meaning. For example, the contents of the contract may be unknown to them, or they may be illiterate or not speak the language. Equally, it would in principle be possible for the law to prescribe uniform meanings for words, expressions, or terms wherever they appeared in a contract, as would be the case with terms and meanings implied by statute.

Observation shows, therefore, that it can be no essential part of the institution of contract that individual contracts be interpreted or construed conformably with the specific and subjective intentions of the parties, or that specific and subjective intentions in respect of particular terms are essential to intention to contract. On the other hand, it could certainly enhance the attractiveness and utility of the institution if, in respect of those matters, the courts were to try and get as close to specifically (and subjectively) held intentions as they could, so far as these could be deduced, and to do so were consistent with such competing considerations as communication, reliance, certainty, and the security of contracts. The next question, then, is: What balance has been struck between objective and subjective intention in the light of these differing considerations?

Objective Intention at Formation

Does Formation Require a Different Approach?

Any discussion of intention in contract in the three areas of intention to contract, the incorporation of terms, and the construction and interpretation of contracts, immediately runs into the problem whether questions of formation should be considered separately from those of construction and interpretation. Formation, involving for the most part an exchange of offer and acceptance made with an intention to contract, is usually thought to be concerned with the intentions of the contracting parties as individuals, in contrast to construction and interpretation of the resulting contract, where joint intentions are supposed to be involved. And intention to contract is commonly regarded as a question of fact,[11] whereas construction and interpretation are questions of law.

On the other hand, it would be odd and potentially inconvenient if the meanings of words used in a written offer should have to change just because the offer had been accepted, and had thereby become the record of the contract. And, while intention to contract might conveniently be a pure matter of fact in systems where

[11] Eg, Lord Wright, 'Ought the Doctrine of Consideration to be Abolished from the Common Law?' (1936) 49 *Harv L Rev* 1225, 1251. To some extent, the position in France would appear to be similar; see Nicholas, above note 8 at 49. And compare *Paal Wilson & Co A/S v Partenreederei Hannah Blumenthal* [1983] 1 AC 854, 913 (abandonment of a contract also a question of fact).

the intention is signalled by the use of distinctive signs and symbols, that may often not be true of simple contracts at common law. The presence or absence of an intention that a communication be an offer or an acceptance, or that an agreement be a contract, has often to be inferred (even if as a matter of fact) from the meaning of the words used, thereby raising questions that ought to receive the same answer at whatever stage they are in issue. As it happens, whether an agreement is a contract and whether a pre-contractual statement has become a term, have both on occasion been characterised as questions of law.

It might be argued that the distinctions between fact and law no longer matter because, nowadays, contract cases are heard by judges sitting alone. But that is really no answer, if only because the fact that a point must be proved by evidence on the balance of probabilities, rather than argued as a question of law, can affect the way in which a case is conducted. In the meantime, observation shows that it is possible for intention to contract to turn at least in part on the meaning of written words, and hence on construction and interpretation.

But even if intention to contract were a pure question of fact, that in itself cannot be conclusive that objective criteria do not apply. The juries who used to decide torts cases, for example, were well used to the test of a reasonable person. And the evidence itself has to be 'objective' in the sense that it is restricted to the actions of, and communications between, the respective parties.[12]

A number of reasons have been given to justify the application of objectivity to questions of formation. There has been much disagreement about the tests by which objectivity should be applied, and there is some uncertainty about how far this actually held or subjective intention can still be taken into account. For example, there have been important suggestions that parties should not be permitted to rely on objectively ascribed intentions unless they should actually hold them.

Justifications for Objectivity in Formation

For those who take an instrumental view of contract, what justifies objectivity is that it enables the judiciary to impose obligations and thereby to pursue their policy objectives.[13] Others have seen objectivity as a corollary to the theory that contract law exists to protect reasonable expectations or reasonable reliance.[14] And there are arguments from the nature of language that find the reality of intention in outward manifestations and appearances. But most of the justifications for contract objectivity in the legal literature relate to the effectiveness of the institution, and that is what would be expected if contract is indeed a facility provided

[12] Eg, *R v Lord Chancellor's Department, ex parte Nangle* [1992] 1 All ER 897, 903–04.

[13] Cf Summers, 'Professor Fuller's Jurisprudence and America's Dominant Philosophy of Law' (1978) 92 *Harv L Rev* 433, 447.

[14] Eg, Pound, 'Promise or Bargain?' (1959) 33 *Tul L Rev* 455, 460 and 471; Waddams, *The Law of Contracts* (4th edn, 1999) paras 141–47; *Corbin on Contracts* (rev edn, 1993) 2, § 1.1.

by society for the general purposes of peace, order, and good government. Even though the protection of reliance or expectations does not explain the existence of the institution, the usefulness of contracts nonetheless frequently depends, at least in the case of executory contracts, on it being possible realistically to make them the basis of forward planning. That puts a premium on certainty, reliability, predictability, and security, which in turn argues for a degree of standardisation and externality, and for a common reference point for the parties in case of disagreement.

It all goes back to contracts being concerned with communication. A party who receives a contractual communication, or who signs a contract document, needs to be able to deduce its significance without having to enquire whether it exactly corresponds with the actual or subjectively held intentions of the other party. That is as true for intention to contract as it is for the constituents of formation. If the deduction could be made by reference to criteria that would give the same answer for both parties, so much the better. Whether that result were achievable would depend on the tests by which objectivity falls to be applied. And in practice a variety of such tests have been proposed.

The Objective Tests Proposed

In the context of formation, as in others, objectivity raises the problem of where the notional reasonable person or persons should be located along the chain of communication between the parties where negotiation has culminated in the acceptance of an offer. In such cases, some commentators locate the reasonable person in the position of the offeree. The offer is to be read as it would have appeared to the offeree if he or she were the reasonable person.[15] On the other hand, whether the offeree's response were an acceptance would doubtless have to be determined as if by a reasonable person in the position of the offeror.[16] Of course, not all contractually relevant communications are offers or acceptances. Not surprisingly, other commentators substitute the addressor and the addressee or the promisor and the promisee.

All of these tests raise problems if regard is had to the rationale of objectivity in contract, particularly if the end result is to be fair. If in respect of particular communications the reasonable person is to be placed in the position of one rather than the other of the parties, it could make for arbitrary results if that party were chosen simply because he or she fell within the category of offeror or offeree, addressor or addressee, or promisor or promisee. For example, offers are frequently made on terms prescribed by the offeree, and a similar situation can exist as between an addressor and an addressee. Again, every offer must contain,

[15] Eg, Corbin, 'Offer and Acceptance and Some of the Resulting Legal Relations' (1917) 26 *Yale LJ* 169, 205.

[16] Murphy & Speidel, *Studies in Contract Law* (4th edn, 1991) 262.

expressly or impliedly, all the terms of the proposed contract, so that the content of a promise may be dictated by the promisee. In such a case, should each provision in the offer be read from a different standpoint, depending on which party was meant to promise it? The more complicated type of objectivity, which asks how a reasonable person in the position of one party would deduce the understandings of the other, could be just as arbitrary in its application as the other tests would be.

Prima facie, what the law should be seeking, if it is going to place the reasonable person in the position of a *single* party and yet be fair, would be the objective meaning and appearance of a given communication that it would have for the party who had not drafted it or put it forward. Only on that basis would the non-drafting party have the (notional) certainty to justify reliance. At least one commentator has suggested a link here with the *contra proferentem* rule.[17] But although that could give a fairer result, it presupposes that the authors of every provision of negotiated contracts can be identified in retrospect. In any event, it might be queried how far the time of the courts ought to be taken up with such enquiries.

Behind these problems lies another. If all that were at issue were the subjectively held intentions of one party and the efforts of that party to convey those intentions to the other, it could be reasonable enough to place the onus of accurate communication on the communicator. But if and when the common law acts on intention objectively determined, both parties are bound by that determination and to each it ought to be equally accessible. Perhaps in recognition of this need there have been suggestions that the hypothetical reasonable person be not a party at all, but rather an observer or bystander. And since the same bystander test could presumably also be applied to the interpretation of the eventual contract, there would be that much less risk of discontinuity as between its formation and its subsequent application.

A test of this last kind would presumably be attractive to those who favour a paternalist function for the law of contract. It would also coincide more closely with the needs of those who have to rely on contracts to which they were not original parties. But it seems to have the disadvantage that it takes no account of the subjective states of mind of the parties, even when they can be shown to be the same, as was the case in *Rose v Pim*.[18] There, the Court of Appeal, applying the observer test, gave a literal interpretation to the word 'feveroles' even though both parties had mistakenly believed at the time that it meant 'horsebeans'. For those who are concerned that objective intention be as close as practicable to actually held intention as the competing requirements of communication and reliance allow, the reasonable person needs to be rather closer than that to the parties. But if so, and the standpoint of a reasonable person in the position of one or other of the parties were chosen, there appears to be the problem that an offer that was read one way during formation might conceivably receive a different interpretation

[17] Kerr, *The Principles of the Law of Contract* (3rd edn, 1982) 253.

[18] *Rose (Frederick E) (London) Ltd v William H Pim Junior & Co Ltd* [1953] 2 QB 450.

when it became a contract, since, at that point, what is sought is their joint intention (so that the reasonable person is placed in the position of them both). The problem would disappear if the two tests were in practice the same. It is submitted that, at least arguably, that is already the case.

The argument depends on what is meant by the reasonable person being in the position of one of the parties. Traditionally, what is meant is that in seeking objective intention the court (through the hypothetical reasonable person) can have regard not only to communicated words and actions, but also to surrounding circumstances of which that party can be taken to have been aware. In principle, those circumstances ought to be confined to the ones known to both parties if each is to be able, at least theoretically, to arrive at common (objective) meanings and hence at the (objective) consensus presupposed by the notion that the resulting contract represents the intentions of both parties.[19] Since the relevant surrounding circumstances would therefore be the same for both, the tests for formation and subsequent interpretation ought also to give the same answer. The objective meaning could therefore remain constant throughout.

Subjective Intention at Formation

Relevance at Formation

To this point, it has been argued that there are good, practical reasons why the law should prefer objective intention in contract, and for the present it is assumed that those reasons apply not only to interpretation but also to formation, including intention to contract. But there are nevertheless some situations where subjective intention (albeit as proved by objective evidence) has been held to be relevant.

One well-recognised example is a corollary to the communication and reliance justifications for objectivity. The argument that each party needs to be able to rely on the objective appearance of what the other intends is negatived if, on the evidence, one party actually knows, or must be taken to know, the subjective intention of the other. When that happens, a result can differ depending on whether the party in the know shares the same subjective intention or has a different one. If the latter, it was at one time thought that no contract could result because the parties were not *ad idem*.[20] That view, of course, reflected the influence of the will theory in the nineteenth century. Nowadays, it would seem that the party not in the know

[19] *Prenn v Simmonds* [1971] 1 WLR 1381, 1384 per Lord Wilberforce ('mutually known facts'); *Inventors Compensation Scheme Ltd v West Bromwich Building Society* [1998] 1 WLR 896, 912–13 per Lord Hoffmann. The test is objective: *Reardon Smith Line Ltd v Yngvar Hansen-Tangen* [1976] 1 WLR 989, 997.

[20] One explanation given for the result in *Raffles v Wichelhaus* (1864) 2 H & C 906; 159 ER 375. The contract, there, would anyway have failed for ambiguity since it was not possible to tell to which vessel the contract referred.

has three options: to seek rectification in terms of her own understandings; to seek relief on the grounds of fraud or misrepresentation, or mistake where applicable; or to submit to the contract as it (objectively) stands. On the other hand, if it can be shown that the subjective understandings of both parties coincide, that common understanding ought in principle to prevail unless a different course is justified by some reason other than the requirements of communication and reliance. Such a justification might, for example, be seen by some to be provided by the Statute of Frauds and its equivalents, or by the desirability of third parties being able to rely on whatever the parties might appear to have done. On the other hand, the bystander objectivists would presumably disallow this particular subjective intentions exception anyway, whether the subjective intention concerned were that of one party or both, on the ground that neither would be known to a notional third-party observer.

A second situation where subjectively held intention can prevail is where a communication or contract is ambiguous. In such cases no objective sense of what has been done is possible. If it were, there would be no ambiguity. If it is the contract that is ambiguous, effect can be given to a subjective intention so long as it was common to both parties,[21] or if one of the parties knew of the meaning ascribed by the other of them. On the other hand, where the ambiguity appears in an instruction from one of the parties, as from a principal to an agent, the latter will ordinarily be protected if she acts upon her subjective understanding if it is a tenable one.[22] A fortiori, regard could also be had to one party's subjective understanding if the other of them induced it.

A much more strongly subjectivist approach would be to suggest that either party should be able to rely on her own subjective understanding provided she had not misled the other in a blameworthy way and that there has been no detrimental reliance. On that approach, objectivity would be justified not as something useful to contract as an institution, but as a protection for reliance, and then only if the party inducing the reliance has been at fault.

Is Subjectivity the Norm?

Unconvincing though this last view might be, it neatly raises the question whether objectivity or subjectivity should be regarded as the norm, or at least as the ideal to be sought wherever possible. Associated with that are two further questions. If a party is to be allowed to rely on an objective meaning, must it coincide with her own subjective intention? And if a contract is to be formed, must both parties have, as distinct from appearing to have, a subjective intention to contract?

If it really were true that objective intentions must subjectively be held before a party could rely on them, most of the usefulness of objectivity would be lost.

[21] Smith, *The Law of Contract* (2nd edn, 1993) 15–16. Compare the *Restatement (Second) of Contracts*, § 212, to similar effect.

[22] *Ireland v Livingston* (1871) LR 5 HL 395.

There would be no common reference point on which both could rely. That would undermine certainty, since the existence of a contract would depend on the accidental circumstance that subjective and objective intentions had coincided. Even so, these subjectivist notions have attracted support. The basis of their appeal has been, on the one hand, the will theory with its emphasis on a meeting of minds as the norm and, on the other, the perception that objectivity in the formation of contracts is primarily a matter of estoppel.

Both of these ideas can be found in *Smith v Hughes*,[23] which, ironically enough, has generally been regarded by many as the leading English case on objectivity in formation. The most famous passage is the following, from the judgment of Blackburn J:[24]

> I apprehend that if one of the parties *intends* to make a contract on one set of terms, and the other intends to make a contract on another set of terms, or, as it is sometimes expressed, *if the parties are not ad idem, there is no contract*, unless the circumstances are such as to preclude one of the parties from denying that he has agreed to the terms of the other. The rule of law is that stated in *Freeman v Cooke*[25] … If *whatever a man's real intention may be*, he so conducts himself that a reasonable man would believe that he was assenting to the terms proposed by the other party, and that other party *upon that belief* enters into the contract with him, the man thus conducting himself would be equally bound as if he had intended to agree to the other party's terms (italics supplied).

What this passage seems to stress as the norm is that, for the formation of a contract, the parties must subjectively be agreed on what terms form the basis of their contract. The only exception mentioned to that requirement is that of (apparently) an offeree whose conduct misleads (apparently) an offeror into believing, subjectively, that she has accepted the terms proposed by the offeror when her real intention was otherwise.[26]

It is now widely agreed that in most contexts objectivity in contract does not depend on estoppel, if only because it does not turn on the detrimental reliance of the party concerned.[27] Moreover, the will theory no longer appears to be a reason why the terms of the contract should not be settled objectively. But that still leaves the possibility of there being something special about offer and acceptance requiring them to be treated differently. As it happens, the notion that a form of subjectivity is essential to offer and acceptance, and hence to formation, was revived in recent times by three members of the House of Lords in *The Hannah Blumenthal*.[28]

[23] (1871) LR 6 QB 597.

[24] Ibid at 607 (italics supplied).

[25] (1848) 2 Ex 654; 154 ER 652.

[26] Samek, 'The Objective Theory of Contract and the Rule in *L'Estrange v Graucob* (1974) 52 *Can Bar Rev* 351, 361, characterises the Blackburn test as purely subjective, according to which it is the viewpoint of the promisor, not that of the promisee, that is crucial.

[27] Eg, Morison, *Rescission of Contracts* (1916) 162–63; de Moor, 'Intention in the Law of Contract: Elusive or Illusory?' (1990) 106 *LQR* 632, 641–42.

[28] *Paal Wilson & Co A/S v Partenreederei Hannah Blumenthal* [1983] 1 AC 854.

The Dicta in *The Hannah Blumenthal*

In this case, one of the subsidiary issues was whether the failure of both parties to prosecute an arbitration had resulted in a contract to abandon it. The House held that while a contract of abandonment might on some facts be implied from inaction, that could not be done on the facts before them. What makes the case significant are obiter comments by some of their Lordships. For Lord Brandon, such a contract of abandonment could be established,[29]

> by showing that the conduct of each party as evinced to the other party and acted on by him, leads necessarily to the inference of an implied agreement between them to abandon the contract.

In the alternative, he suggested, the conduct of one party might lead the other reasonably to believe that the former had abandoned the contract in consequence of which the latter had altered his position in reliance on that belief thus giving rise to an estoppel.[30] But in the case of an inferred contract, he seems to have thought *both parties* should have acted *in reliance on the conduct of the other*, which presumably means that each must have had the same subjective intention not just to agree on an abandonment, but also to contract for it.

For Lord Diplock, it was necessary to the creation of the contract that the intention of each party '*as it has been communicated to and understood by the other* (even though that which has been communicated does not represent the actual state of mind of the communicator) should coincide'.[31] For him, then, the formation of a contract would depend on both parties having identical perceptions of what the other of them appeared to have intended.

For Lord Brightman, a party claiming that a contract had been made must show that the other party 'so conducted [itself] as to entitle the [claiming party] to assume, *and that [that party] did assume*, that the contract was agreed to be abandoned sub silentio'.[32] While his reference was thus to the actual belief of one party only, there is nothing to suggest that a similar burden would not have applied had it been the other party who was making the claim.

While their Lordships expressed what they meant in different ways, all three seem to have thought that before a contract of abandonment could come into existence both parties must, at the least, subjectively have believed that the other of them so intended. That, presumably, could come about if the subjective intentions that prompted their respective actions and the subjective apprehensions that those actions prompted should both coincide. Alternatively, the coincidence might be of the respective apprehensions themselves. In thus requiring the subjective belief of both parties, their Lordships seem to be taking the same view as Blackburn J

29 Ibid at 914.
30 Ibid.
31 Ibid at 915 (the italics are Lord Diplock's).
32 Ibid at 924 (the italics are Lord Brightman's).

in *Smith v Hughes*,[33] who appeared to require the subjective belief of both parties except in the case of an estoppel, in which case the subjective belief was to be only that of the one proposing the terms. Obviously enough, a requirement that at least the subjective *apprehensions* of the parties should coincide would be a serious threat to objectivity in formation, unless it could be confined within a narrow compass.

The Scope of the Dicta

One possible way of so confining the three dicta would be to read them in the particular factual context to which they were directed, that being a situation where an attempt was being made to imply a contract from the inaction of both parties. As Robert Goff LJ pointed out soon afterwards in *The Leonidas D*,[34] only in very special circumstances could silence and inaction constitute either an offer or an acceptance. This was because, in the absence of such special circumstances, inaction, when considered objectively, is consistent with other explanations.

The Hannah Blumenthal being a case where there were no communications or actions to which objective tests could refer, it could be argued that only a coincidence of subjective intentions could have created a contract. (That possibility had been excluded by the fact that, during the relevant period, at least one of the parties had continued to seek evidence for the arbitration.)[35] Under this explanation, the dicta of all three of their Lordships were directed exclusively to the circumstances in which contracts of abandonment could be implied. As against that, Lord Diplock asserted that to the formation of contracts of abandonment the ordinary principles of the English law of contract applied.[36]

A second explanation has been advanced by the late Anne de Moor.[37] It depends on distinctions she made between meaning and interpretation, intention to assume contractual obligations, and what she called 'formal' intention, by which she meant subjective intention to assume contractual obligations. The first of these, she argued, are properly to be determined objectively. But the last requires that subjective intention exist so far as that can be deduced from the evidence, on the balance of probabilities.[38]

Objectivity, she suggested, is the natural, appropriate way of dealing with interpretation. But 'formal' intention must be subjectively held (so far as that can be deduced on the evidence) because it is impossible to assume an obligation without (subjectively) intending to do so. In support, she cited, inter alia, the established rule (at least of classical contract law) that a party alleging an acceptance will be

33 (1871) LR 6 QB 597.
34 *Allied Marine Transport Ltd v Vale de Rio Doce Navegacao SA* [1985] 1 WLR 925, 937.
35 [1983] 1 AC 854, 914.
36 Ibid at 915.
37 de Moor, above note 27.
38 Ibid at 646–49.

defeated if it can be shown that the acts she relies on as an acceptance were not done in response to the offer.[39] Indeed, that rule could hardly be otherwise if contracts are in any real sense to constitute a relationship between the parties.

With respect, however, it would be quite another matter to extrapolate from requirements such as that an acceptance be a response to the offer to the further requirement that both parties must, on the evidence, have an actual, as distinct from imputed, subjective intention to assume contractual obligation. If that were so, offers, also, would in that sense subjectively have to be intended to be such since, by definition, they also must show a willingness to assume obligation thereby if accepted. Yet such leading cases as *Carlill v Carbolic Smoke Ball Co*[40] and *Pharmaceutical Society of Great Britain v Boots Cash Chemists (Southern) Ltd*[41] appear to proceed on the basis that whether an act or a statement is to be characterised as an offer is to be determined objectively, independently of the actual intentions of the parties.

A further problem for Ms de Moor's thesis is that even the requirement that an acceptance be a subjective response to an offer can be displaced. It is true that an alleged acceptance can be defeated if the offeror shows affirmatively that it was not made in response but, short of that, an offeree who appears to know of the existence of the offer can rely on a presumption in her favour.[42] Doubtless, Ms de Moor's test of agreement would accommodate this. But if it is the offeror who seeks to establish a contract, it will not avail the alleged offeree to deny that she had accepted if her actions, regarded objectively, appeared to be in response, particularly if the offeror had acted in reliance on that appearance.

With some trepidation, it is submitted as a possible third explanation that their Lordships' insistence on the subjective agreement of each party with the objective intentions of the other was misconceived. Almost certainly, they had in mind the already-cited dictum of Blackburn J in *Smith v Hughes* and had extended to both parties his requirement that a party relying on the objective sense of what the other had done should have acted on the belief that the other had assented to the terms proposed. In the language of offer and acceptance, the Blackburn dictum can be read in two ways. If the party proposing the terms is the offeree, the offeror must appear to have offered to be bound on the offeree's terms. The offeree must then accept in the belief that an offer had been made. That would be consistent with the 'response' requirement, but it does not necessarily determine what would be the position of the offeror if she should subsequently wish to enforce the resulting objective or apparent contract against the offeree. On the other hand, if by the party proposing the terms Blackburn J meant the offeror, which would seem to be the more natural reading of the two, his dictum requires of an offeror some action

[39] Ibid at 651, citing *R v Clarke* (1927) 40 CLR 227. She also relied on *Harvela Investments Ltd v Royal Trust Co of Canada (CI) Ltd* [1986] AC 207, 226, 234–35.

[40] [1893] 1 QB 256.

[41] [1953] 1 QB 401.

[42] *R v Clarke* (1927) 40 CLR 227.

subsequent to the acceptance by the offeree in order to complete formation. Since such additional acts are not required by the principles of offer and acceptance, they must go back to the estoppel on which the learned judge based his conclusions and a subjective reliance required for an estoppel to operate. Assuming estoppel does require subjective reliance by the party claiming its protection, it would be an odd result if there were then no contract at all and the offeror's reliance were to no avail unless the offeree herself had subjectively believed the offeror to have understood her to have accepted, as would seem to follow from *The Hannah Blumenthal* dicta.

The better solution, it is submitted, is that objectivity in formation, as in interpretation, should not depend on estoppel and, on that account or any other, require either proven subjective belief, or an acting in reliance. To apply such requirements to both parties, as their Lordships appear to have done, is only to compound the problem. If the purposes of objectivity are to be served, each party needs to be able to rely (whether in relation to formation or interpretation) on the objective sense of what the other of them has said and done, unless at the time of formation she was aware of the other's subjective intention.[43] To put the matter another way, just as Monsieur Jourdain found that he had been speaking prose without knowing it, it should in principle be possible to have accepted contractual obligation without subjective belief, at the time, that that was what one was doing. This does not mean that subjective intention at formation should otherwise be irrelevant. To the circumstances such as ambiguity listed at the beginning of this section should now be added the rules requiring acceptance to be a response. Should it prove impossible to confine the three dicta in *The Hannah Blumenthal* to the implication of contracts from inaction, it is respectfully submitted that they should not be followed, at least in jurisdictions not bound by English law.

Meaning, Interpretation, and Construction

Objectivity as the Norm

Considerations of reliance, certainty, and even the expedition of cases in court require that the parties ordinarily be bound by what they have expressed rather than by what they may actually or subjectively have meant, and by what they appear to have agreed rather than by their subjectively held intentions where the two fail to coincide. The practical pressures are such that even in systems that derive from Roman law such as those of Europe,[44] Scotland, and South Africa, where the will theory still predominates, the objective approach has, to varying degrees, been followed. At common law, the courts seek the 'common intention' of

[43] Cf Treitel, *The Law of Contract* (11th edn, 2003) 1; *Chitty on Contracts* (29th edn, 2004) vol 1, 123–24 and 200–01.

[44] Eg, Pound, 'The Role of Will in Law' (1954) 68 *Harv L Rev* 1, 14.

the parties but, as stated previously, it is intention as deduced, for the most part, from the ordinary meanings of the words used, read in the light of the contract as a whole and of such of the surrounding circumstances as were known to both parties at the time the contract was made.[45] The courts may be further limited, and objectivity to some extent reinforced, by the exclusion under the parole evidence rule of evidence that would add to, vary, or contradict a written instrument.

Despite the obvious utility of the objective approach to interpretation and construction, it is open to criticism for its seeming artificiality, particularly in relation to common-form contracts and to the implication of terms. In both cases that criticism might be based on one or both of two premises, one being the view that, ideally, intention in contract ought to be no different in principle from actual intention, or at least from the subjective intention that prevails in the criminal law.

Nominalism

The second suggested premise stems from the phenomenon called nominalism to which Professor Lon Fuller drew the attention of contract scholars.[46] In the strict philosophical sense, nominalism is the contention that all things existing are only particulars. It denies any generic identity to things that are not identical. In Fuller's use of the term, it involves a denial that anything can have been intended that was not specifically present in the mind of the person concerned at the time the intention was formed. An intention may refer to a genus but, if so, it can include only those members of the genus that the intending party would have had in mind at the time and thus can have no reference to members of a genus not invented or coming into existence until a later date. On this view, for example, a mid-nineteenth-century ban of offensive weapons could not apply (say) to a modern laser gun since, it would be said, the degree of foreknowledge necessary to form an intention would be lacking. The same could be said of events that had not specifically been foreseen. Similar issues were raised in relation to a New Zealand controversy over whether the 1840 Treaty of Waitangi could have been intended to apply to radio and television broadcasting channels, or to the transmission of electricity. It may be that nominalism amongst lawyers owes less to philosophy than to the personalities of those who prefer concrete to abstract thought. Nor, in principle, need it be confined to subjectivists. Be that as it may, the common law has in practice proceeded on the basis that one can intend to be bound by the contents of a document, while taking the risk of what they might be. Those who sign contract documents will ordinarily be bound by all of their contents, unless those contents have been misrepresented. The misrepresentation may be external to the contract

[45] *Rose (Frederick E) (London) Ltd v Williams H Pim Junior & Co Ltd* [1953] 2 QB 450.

[46] Fuller, 'American Legal Realism' (1934) 82 *U Pa L Rev* 429, 444–46; Fuller, *The Morality of Law* (1963) 82–83. Both of these passages are reproduced in Evans, *Statutory Interpretation: Problems of Communication* (1988) 25–29. See generally, Evans, ibid at 14–48.

document or be contained within it, or it may be a matter of implication if the document has been presented as having normal content when that is not so in fact.

The Possible Coincidence of Objective and Subjective Intention

An obvious consequence of nominalism is that it exaggerates potential differences between subjective and objective intention. If it is once allowed that it is possible to intend to be bound by a set of terms whatever they might be, it becomes apparent that a signature to a contract document could more often than not express a subjective as well as an objective intention to the effect.

This tendency to exaggerate the difference between the subjective and the objective is also apparent in relation to implied terms, in which context it is also compounded by the propensity of common lawyers to think of exceptions and qualifications not as essential components of rules, promises, or statements but as, in effect, contradictions of them.[47] This cast of mind can be observed, for example, in the refusal to accept that exception clauses help define obligation rather than merely excuse breach.[48] It can be seen, too, in the bald and unqualified account of the rules of 'classical' contract law given by some of its modern critics.[49] In particular, treatment of exceptions and qualifications as negations makes it difficult under the common law to imply terms. It also leads to the inference that qualifications implied by the courts have been imposed *ab extra* rather than as reflecting the intentions of the parties, actual or ascribed. It obscures the fact that most statements tend to carry unspoken qualifications that are nonetheless real and intended for being unexpressed or even unformulated in the mind of the person making them.

Two examples may help to make this last point clearer. If I ask a builder to supply a replacement roller door for my garage, I would rightly say 'I did not intend that' if he should supply a broken-down used one that did not fit. Again, if I should tell my tenant she could keep a pet on the premises, I could justifiably complain that I had not intended she keep a savage dog, let alone a poisonous snake, or a baby elephant.

In a number of ways, therefore, 'implied' words and terms may in fact be no more than is implicit in what has been agreed. Implications may also be necessary as a matter of logical necessity or as the inevitable consequence of what has been expressed. They may be necessary in order to give sense to a contract or to ensure it has its intended effects. They may simply express what was so obvious and expected as to go without saying, or was known to form an invariable part of contracts of the particular kind. There may even be cases where no implication of

[47] Cf Nicholas, 'Rules and Terms—Civil Law and Common Law' (1974) 48 *Tul L Rev* 946, especially at 955–56 and 961–63.

[48] This despite the judgment of Lord Diplock in *Photo Production Ltd v Securicor (Transport) Ltd* [1980] AC 827 (let alone Coote, *Exception Clauses* (1964))!

[49] Eg, Reiter & Swan, 'Contracts and the Protection of Reasonable Expectations' in Reiter & Swan (eds), *Studies in Contract Law* (1980) 3.

any kind is needed because rights and obligations have on analysis already been expressed. A good example of a failure to recognise a situation of this kind was section 13 of the original Sale of Goods Act 1893 (Imp), which provided that, where goods were sold by description, a term should be implied that the goods would correspond with the description. Provided the goods were in fact sold by description (which would necessarily be the case if they were not specific), there would be no need whatever for a term to be implied. The goods would have to comply with description because that would be inherent in what the seller had undertaken. It would be what she had already contracted to do.

Nominalist criticism has been at its most insistent in relation to the implied term theory of frustration. How, it is asked, could the parties have intended what the law implies if the frustrating event were neither expected nor foreseen?[50] Hence Lord Sands' protest that it would hardly be reasonable to imply the clause 'tiger days excepted' into contracts for the delivery of milk.[51] Three things are likely to have influenced this perception. One is the already mentioned difficulty that common lawyers have of seeing exceptions as qualifications. A second is the nominalist insistence on the particular (for example, tiger days) rather than the generic. The third is the way Lord Loreburn put the matter in a very influential dictum in *Tamplin (FA) Steamship Co Ltd v Anglo-Mexican Petroleum Products Co Ltd.*[52] For him the test was, in part:[53]

> Were the altered conditions such that, had [the parties] thought of them, they would have taken their chance of them, or such that as sensible men they would have said 'if that happens, of course, it is all over between us'?

Quite unfairly, that formula has been taken to mean that the law ascribes to the parties an intention in respect of the precise events that have occurred and, if that were indeed so, the artificiality would be obvious. It would justify the criticism that the law presumed the omniscience of the parties,[54] or their '100 per cent presentiation', which would be a matter of pure fiction. In large measure because of that perception, the implied term theory of frustration has tended to be replaced by the construction theory or some variant of the notion that the courts impose a just solution.

It is ironic that an earlier part of Lord Loreburn's speech was very much closer to an original version of the implied term test, that of Blackburn J in *Taylor v Caldwell*,[55] who put the matter in this way:[56]

> [W]here, from the nature of the contract, it appears that the parties must from the beginning have known that it could not be fulfilled unless when the time for the fulfilment

[50] *Davis Contractors Ltd v Fareham Urban District Council* [1956] AC 696 per Lord Radcliffe.
[51] *James Scott & Sons Ltd v Del Sel*, 1922 SC 592, 597.
[52] [1916] 2 AC 397.
[53] Ibid at 404.
[54] Collins, above note 1 at 93.
[55] (1863) 3 B & S 826; 122 ER 309.
[56] Ibid at 833–4; 312.

> of the contract arrived some particular specified thing continued to exist, so that, when entering into the contract, they must have contemplated such continuing existence as the foundation of what was to be done; there, in the absence of any express or implied warranty that the thing shall exist, the contract is not to be construed as a positive contract, but as subject to an implied condition that the parties shall be excused in case, before breach, performance becomes impossible from the perishing of the thing without default of the contractor.

It is unfortunate that the implied term test thus propounded should subsequently have been overtaken by the perception that the intention must be specific rather than generic. When they made their contract, the proprietors of the Surrey Music Hall and their customers may not have had in mind the precise manner in which the hall might be destroyed. But since there was no warranty as to existence, there is nothing unreal in ascribing to them the unstated assumption that all would be over between them if, when the time came, the hall should no longer exist, provided neither party were to blame.

On a similar line of reasoning it seems likely that arguments for the implication of terms under *The Moorcock*[57] are from time to time denied by the courts simply because the term proposed was formulated so narrowly that it was thought impossible to say that both parties must necessarily have intended it, whereas something more general (like the continued existence of a subject matter) could have been treated quite differently.

Conclusion

What the law means by intention varies with subject matter and context. In the criminal law, for example, where the focus is on the guilt and punishment of the offender, the concern is for the most part with subjective intention, the guilty mind, so far as it can be deduced from the evidence. In contract, by contrast, where the focus is on the incidents of a legal relationship that, again for the most part, the parties have prescribed for themselves, the concern has had to be with problems of communication and meaning, and with ensuring a degree of certainty sufficient to enable reliance. The result has been that, in contract, intention usually means objective intention since, at least in theory, objective intention is more accessible to the parties and to third persons than subjective intention would be.

These practical considerations have had to contend with at least two main factors. One is the lingering influence of the will theory. The other is the nominalist notion that for an intention to be held it must be specific rather than generic, with the tendency of that notion to reinforce a subjectivist position. In the event, however, the preference of the law for objective intention in contract has been amply

[57] (1889) 14 PD 64.

demonstrated. Quite clearly, parties can be bound in law to contractual provisions to which subjectively they have not intended to agree.

While convenience and practice are on the side of objective intention, there remains uncertainty as to the location of the reasonable person postulated by the objective test. It is also still unclear whether different meanings may be ascribed to contractual provisions depending on whether questions arise in relation to formation or thereafter. And, rather strangely, there is, on the evidence of some fairly recent dicta in the House of Lords, still a lingering suggestion that even an objective intention will not bind unless it is also subjectively held.

Although, for the reasons given, intention in the law of contract normally means objective intention, that sort of intention may in practice come rather closer to intention actually held than some might be prepared to allow. Once it is allowed that intention does not require that the specific be actually present in the mind at the time the intention is formed, and that intention can cover the general, it becomes much more likely that what a reasonable person in the position of the parties would have intended in the light of mutually known facts will correspond with what the parties themselves actually did intend.

3

The Instantaneous Transmission of Acceptances

Introduction

General

Ask any law student when an acceptance, sent by an instantaneous mode of transmission, takes effect and he will almost certainly say 'when it is actually received by the offeror'.[1] He will cite *Entores v Miles Far Eastern Corporation*[2] as his authority. On analysis though, it is very doubtful whether the *Entores* case really goes as far as that. If the law is in truth as the law student would state it (and he could possibly be right) it would be fair to say that it has become so by default and on no very clear ground of principle. All of which seems a little strange when it is remembered that questions of offer and acceptance are basic to contractual theory. Nor are they of merely academic interest for, as is illustrated by the recent case of *D'Oyly Downs Ltd v Galloway*,[3] the binding effect of quite large transactions can turn on such questions as whether or not a telephoned acceptance must come to the actual knowledge of an offeror before a contract can come into existence.

The *D'Oyly Downs* Case

In the *D'Oyly Downs* case, an intending purchaser of a farm property had caused his land agent to telephone an offer to the effective seller. The seller had telephoned his acceptance to the land agent and had subsequently sent him a confirming letter. The land agent had in turn telephoned the offeror at his house. The offeror was out at the time, so the land agent left a message with the offeror's family, to the effect that his offer had been accepted. It was the offeror's case that he had still not received this message when, next day, he sent a telegram to the seller in which he purported to revoke the offer. Richmond J had no difficulty in finding, on the

[1] See, eg, Treitel, *The Law of Contract* (3rd edn, 1970) 24.
[2] [1955] 2 QB 327 (CA).
[3] [1970] NZLR 1077.

facts, that the intending buyer did know of the acceptance before he dispatched the revocation. Accordingly, he held that a contract had come into being.

Had he accepted the buyer's version, however, it would have been necessary for him to decide whether the offeror must have had actual knowledge of the acceptance or whether the seller's telephone message and letter to the land agent, or the message left by the land agent with the offeror's family, would have sufficed. The problems associated with instantaneous transmission of an acceptance would have been raised.

The Problem

Some Preliminary Considerations

Of course, it would be a mistake to exaggerate the extent of the difficulties. Certain aspects of the law are clear enough. But before the 'grey areas' of doubt are identified, three points need to be stated by way of introduction. The first is that the parties negotiating a contract may be together at the time, or apart. Because these alternatives pose different problems in fact, different solutions may be called for. The second is that there are four types of communication relevant to the formation of a contract: offer, acceptance, revocation of offer, and revocation of acceptance. Here again different problems may, ideally at least, call for different solutions and it may therefore be inappropriate to argue from the one to the other. The third point is that if the common law of contract were really concerned with *consensus* or a 'meeting of minds' between the parties, there would be no problem at all, since in every case actual receipt of a communication and knowledge of its contents would have to be established. But the concept of a meeting of minds is an importation from Continental jurisprudence, to which it more appropriately belongs. The common law is usually more interested in what a party says and does than in what he thinks. There is no theoretical objection, at common law, to a concept of constructive notice or knowledge.

The Doctrinal Basis for Notice

So far as an offer is concerned, it makes no difference in law whether the parties are together or at a distance. In both cases the offer must come to the actual knowledge of the offeree before he can accept it. The doctrinal reason for this is clear enough. It is of the essence of an acceptance that it be a response to an initial offer.[4] In consequence, letters crossing in the post cannot create a contract, even if

[4] *R v Clarke* (1927) 40 CLR 227 (HC); *Taylor v Allon* [1966] 1 QB 304 (DC).

they should be in identical terms.[5] Similarly, the finder of a lost watch has no claim in law to a reward if he was unaware that a reward had been advertised.[6]

In the case of an acceptance, however, the position is quite different. No question of response is involved, so that that particular need for actual knowledge does not exist. Conceptually, at least, the mere act of acceptance could be enough to constitute a contract.[7] The question at issue is the rather different one of whether the offeror needs to have notice that the act of acceptance has occurred as an *additional* requirement before the contract can come into being. If one accepts that an actual meeting of minds is not of the essence of a common law contract, the question whether actual notice of acceptance is necessary falls to be answered, not on doctrinal grounds, but by reference to standards of fairness and practical convenience.[8] Accordingly, while in respect of offers the common law is unable, for doctrinal reasons, to take into account whether the parties are present together at the relevant time or apart, it can and does regard such considerations as very relevant to the question whether actual notice of an acceptance must be given.

Together or Apart

It is quite clear that when the parties are together, face to face, actual communication of the acceptance must occur or at least appear to occur. In this respect the common law rule is the same as that in Continental jurisdictions[9] and hardly needs any justification. Fairness and convenience require as a norm that both parties should know when a contract has been formed. In the face-to-face situation, there are no other considerations present which might compete with that norm. On the other hand, when the parties are apart, additional elements are introduced. The risks attending transmission from a distance may make it uncertain when a message will be received or, indeed, whether it will be received at all. Even if it is received, there may be uncertainty whether it has actually come to the mind of the person to whom it was addressed. Here it becomes a question of whether the advantages to the offeror in requiring actual communication of the acceptance to him outweigh the disadvantages to the offeree and, if so, whether a balance should be struck as between them.

For reasons which will be considered later in this article the common law has decided that in the case of acceptance by post or telegraph, acceptance is deemed to be complete when the letter is posted or the telegram is left with the Post Office for

[5] *Tinn v Hoffman & Co* (1873) 29 LT 271.

[6] *R v Clarke* (1927) 40 CLR 227 (HC).

[7] Thus, it is possible for the offeror to waive communication of acceptance (*Carlill v Carbolic Smoke Ball Co* [1893] 1 QB 256) though he is, of course, not able to *impose* liability on the offeree by such means (*Felthouse v Bindley* (1862) 11 CB (NS) 869).

[8] Cf Treitel, above note 1 at 20.

[9] Schlesinger (ed), *Formation of Contracts*, vol I (1968) 157.

transmission provided that, in the words of Lord Herschell in *Henthorn v Fraser*,[10] it was 'within the contemplation of the parties' that that mode of communicating acceptance might be used. In such cases actual communication is dispensed with. On the other hand, where the parties are physically apart but in simultaneous communication with each other, as by telephone or telex, actual communication is required.[11] This is hardly surprising, since parties at each end of a telephone link are substantially in each other's presence and the risks attending communication are correspondingly similar. The grey area, for present purposes, involves those circumstances where an instantaneous mode of transmission is employed, but the parties themselves (and in particular, the offeror) are not present or available to transmit or receive messages and hence are not in instantaneous communication with each other. An example would be an acceptance transmitted by a teleprinting machine of a kind needing no operator at the receiving end, where the messages were recorded on ticker tape. A similar situation would exist where a telephoned message of acceptance was recorded by an automatic answering device attached to the offeror's telephone. Another example would be an acceptance transmitted by telephone or radio and written down by an operator at the offeror's address, but at a time when the offeror was absent from that address. In respect of this type of situation there is no direct authority and accordingly the problem is one of finding the appropriate analogy. There would seem to be four lines of authority potentially available.

Four Possible Analogies

The *Entores* Analogy

The first and most obvious approach to the question would be by reference to *Entores v Miles Far East Corporation*.[12] There, the English Court of Appeal had to decide in which country the contract had been formed in a case where an acceptance transmitted from Holland had been received on a telex machine in the London office of the offeror. The Court decided that the contract had been formed in London, the place where the acceptance had been received. In reaching this conclusion, all three Lords Justices drew heavily on the analogy of parties present together in the same place. Denning LJ also drew on the *inter praesentes* analogy, but seemed to envisage circumstances where an offer, having been received by the telex operator, would have to be conveyed subsequently to the offeror. It is perhaps a fair inference (though not a necessary one) from his judgment that in his view there would be no contract until actual receipt of the message of acceptance by the

[10] [1892] 2 Ch 27 at 33.
[11] *Entores v Miles Far East Corporation* [1955] 2 QB 327 (CA).
[12] [1955] 2 QB 327 (CA).

offeror. Nevertheless, none of the Lords Justices actually went as far as saying that this would be the case.

What seems to have happened in the *Entores* case is that two types of fact situation were confused. If, say, the parties are at either end of a telephone link it is clearly true to say that they are effectively in each other's presence. Communication between them is instantaneous and the *inter praesentes* analogy is a nearly total one. On the other hand, if it is not the parties but only telex operators who are at each end of the link, the analogy is much slighter. The operators are in instantaneous communication and consequently the risks of faulty transmission as between them are those of persons *inter praesentes*, but unless the parties themselves are on the premises, or otherwise close at hand, communication between them is neither instantaneous nor even 'almost instantaneous' and the message of acceptance must be retransmitted before it reaches the offeror. The analogy breaks down completely when there is neither a party nor even an operator present at the receiving end of the line, as in the case of an answer phone message.

The Postal Analogy

The next most obvious analogy is that of acceptance sent by post or telegraph. In the case of a telegram, indeed, the physical conditions are very similar to those which exist when a telex message is sent to the premises of an offeror who happens to be absent at the time. In each case the message is sent by an instantaneous mode of transmission and then has to be conveyed to the offeror. The only difference is that in the case of a telegram, the Post Office intervenes to handle the message at two additional points, ie, between the writing and transmission of the message and between its reception and delivery to the offeror. Transmission by telegraph may therefore increase the amount of risk but it might be questioned whether it did so sufficiently to break the analogy.

A few years ago, one learned writer was able to identify no fewer than 11 *rationales* which have been put forward for the rule in Anglo-American law that an acceptance sent by post or telegraph takes effect from receipt.[13] They included such well-known justifications as the supposed agency of the Post Office, a wish to obviate the need for an endless series of acknowledgements of receipt as between the parties, the evidential argument from the comparatively greater ease of establishing dispatch as against receipt by post, and the fact that it is in the power of an offeror to prescribe that acceptance shall take effect only on receipt, if he wishes to do so. The only *rationale* which stands analysis is the need to protect an offeree from revocation of the offer after dispatch of the acceptance.[14]

An offeror is aware until he receives some communication, or until his offer lapses from effluxion of time, that he may have a contract and he can take

[13] DM Evans, 'The Anglo-American Mailing Rule' (1966) 15 *ICLQ* 553, 558–61.

[14] Ibid at 561.

precautions accordingly. But an offeree, having posted his acceptance, has done all he can to ensure a contract and will want to be able to rely on having one. He needs to be protected from any subsequent revocation by the offeror. This *rationale* draws confirmation from the realms of comparative law. The acceptance-on-posting rule is found usually in those jurisdictions where an offer is regarded as revocable. In jurisdictions where an offer is ordinarily irrevocable, actual receipt of the acceptance is usually required. By these contrasting means, a balance of advantage is kept between offeror and offeree.[15]

On this reasoning, in cases where the use of instantaneous methods of transmission is contemplated by the parties, actual communication to the offeror ought not to be an invariable prerequisite to the formation of a contract in common law jurisdictions. True, the mere dispatch of a message ought not to be enough where there is an operator at the receiving end of the link. As Denning LJ pointed out in the *Entores* case, for the purposes of transmission, the sender and the receiving operator would effectively be dealing *inter praesentes*. But acceptance should take effect on receipt by the operator, for at that point the offeree would have done all he could to ensure communication to the offeror. By similar reasoning, an acceptance spoken into a telephone recording device should take effect at the time it ought to have been recorded at the receiving end of the link.

The Argument from the General Rule

The third possible line of approach to the problem would be by a literal reliance on a general rule that acceptances must be communicated unless waived, to which the post and telegraph rules would be seen as exceptions.

The rule that acceptances must be communicated, however, does not answer, but merely begs, the main question. The issue is not whether an acceptance must be communicated but what acts on the part of the offeree will fulfil that requirement. The post and telegraph rules are not exceptions to the requirement but applications of it.[16] Moreover, they represent the only binding authority where the parties are truly apart, and not in instantaneous communication with each other.

In other words, that acceptances must be communicated does not necessarily infer that they must come actually to the mind of the offeror and in the *inter absentes* situation there is the clear precedent of the postal and telegraph rules for requiring something much less than that.

The Analogy of Delivery

The fourth and final analogy to which recourse might be had would be that of the delivery of an acceptance by hand to the offeror's address or to a messenger

[15] Schlesinger, above note 9 at 162.
[16] Cf RN Gee (1959) 2 *Syd LR* 357, 359–60.

sent by him. So far as the first of these alternatives is concerned, there seems to be no direct authority as to whether, or in what circumstances, actual communication to the offeror is required. As to delivery to an agent nominated or sent by the offeror, a distinction has been drawn between an agent with authority to receive an acceptance and an agent having authority only to transmit it.[17] In the former case, acceptance dates from delivery to the agent; in the latter, from receipt by the offeror.

If one once accepts the existence of the postal rule, it would seem rather odd if delivery at the offeror's address should be ineffective without actual receipt in cases where posting at the post office next door would be sufficient by itself. Similarly, if delivery of an acceptance to the Post Office (over whose actions the offeror has no control) is a sufficient communication, it may seem strange that delivery to the offeror's own agent (over whom he does have control) may not be enough. The real truth about situations of this kind, it is submitted, lies in the contemplation of the parties in the particular circumstances of the case. The offeror, after all, has it in his power to prescribe actual receipt on his part as a condition of acceptance and, if he sends a messenger whose authority is clearly restricted to transmitting the acceptance, he may effectively be exercising that power. On the other hand, in cases where acceptance by posting is within the contemplation of the parties, an actual delivery of the acceptance by the offeree at the offeree's address ought to be a sufficient communication.

A Possible Solution

Available Criteria for General Rules

In the light of all this, it is submitted that there is no universal rule that an acceptance must in fact be received by the offeror before a contract can be formed, to which rule communications by post and telegraph form the only exceptions. There are gaps in the law, but there are also available well-established elements from which a general system of rules could be constructed and the gaps filled. Those elements are:

1. The prima facie requirement that an acceptance should be (or appear to have been) communicated to the offeror before a contract can come into being, unless communication has been waived.[18]
2. The right (and opportunity) an offeror has to prescribe actual receipt if he so desires.[19]

[17] *Henthorn v Fraser* [1892] 2 Ch 27 at 35–36; cf *Wright v Bigg* (1852) 15 Beav 592; *Re National Savings Bank Association* (1867) LR 4 Eq 9.

[18] *Carlill v Carbolic Smoke Ball Co* [1893] 1 QB 256, 269.

[19] Evans, above note 13 at 560.

3. A recognition that different considerations may apply depending on whether or not the parties are in each other's presence.[20]
4. The desirability, in a legal system where offers are ordinarily revocable, of redressing the balance in favour of the offeree.[21] At common law this could be said to mean that, where the parties are apart, an offeree should ordinarily have to bear the risks of transmitting the acceptance only so long as transmission is under his control.[22]
5. A recognition that the risks of transmission should pass to the offeror only if, and to the extent that, the mode of transmission used is one which the parties contemplate may be used for the purpose.[23]

Suggested General Rules

From these elements the following rules can be posited:

1. Where offeror and offeree are face to face or in instantaneous communication with each other, an acceptance must either actually be received by the offeror or reasonably appear to the offeree to have been so received.
2. Where the offeror and offeree are apart and not in instantaneous communication with each other then, unless the offeror has stipulated for actual receipt, the contract will be formed once the offeree, using a mode of transmission contemplated by the parties for the purpose, has done all he can to ensure communication to the offeror.[24]

The Rules Applied

Applying these rules, an acceptance by post or telegraph, if correctly addressed, would take effect as hitherto when posted or lodged, because this would be as far as the offeree could control its transmission. Should the parties be at each end of a telephone link, acceptance would take effect, again as hitherto, once the offeror had appeared to hear and understand it.

In the case of a telex link, the contract would be formed at that point in time when the party transmitting the acceptance (or his operator) could reasonably

[20] The reliance in the *Entores* case on the *inter praesentes* analogy is in itself evidence of this.

[21] Schlesinger, above note 9 at 162; Evans, above note 13 at 561.

[22] Compare, for example, the emphasis placed by Denning LJ in the *Entores* case on the ability and duty of an offeree at the end of an instantaneous link to check to make sure that his message has been received.

[23] Cf *Henthorn v Fraser* [1892] 2 Ch 27 at 33.

[24] Compare the Restatement of Contract (Second) Art 64, under which the contract is said to be formed as soon as the acceptance is 'put out of the offeree's possession'. This formula seems to express the same object as the rule suggested in the text, but is too narrow to cover instantaneous modes of transmission. And cf also Treitel, above note 1 at 24 in relation to telegrams.

assume that the message had been received (if there were an operator at the other end) or recorded (if there were no such operator). It would follow in such a case that the acceptance could be binding even though not in fact received by the operator or recorded and this, too, would be consistent with the dicta of Denning LJ in the *Entores* case.[25] The *rationale* would, however, be different. The acceptance would take effect even though not received or recorded, not, as Denning LJ suggested, as a consequence of the offeror's fault or neglect, but because the offeree would have given the degree of notice required by the law and the risks would accordingly have passed to the offeror. Similarly, the acceptance could take effect when received by the operator, or recorded, even though it did not subsequently come to the mind of the offeror himself. The same would apply in the case of acceptances dictated into a telephone recording device at the offeror's address provided the offeree could not reasonably have been aware of any defect in the recording apparatus, if any should exist.

Under these same rules, an acceptance delivered by hand at the offeror's ordinary address for service would take effect from delivery to his door if the post were a contemplated mode of transmission. If it were not, the result would depend on the mode of transmission contemplated in the particular case. Delivery to a receptionist at the offeree's address would, for example, ordinarily be sufficient, unless the parties had in the particular circumstances contemplated delivery into the hands of the offeror. Rather similar considerations would apply to transmission of an acceptance by telephone, where the offeror himself was not available to take the call. A message left with a member of his staff or a responsible member of his family might be taken to fall within the contemplation of the parties in the ordinary case. On the other hand, a message left with a child or with an office cleaner clearly would not. In practical terms, what the 'contemplation of the parties' would require of the offeror in the ordinary case would be simply that he acts reasonably in the circumstances.

The Place of Formation

The discussion so far has been directed to the time when a contract is formed. Another question, relevant in private international law, is the place at which it is formed. The rule adopted by the common law is in effect that a contract is formed at the place where the last fact occurs which is necessary for its formation. In the case of acceptance by post or telegraph, this means the place of posting or dispatch.[26] In the case of telex, the *Entores* case established that it is the place of receipt. Again, in the case of telephoned acceptances, Canadian and Australian

[25] [1955] 2 QB 327, 332 (CA).
[26] Evans, above note 13.

courts have held, in circumstances where the parties were at either end of a telephone link, that the place of receipt is the place where the contract is formed.[27] There is still, however, no direct authority on cases such as those where instantaneous modes of transmission are used but the offeror is absent at the time the acceptance is transmitted. Accordingly there is still room for the application, to this particular problem, of rules such as the two suggested above in relation to the time of formation.

Under those rules, where the parties are apart, the contract is formed when the offeree has done all he can to ensure communication to the offeror. On that basis, applying the ordinary common law rule, the place at which the contract would be formed would be the place where the message of acceptance is received, or appears to have been received, at that point in time when the offeror has fulfilled the requirements for communication resting upon him.

In practice, this would mean, as hitherto, that contracts by post or telegraph would normally be formed at the place of posting or lodging and, in the case of parties in simultaneous communication with each other, at the place of receipt. But in the case, say, of a message recorded on an automatic answering device, the place of formation would be the place where the message is recorded, even if, at that particular time, the offeror should happen to be in another jurisdiction. This would follow because the offeree would be in a position to control its transmission only thus far. Accordingly, to the two rules already posited is added another:

3. The place at which a contract is formed is that point in the line of transmission between offeree and offeror which the acceptance reaches, or can reasonably be expected by the offeree to have reached, at the moment transmission passes beyond his control.

Summary

A general rule that acceptances must always come to the mind of the offeror (the post and telegraph rule being the only exception) before a contract can be formed would be unduly restrictive and, moreover, has no overwhelming authority to support it. There being no doctrinal necessity for actual communication, the requirements of the law fall to be assessed by other criteria. The basic purpose should be to give the offeree reasonable protection from the risk that the offer will be

[27] *Re Viscount Supply Co* (1963) 40 DLR (2d) 501; *Aviet v Smith and Carls Pty Ltd* (1956) 73 WN (NSW) 274; *Dewhurst v Cawrse* [1960] VR 278. This last case illustrates the impossibility, in some instances of oral communication, of determining who was the offeror and who the offeree.

revoked before his acceptance comes to the notice of the offeror. Where there is no such risk, as where the parties are face to face or in instantaneous communication with each other, nothing stands in the way of requiring actual communication. But where such a risk does exist, it is proper that the offeree bear it only so long as he can control the transmission of the acceptance, subject always to the offeror's right to stipulate for actual receipt and to the overall contemplation of the parties. By the same token, the place of formation should be the point the acceptance has reached at the time the contract is formed. It follows that the mere use of an instantaneous mode of *transmission* would never by itself be decisive. It would always be necessary to know in addition whether the parties were thereby placed in instantaneous *communication* with each other.[28]

[28] This article has been concerned only to generalise from existing principles. Much more thoroughgoing reforms, particularly of the postal rule, have been advocated elsewhere. See, eg, Ian R Macneil, 'Time of Acceptance' (1964) 112 *U Pa L Rev* 947; Evans, above note 13 at 562 *et seq*.

4

Dunlop v Lambert: The Search for a Rationale

Introduction

In has been one of the givens of the common law that if a promisor (A) contracts with a promisee (B) to confer a benefit on a third person (C) who is not a party, and if A then commits a breach, neither B nor C can recover substantial damages in contract. In C's case, this is because of the privity rule and in B's, because he is taken to have suffered no loss. The result, to adapt words used by Lord Keith of Kinkel in *GUS Property Management v Littlewoods Mail Order Stores Ltd*,[1] can be that potential claims disappear into some legal black hole, so that the wrongdoer escapes scot-free.

The challenge posed by that result has been to find ways of avoiding it. One such way has been through a revival in modern times of the rule in *Dunlop v Lambert*.[2] That was a case where the House of Lords held a plaintiff consignor could recover substantial damages from a carrier for goods lost at sea, notwithstanding that, by the time of the loss, they had become the property of the consignee. That decision was in 1977 applied to another carriage contract by the House of Lords in *The Albazero*,[3] though with the qualification that the rule would not assist the consignor if the contracting parties had contemplated a second contract, such as a bill of lading, coming into existence between the carrier and the actual owner, which regulated the liabilities between them in relation to the goods carried. The rule in this qualified form has since been applied to building contracts by the House of Lords in *St Martins Property Corporation Ltd v Sir Robert McAlpine Ltd*[4] and by the Court of Appeal in *Darlington Borough Council v Wiltshier Northern Ltd*[5] and (more recently) in *Alfred McAlpine Construction Co Ltd v Panatown Ltd*.[6]

1 1982 SLT 533, 538.

2 (1839) 6 Cl & F 600; 7 ER 824. Another analysis of the *Dunlop v Lambert* line of cases, from a different point of view and with a different conclusion, can be found in ch 2 of Cashmore, *Parties to a Contract of Carriage* (Lloyds of London Press Ltd, London, 1990).

3 [1977] AC 744.

4 *Sub nom Linden Gardens Trust Ltd v Lenesta Sludge Disposals Ltd* [1994] 1 AC 85.

5 [1995] 1 WLR 68.

6 [1998] CLC 636 (reversed [2001] 1 AC 518, three of their Lordships nevertheless treating *Dunlop v Lambert* as applicable). See also Coote, 'The Performance Interest, *Panatown*, and the Problem of Loss' (2001) 117 *LQR* 81–95 reprinted as Chapter 9 of *Assumption*.

Agency and Trust

In the modern cases on the rule in *Dunlop v Lambert*, it has been taken for granted that a promisee who recovers substantial damages must account for them to the third-party owner. If this were because the promisee had contracted as an agent or trustee for the owner, the *Dunlop v Lambert* rule would be easily explained but, by the same token, it would not be a separate rule. Some of the cases on carriage during the period leading up to *Dunlop v Lambert* were, in fact, decided on the basis of the consignor's having been an agent. But they were distinguished on that very ground by Brandon J at first instance in *The Albazero*.[7] In the Court of Appeal, Roskill LJ dismissed an argument that the early cases supporting the rule were based on agency as a mere 'ex post facto rationalisation' finding 'no shadow of support from the language used in the decided cases'.[8] And as Lord Diplock said when the case reached the House of Lords[9] the rule 'does not fit easily into the law of trusts as it [has] been developed by the courts of equity'. For one thing, the third-party beneficiary is unable to compel the promisee to sue on his behalf, a point also made by Lord Goff in *White v Jones*.[10] The rule is, after all, an invention of the common law.

The Cases before *Dunlop v Lambert*

The various cases on carriage of goods which immediately preceded *Dunlop v Lambert* were, like that case itself, decided at a time when delivery by the consignor to a common carrier was treated as delivery to the consignee. Accordingly, both property in the goods and risk ordinarily passed to him at that point. To this general rule, though, there were exceptions.[11] It was open to a consignor to contract on the basis that both property and risk remained with him throughout the carriage. He could also contract on the basis that, though property passed to the consignee, he retained the risk. In both those cases, loss of the goods would mean a resulting loss to the consignor.

The case of *Davis and Jordan v James*,[12] decided by the Court of King's Bench in 1770, marked what seems to have been a departure from the usual pattern.

[7] [1977] AC 744, 786.

[8] [1977] AC 744, 815, though see, also, the suggestion by Lord Diplock at 843 that they 'could have been explained on the ground of agency and that one of them was so explained by the writer of the head note'.

[9] [1977] AC 744, 845.

[10] [1995] 2 AC 207, 267.

[11] It was on this point that Lord Cottenham LC, in *Dunlop v Lambert* (1839) 6 Cl & F 600, 626; 7 ER 824, 834, thought *Joseph v Knox*, below note 15, to be a 'very strong' case.

[12] (1770) 5 Burr 2680; 98 ER 407.

The carrier there had urged that, on ordinary principles, property in the goods had passed to the consignee when the consignor had handed them over to the carrier and that the action ought therefore to have been brought in the name of the consignee. That argument was not accepted. Lord Mansfield, with whom Willes and Ashford JJ agreed, declared that vesting of the property 'does not enter into the present question'. He continued:[13]

> This is an action upon the agreement between the [consignors] and the carrier. The [consignors] were to pay him. Therefore, the action is properly brought by the persons who agreed with him and were to pay him.

Subsequently, a similar approach was followed by the Court of King's Bench in *Moore v Wilson*[14] and by Lord Ellenborough in *Joseph v Knox*,[15] though the latter added that he thought the consignors would hold the sum recovered 'as trustees' for the real owner.[16]

A modern lawyer would readily agree that a contracting party will, by reason of that very fact, qualify to recover damages against another party in breach. What makes the three cases unusual is the apparent assumption, evidenced by Lord Ellenborough's reference to 'trustees', that the damages recoverable by the consignor were to be substantial and not merely nominal, whoever might own the goods. One suggested explanation has been that, at the relevant period, the law of damages was still in a primitive state, in that the distinction between the two kinds of damages had not yet emerged.[17] Whether that was so or not, the modern cases take it for granted that in *Dunlop v Lambert*, the House of Lords approved and confirmed the three earlier cases. Reliance has been placed particularly on the following passage from the penultimate paragraph in the speech of Lord Cottenham LC:[18]

> [I]f the consignor made a special contract with the carrier, and the carrier agreed to take the goods from him and to deliver them to any particular place, the special contract supersedes the necessity of showing the ownership in the goods; and that, by the authority of the cases of *Davis v James* and *Joseph v Knox* the consignor, the person making the contract with the carrier, may maintain the action, though the goods may be the goods of the consignee.

Bailment as an Explanation

Assuming for the present that the received reading of *Dunlop v Lambert* is correct, one reasonably plausible explanation for the rule might have been found

[13] Ibid at 2681; 98 ER 407, 408.
[14] (1787) 1 Term Rep 659; 99 ER 1306.
[15] (1813) 3 Camp 320; 170 ER 1397.
[16] (1813) 3 Camp 320, 322; 170 ER 1397.
[17] *The Albazero* [1977] AC 744, 841 per Lord Diplock.
[18] (1839) 6 Cl & F 600, 626–27; 7 ER 824, 834.

in the law of bailment, as was pointed out by Lord Diplock in *The Albazero*.[19] A carrier of goods is a bailee and, as such, is estopped from denying his bailor's title. According to Lord Diplock, there was at the time a presumption that it was the consignee who was the bailor, and that the consignor was the bailor's agent to make the contract of carriage. But that presumption could be rebutted, and action could be brought by a consignor who had contracted as bailor on his own account. As between the parties to that bailment, the true ownership of the goods would, because of the estoppel, be irrelevant. Brandon J, at first instance in *The Albazero*,[20] was doubtless thinking along those lines when he ascribed the *Dunlop v Lambert* rule to the operation of an estoppel. On the other hand, in the Court of Appeal in that case, Roskill LJ, with whom the other members of the Court agreed, rejected the estoppel explanation as a mere 'ex post facto rationalisation' which, like agency, found 'no shadow of support' from the language used in the decided cases.[21] For his part, Ormrod LJ thought that what underlay the rule was the principle *res inter alios acta*.[22] In the end, even Lord Diplock failed to adopt the bailment explanation for the rule. Moreover, if bailment was indeed the justification, it could have no application to the cases which have since applied the rule to building contracts.

Lord Diplock's Explanation

For his part, Lord Diplock found the reasoning in Lord Cottenham's speech in *Dunlop v Lambert* 'baffling'.[23] His concern was not with the bulk of the speech but with the final two paragraphs, and in particular with the passage quoted above which ends with the statement that the person making the contract with the carrier might maintain the action even if the goods were those of the consignee. Because it was so long-standing and well established, Lord Diplock was not prepared to depart from 'the broad proposition' that the consignor might recover substantial damages if there were privity of contract with the carrier though, if the goods were not his property or at his risk, he would be accountable to the true owner for the proceeds.[24] However, he considered the rule to be necessary only where there was no contract between the carrier and the person who sustained the loss. In sum, he concluded:[25]

[19] [1977] AC 744, 841–42. See also NE Palmer, *Bailment*, 2nd edn (Sweet & Maxwell, London, 1991) 377–78.

[20] [1977] AC 744, 792–93.

[21] [1977] AC 744, 815. And see 803–04 per Cairns LJ.

[22] [1977] AC 744, 824.

[23] Ibid at 843.

[24] Ibid at 844, 847.

[25] Ibid at 847 (italics added).

> The only way in which I find it possible to rationalise the rule in *Dunlop v Lambert* … is to treat is as an application of the principle that … where it is in the contemplation of the parties that the proprietary interests in the goods may be transferred from one owner to another after the contract has been entered into and before the breach which causes loss or damage to the goods, an original party to the contract, if such be the intention of them both, *is to be treated in law* as having entered into the contract for the benefit of all persons who have or may acquire an interest in the goods before they are lost or damaged, and is entitled to recover by way of damages for breach of contract the actual loss sustained by those for whose benefit the contract is entered into.

His Lordship drew an analogy with *Waters v Monarch Fire and Life Assurance Co*[26] where it was held that a warehouseman could insure goods as being in his possession, and recover the full amount of any loss, for the benefit of those who owned them.

On the face of it, that might well appear to support the notion that a consignor could recover damages for the benefit of everyone who had an interest in the goods. There is the problem, though, that in the *Waters* case, Lord Campbell CJ saw the result as turning on ratification by the owners and, hence, presumably on the existence of an agency.[27] Lord Diplock,[28] by contrast, seems to have seen the *Dunlop v Lambert* rule as depending on some sort of fiction ('treated in law') quite independently of any ratification, albeit a fiction conditioned by the contemplation and intention of the parties. It was on this reasoning, he said, that the rule would not extend to cases where it was contemplated that the carrier would also enter into separate contracts with subsequent owners of the goods. There could be no sensible business reason for inferring that a carrier would intend to accept concurrent liabilities to be sued by both or all of the parties with whom he had contracted for a loss or damage which only one of them had sustained.

The *St Martins* Case

In the *St Martins* case,[29] Lord Browne-Wilkinson also thought it proper,

> to treat the parties as having entered into the contract on the footing that [the promisee] would be entitled to enforce contractual rights for the benefit of those who suffered from defective performance but who, under the terms of the contract, could not acquire any right to hold [the promisor] liable for breach.

[26] (1856) 5 El & Bl 870; 119 ER 705.

[27] (1856) 5 El & Bl 870, 881; 119 ER 705, 709. Reference was made to the goods being 'entrusted' but not in the sense of an equitable trust.

[28] *The Albazero* [1977] AC 744, 847–48.

[29] *St Martins Property Corporation Ltd v Sir Robert McAlpine Ltd* [1994] 1 AC 85, 115.

He saw the rule as providing a remedy where no other would be available, one which a rational system ought to make available. He did, though, add the comment that:[30]

> If *pursuant to the terms of the original building contract*, the contractors have undertaken liability to the ultimate purchasers to remedy defects appearing after they acquired the property, it is manifest the case will not fall within the rationale of *Dunlop v Lambert*. If the ultimate purchaser is given a direct cause of action against the contractor (as is the consignee or endorsee under a bill of lading) the case falls outside the rationale of the rule. The original building owner will not be entitled to recover damages for loss suffered by others who can themselves sue for such loss.

The words italicised are a little puzzling since, if the ultimate purchaser had a direct cause of action under a separate contract, it ought not to matter whether or not that separate contract was entered into pursuant to the original building contract. Contemplation is all that is required, at least according to Lord Diplock's formulation. And his Lordship can hardly have meant an undertaking by the contractors as part of the original contract, unless he had in mind cases where the ultimate purchaser was also a contracting party to that original contract. Any claim the latter might make would, of course, otherwise fail for want of privity and consideration.

The *Panatown* Case

The most recent discussion of the rationale for the *Dunlop v Lambert* rule was by the Court of Appeal in *Alfred McAlpine Construction Co Ltd v Panatown Ltd.*[31] That case arose out of a contract to design and build an office block and multistorey car park on JTC standard terms, on a site in Cambridge, McAlpine being the contractor and Panatown, the employers. The latter alleged that the building as completed was seriously defective and might have to be demolished. However, at no stage had they owned the building site, which belonged to an associated company, Unex Investment Property Ltd, the actual developers.

The case came before the Court of Appeal on an issue of law under the Interim Award of an arbitrator. The judgment of the Court (Evans, Hutchison and Mantell LJJ) was delivered by Evans LJ who defined the question for decision as being:[32]

> Are Panatown debarred from recovering substantial as opposed to nominal damages, by reason of the fact that they were not and are not, owners of the land?

It was held that the employers were entitled, prima facie, to rely on the *Dunlop v Lambert* rule. Nor were they debarred from doing so by the existence of a separate

30 Ibid (italics added).
31 [1998] CLC 636.
32 Ibid at 638.

'Duty of Care Deed' which the site owners and the contractors had entered into on the same day as the building contract. It had imposed a limited liability for want of care quite different from the liability accepted by the contractors under the building contract itself. The parties could not have intended that a deed in those terms would deprive the employers of their contractual rights.

After a review of the cases, Evans LJ concluded that the rationale of the *Dunlop v Lambert* rule was 'contract based' and that the promisee's right to substantial damages arose because the parties to the contract intended or contemplated that it should. In his view, the general rule that a plaintiff cannot recover damages in respect of another person's loss 'can be modified by agreement, express or implied, between the parties concerned'.[33]

This formulation obviously derives from the speech of Lord Diplock in *The Albazero* but with, it is submitted, at least one vital difference. It is true that, according to Lord Diplock, much depends on the contemplation and intention of the parties. But ultimately, on his reasoning, the right of the consignor to substantial damages arises because he is 'treated in law', by what one takes to be a kind of fiction, as having entered into the contract for the benefit of third persons who might acquire an interest.[34] In other words, the right to recover substantial damages is derived by force of law.

By contrast, and on the assumption that the promisee in this type of case does suffer no loss because the loss is that of the third party, Evans LJ seems to be saying that the contracting parties themselves are able to impose a liability in damages upon one another which would necessarily go well beyond a genuine pre-estimate of the promisee's loss. In any other context, that would be a penalty.[35] Moreover, though the learned Lord Justice referred to the promisee's being liable to account for his damages to the third-party owners, his actual formulation would seem to allow the possibility of the parties also agreeing that he should be able to recover substantial damages without having to do so. On both counts, those views would have to be novel, always provided it is really true that in such cases the promisee himself suffers no loss.

Thus far, we have seen that the rule in *Dunlop v Lambert* cannot be based on agency or trusts. We have also seen it explained with varying degrees of plausibility as:

(a) an incident of privity of contract, antedating the emergence of a modern law of damages;
(b) an incident of the law of bailment;
(c) the result of an estoppel;
(d) the result of the principle *res inter alios acta*;
(e) a rule of law depending on what appears to be a fiction conditioned by the contemplation and intention of the parties; and, most recently
(f) a creation of the parties' own agreement.

[33] Ibid at 644.
[34] Quoted above at note 25.
[35] Cf Palmer, above note 19 at 380–81.

In the face of this degree of uncertainty, two questions spring to mind. 'Can *Dunlop v Lambert* really have decided what has since been ascribed to it?' and 'Is it really correct that a contracting party such as a consignor or building employer suffers no loss just because he does not own the relevant goods or land respectively?'

What did *Dunlop v Lambert* Really Decide?

If we refer back to the previously cited passage from Lord Cottenham's speech,[36] it will be noticed that the contract which is said to supersede the necessity of showing ownership, and to enable the contracting party to maintain the action, is not just any contract but is denoted specifically as a 'special contract'.

At the time at which his Lordship spoke, the ordinary significance of a 'special' contract with a carrier was that it introduced specially agreed terms and for that reason could have the effect of altering the status of the carrier in respect of the particular goods to be carried. His liability could cease to be the 'insurer's' liability of a common carrier and, subject to the specially agreed terms, become that of an ordinary carrier, for negligence only. But if that were what Lord Cottenham had in mind when he used the word 'special', it is difficult to see how the distinction between the two types of liability could be relevant to the consignor's right to maintain his action. Nor could that distinction have any bearing on the question whether recovery by the consignor would be for his own benefit, or for the benefit of others.

It is believed that an indication of what his Lordship actually meant can be drawn from the final paragraph of his speech, immediately following the passage already quoted. The relevant part reads:[37]

> But further, the authorities seem to me to establish that the consignor is entitled to maintain the action where there is a contract to deliver at a particular place, provided the risk appears in fact to be still on him. The circumstances of paying the freight or insurance, though a circumstance to be taken into consideration, is not in itself conclusive on the question of property, nor is it conclusive on the right to sue. The Lord President held it to be conclusive on these points, and therefore shut out from the jury the consideration of other facts in the case. In so doing, I think that his direction was erroneous. I think that there are two objections to the mode at which he left the case to the jury: first, that he withdrew from their consideration the question, whether, in fact, the goods had been delivered to the carrier on the risk of the consignors or the consignee; and secondly, that he directed the jury to find a verdict without previously determining the question, whether there was a special contract between the consignors and the consignee, which might have enabled the pursuers to recover in the action.

[36] (1839) 6 Cl & F 600, 626–27; 7 ER 824, 834, quoted above at note 18.
[37] (1839) 6 Cl & F 600, 627; 7 ER 824, 834.

The concern in that paragraph is with the allocation of risk. Two questions are identified. The first is at whose risk, on the facts, the goods had been delivered to the carrier. That is something which does not depend exclusively on ownership and which could, for example, be settled by a specially agreed term of the contract with the carrier. The second question concerns the possible existence of a separate special contract between the consignor and the consignee which, in its turn, might also have had the effect of enabling the consignor to recover in its action against the carrier.

In *The Albazero*,[38] Lord Diplock thought there must have been a misprint in Clark and Finelly's report and that, in respect of the second of these questions, the Lord Chancellor had actually intended to refer to a contract between the consignor and the carrier. With respect, it is submitted that that was not the case and that what was printed was what was meant. That becomes much clearer, as does the meaning of both paragraphs and the significance of the allocation of risk, if reference is made to an earlier portion of Lord Cottenham's speech. After stating the then general rule that delivery to the carrier was to be regarded as delivery to the consignee, to whom risk thereupon passed, his Lordship continued:[39]

> But though the authorities all establish the general inference I have stated, yet that general inference is capable of being varied by the circumstances of any special arrangement between the parties, or of any particular mode of dealing between them. If a particular contract be proved *between the consignor and the consignee*, and the circumstance of the payment of the freight and insurance is not alone a conclusive evidence of ownership, as where the party undertaking to consign, undertakes to deliver at a particular place, the property, till it reaches that place and is delivered according to the terms of the contract, *is at the risk of the consignor*. And again, though in general the following the directions of the consignee, and delivering the goods to a particular carrier, will relieve the consignor from the risk, he may make such a special contract, that, though delivering the goods to the carrier specially intimated by the consignee, *the risk may remain with him; and the consignor may, by a contract with the carrier, make the carrier liable to himself.* In an infinite variety of circumstances, the ordinary rule may turn out not to be that which regulates the liabilities of the parties.

What, it is submitted, the Lord Chancellor was doing here was indicating what, in the context of the case before him, he meant by 'particular' or 'special' contracts, in effect providing an internal dictionary. The passage confirms that he had in mind two particular categories of special contract, one with the consignee and the other with the carrier, and both of them concerned with the allocation of risk to the consignor. The connection between that paragraph and the final paragraph of the speech is unmistakable. Property and risk being severable, that explains why, as his Lordship stated in his penultimate paragraph, the sort of special contracts to which he referred superseded 'the necessity of showing the ownership in the

[38] [1977] AC 744, 843.
[39] (1839) 6 Cl & F 600, 620–21; 7 ER 824, 832 (italics added).

goods'. And, of course, it confirms that there was no misprint of the kind suggested by Lord Diplock.

If this analysis is correct, it would follow that there is, after all, nothing very radical or mysterious about the actual *Dunlop v Lambert* decision. It would also follow that the purported 'rule' far from being based on principle, is actually the result of a misunderstanding of Lord Cottenham's speech. No wonder, therefore, that the explanations so far advanced for the rule carry so little conviction.

Does the Promisee Really Suffer No Loss?

That, then, raises the question whether there exists any other principle on the basis of which the rule could be justified, independently of the actual decision in *Dunlop v Lambert*. Since the governing principle is that damages in contract are compensatory, that seems unlikely so long as it is maintained that the loss is suffered by the third party and not by the promisee. But is it really true that the consignor or building employer does not suffer the loss?

In an article in the *Cambridge Law Journal*,[40] I made the point that the problem in these fact situations stems from the reluctance of common lawyers to accept in this context something they are quite prepared to accept in other contexts. It is that the performance of a contractual promise, and the contractual right to that performance, are themselves of economic value, the measure of which is at least the cost of obtaining alternative performance or of making good any defects, but which can also include consequential loss. What has happened is that contractual loss, the loss of the contracted performance, has been confused with loss, de facto, of the enjoyment of the benefits of contracted performance. It is a confusion between benefits in law and benefits in fact.

The difference between the two becomes obvious if one takes, for example, the case of a father who wishes to purchase a new refrigerator for the use of his daughter who is about to set up house for herself. If the refrigerator is defective, or if it is not delivered, the daughter's enjoyment of the benefits of its use will be affected. But it is the father who suffers contractual loss and it is he who is contractually entitled to the performance for which, after all, he has paid by providing consideration for the contract. The fact that the performance may be to what is, or may become, the property of a third party is, in the contractual sense, merely accidental. The third party loses only the practical benefits of the performance. In some circumstances, this might entitle her to a claim in tort for damage or for loss of enjoyment. But loss of enjoyment, per se, is not a recognised head of damages in contract unless it has been specifically contracted for. In turn, it is the contracting party who, in the words of Parke B in *Robinson v Harman*,[41] should 'be placed in the same situation

[40] 'Contract Damages, Ruxley, and the Performance Interest' [1997] *CLJ* 537, 550 *et seq*, reprinted as Chapter 8 of *Assumption*.

[41] (1848) 1 Exch 850, 855; 154 ER 363, 365.

with respect to damages, as if the contract had been performed'. It is he who ought to be able to recover the damages equivalent of what he bargained for.

In the *St Martins* case,[42] Lord Griffiths appeared, at least on one view, to have grasped the nettle and to have accepted that the right to performance has a value equivalent at least to the cost of obtaining performance. He pointed out[43] that, in everyday life, contracts for work and labour are constantly placed by those having no proprietary interest in the property on which the work is done. He instanced a husband contracting for work to be done to a matrimonial home belonging to the wife. Should the work be done ineffectively, the husband would suffer loss because he would not have received 'the bargain for which he had contracted', the measure of damages being the cost of having the defects made good. Any other result would, in his view, be 'absurd'.

On the other hand, it has to be admitted that, while the other members of the House expressed sympathy with this approach,[44] none of them accepted it as part of his ratio. Moreover, there may be a certain degree of ambiguity in Lord Griffiths' discussion of his principle. At one point, he said:[45]

> In cases such as the present the person who places the contract has suffered financial loss because he has to spend money to give him the benefit of the bargain which the defendant had promised but failed to deliver.

And four sentences later he added:[46]

> The Court will of course wish to be satisfied that the repairs have been or are likely to be carried out but if they are carried out the cost of doing them must fall upon the defendant who broke his contract.

In his textbook, *The Law of Contract*,[47] Professor Treitel has taken these references to mean that Lord Griffiths was saying no more than that the promisee recovers damages in respect of his own loss in making alternative arrangements for the third party to receive the intended benefit. He points out that that reasoning would be consistent with something said in *Beswick v Beswick*.[48] Arguably, it might also gain support from *Dunlop v Lambert* itself, in that the consignor there had, before the hearing, reimbursed the consignee for its loss.[49] But, if this were all Lord Griffiths meant to convey, why should the other members of the House have thought his principle a novel one and have chosen to apply the *Dunlop v Lambert* rule instead? Why, too, Lord Griffiths' reference to the husband having suffered loss, not because he had paid the cost of making good, but because he did not receive the bargain for which he had contracted? Certainly, Dillon and Steyn LJJ, in *Darlington Borough*

[42] [1994] 1 AC 85, 96–98.
[43] Ibid at 96–97.
[44] Ibid at 95 per Lord Keith ('much force'), at 96 per Lord Bridge. And see at 112 per Lord Browne-Wilkinson.
[45] [1994] 1 AC 85, 97.
[46] Ibid.
[47] 9th edn (Sweet & Maxwell, London, 1995) 546.
[48] [1968] AC 58, 102.
[49] A similar point was made by Ormrod LJ in *The Albazero* [1977] AC 744, 823.

Council v Wiltshier Northern Ltd,[50] cannot have thought that the promisee's right to substantial damages turned on his benefiting the third party. Both thought that what he did with his damages should be no concern of the law.[51]

Ought the Promisee to be Accountable?

Merely as a matter of principle, the ordinary rule would require that any damages recovered by the contracting party should be his to do with as he wills. The fact that the supposed rule in *Dunlop v Lambert* went the other way is hardly conclusive if it is accepted that that rule was itself based not on principle but on a misunderstanding. After all, it is the promisee who has paid for the performance and he who, in the contractual sense, has suffered the loss. Whether, having recovered the damages equivalent of performance, he should decide not to pass on those damages should be a matter between the third party and himself. In the absence of any collateral contract between them to the contrary, he should be as free to withhold substitute performance as he would be free to withhold any other form of gift. It is reassuring to find that a party's right freely to dispose of his damages has had the support of such authorities as Lord Goddard CJ,[52] the High Court of Australia,[53] and Kerr[54] and Staughton LJJ[55] as well as Steyn and Dillon LJJ.

No doubt the contrary view stems largely from a reluctance (again, in some contexts but not in others)[56] to allow a contracting party to collect a 'windfall'. The short answer to that objection is that to receive the damages equivalent of what one has bargained and paid for cannot be a windfall in any ordinary sense of that term.

It has to be admitted, though, that this last assertion is not so easily made where the damages claimed are for consequential losses which have befallen the third-party beneficiary. In carriage cases like *Dunlop v Lambert* and *The Albazero*, the loss was not of the cost of obtaining alternative performance, but of the goods themselves. If the consignor does not own the goods, and if they are not being carried at his risk, it might understandably be questioned how their loss could be accounted a loss to him rather than to their actual owner.

In the already mentioned article on the performance interest,[57] I suggested that a promisor's responsibility for consequential loss is just as much a part of the contractual bargain as is the duty to perform. Thus, in contracts of carriage, the carrier contracts to avoid loss of the goods, or to take care to do so, just as

[50] [1995] 1 WLR 68.
[51] [1995] 1 WLR 68, 75–76 and 80–81 respectively.
[52] *James v Hutton and Cook Ltd* [1950] 1 KB 9, 15.
[53] *Bellgrove v Eldridge* (1954) 90 CLR 613, 620 per Dixon CJ, Webb and Taylor JJ.
[54] *Dean v Ainley* [1987] 1 WLR 1729, 1737–38.
[55] *Ruxley Electronics Ltd v Forsyth* [1994] 1 WLR 650, 657.
[56] Coote, above note 40 at 548–49.
[57] Ibid at 551–52.

much as he contracts to carry them. The carrier's failure ought, therefore, just as much to sound in substantial damages to the promisee. Once again, if it does not, the carrier may escape scot-free since, absent a right of action in tort, the third party could not bring a claim. The carrier would be unable, in any realistic sense, to assume contractual liability for the loss. Lord Griffiths himself[58] distinguished between the loss by a husband who had contracted for repairs to a roof and the loss of a cargo in *The Albazero*. But the point he made about that case was that, because of its separate contract with the carrier, the goods owner was itself in a position to sue.

On the other hand, the recovery of damages, at least for consequential loss by the promisee, would obviously be rather more broadly acceptable if it were held to be for the benefit of the true owner. And for that result in the context of contracts of carriage, the rule in *Dunlop v Lambert*, principled or not, can be regarded as authority. It would also give special point to the distinction that was recognised in the *Panatown* case between the building employer's right to substantial damages for defective performance and the site owner's rights to be indemnified in respect of its own separate losses under the 'Duty of Care Deed'.

Conclusion

In the *Panatown* case, Evans LJ saw Lord Griffiths' principle not as an alternative route to the same result as the rule in *Dunlop v Lambert*, but as being itself the underlying basis for the rule. It has been suggested in this article that the actual decision in *Dunlop v Lambert* has been misunderstood and provides no principled basis for the rule ascribed to it. It has also been suggested that a possible alternative justification for the rule might be found in the performance principle, though, in the case of consequential loss, the damages might have to be treated as being recovered for the benefit of the third party.

If this were so, it would follow that, at least in respect of the performance interest, Evans LJ and the Court of Appeal were right, after all, to say that the rationale of the rule is 'contract based'. In consequence, no question of penalty would arise. It would also mean that, since those three early cases which preceded *Dunlop v Lambert*, the law had virtually come full circle. In *Davis and Jordan v James*,[59] *Moore v Wilson*,[60] and *Joseph v Knox*,[61] it will be remembered, the judges seem to have agreed that the consignor's right to recover substantial damages for breach followed from the mere fact of his being the contracting party, quite independently of any questions of ownership and risk.

[58] [1994] 1 AC 85, 97.
[59] (1770) 5 Burr 2680; 98 ER 407.
[60] (1787) 1 Term Rep 659; 99 ER 1306.
[61] (1813) 3 Camp 320; 170 ER 1397.

5

Sale of Goods at Auction Without Reserve

There has long been argument over the legal position when an auctioneer, having announced that a sale of goods would be 'without reserve', fails to sell to the highest bona fide bidder. This article explores the extent to which that question has been answered by the English Court of Appeal in the case of *Barry v Davies*.

Sales of goods at auction without reserve can hardly be rare events. Yet on the evidence of the text books, the legal effect of such sales seems never to have been fully tested in the reported cases of England,[1] Canada,[2] Australia,[3] or New Zealand[4] and has rested, essentially, on the obiter dicta of a single reported case.

Two Nineteenth-Century Cases

Warlow v Harrison

In all four countries, the starting point has been the judgment of the Court of Exchequer Chamber delivered by Martin B in *Warlow v Harrison*[5] some 140 years ago. The defendant, an auctioneer, had advertised the sale 'without reserve' of a mare, 'the property of a gentleman'. The plaintiff, Warlow, bid 50 guineas, whereupon the owner bid an additional guinea. Having been told the last bidder was the owner, Warlow declined to bid further and the auctioneer, having accepted the owner's bid, knocked down the lot to him. There was no question of the plaintiff's being able to claim ownership of the mare since it had not been knocked down to him. Accordingly, his claim was made against the auctioneer. Both before the Court of Queen's Bench[6] and on appeal to the Exchequer Chamber,[7] his case was

[1] Eg, Furmston, *Cheshire, Fifoot and Furmston's Law of Contract* (13th edn, 1996) 32–33; *Benjamin's Sale of Goods* (5th edn, 1997) para 2-005, 107–08; Treitel, *The Law of Contract* (10th edn, 1999) 142.
[2] Eg, Waddams, *The Law of Contracts* (4th edn, 1999) 26–27.
[3] Eg, Carter and Harland, *Contract Law in Australia* (3rd edn, 1996) 31–32.
[4] Eg, Burrows, Finn and Todd, *Law of Contract in New Zealand* (1977) 44–46.
[5] (1858) 1 El & El 295; (1859) 1 El & El 309.
[6] (1858) 1 El & El 295.
[7] (1858) 1 El & El 309.

based on a plea that the auctioneer had become the agent of the plaintiff, as bidder, to complete the sale.[8] On this point he failed, but the Court of Exchequer Chamber gave him leave to amend his pleadings so as to enable 'the real question in controversy between the parties' to be determined.

Delivering judgment, Martin B referred to cases on such unilateral-type contracts as those promising a reward for the return of lost property, and continued:[9]

> Upon the same principle, it seems to us that the highest bona fide bidder at an auction may sue the auctioneer as upon a contract that the sale shall be without reserve. We think the auctioneer who puts the property up for sale upon such a condition pledges himself that the sale shall be without reserve; or, in other words, contracts that it shall be so; and that this contract is made with the highest bona fide bidder; and, in case of a breach of it, that he has a right of action against the auctioneer ... We think the auctioneer has contracted that the sale shall be without reserve; and that the contract is broken upon a bid being made by or on behalf of the owner, whether it be during the time when the property is under the hammer, or it be the last bid upon which the article is knocked down; in either case the sale is not 'without reserve,' and the contract of the auctioneer is broken.

In other words, if the pleadings were changed, the Court indicated it would have been prepared to hold that the plaintiff, as the highest bona fide bidder, could recover damages against the auctioneer for breach of a collateral contract by the auctioneer to sell without reserve.

Mainprice v Westley

Warlow has to be contrasted with the decision of three judges of the Court of Queen's Bench in *Mainprice v Westley*,[10] heard only a few years later. There, land and a shop had been advertised for 'peremptory sale' by public auction, and it seems not to have been disputed that that expression meant the sale was to be without reserve. Certainly, Blackburn J, delivering the judgment of the Court, was clear that, if there had in fact been a contract on the auctioneer's part that the sale should be peremptory, it had been broken by his allowing the property to be bought in.[11] The plaintiff had been the highest bona fide bidder but the lot had been knocked down to a Mr Hastwick, a solicitor, who was selling (either as a principal or as an agent) under a mortgagee's power of sale. During the argument, Blackburn J made the point that only three of the five judges in *Warlow* had been of the opinion that the auctioneer there had made a contract. The other two judges had based their decision on the ground that the defendant had, contrary to the evidence, undertaken that he had authority to sell without reserve. What that meant, according to Blackburn J, was that 'we have three Judges of the Exchequer

[8] Cf *AGC (Advances) Ltd v McWhirter* (1977) 1 BPR 9455.
[9] Ibid at 316–17.
[10] (1865) 6 B & S 420.
[11] Ibid at 428.

Chamber against three Judges of this Court'.[12] The view taken by Blackburn J and the other members of the Court in *Mainprice* was that had there, in the case before them, been any contract to sell to the highest bidder, it would have been one made by or on behalf of the seller and not one made by the auctioneer as principal. *Warlow* was distinguished on the basis that the vendor there had been described by Martin B as a 'concealed principal'. By contrast, in *Mainprice*, the identity of the seller had been disclosed in the initial advertisement. Accordingly, there was no reason why the ordinary rules of agency should not apply with the result that, if there were any liability, it would have rested with the seller as principal. Since the seller was not a party to the suit, the question did not have to be decided.[13] That being so, it might be argued that *Mainprice* and *Warlow* are not necessarily inconsistent.

A Possible Reconciliation

In distinguishing *Warlow*, their Lordships may well have had in mind the cases of *Franklyn v Lamond*[14] and *Hanson v Roberdeau*,[15] which had been cited to them in argument and which appeared to show, at least in respect of the contract of sale, that auctioneers who sold without disclosing on whose behalf they were acting would be personally liable. There had been such disclosure in *Mainprice* but not in *Warlow*. In that light, and at least at first sight, *Warlow* and *Mainprice* might therefore be reconciled on the basis that, in the absence of any indication to the contrary, the collateral contract to sell to the highest bidder would be made with the seller if named, but otherwise would be with the auctioneer.[16] Support for making identification a distinguishing factor could be found in statements in *Hanson* and *Franklyn* respectively. In the former, Lord Kenyon said:[17]

> Though where an auctioneer names his principal, it is not proper that he should be liable to an action, yet it is a very different case when the auctioneer sells the commodity without saying on whose behalf he sells it; in such a case the purchaser is entitled to look to him personally for the completion of the contract.

In the latter, Wilde CJ said to similar effect:[18]

> I apprehend it to be very old law, that an auctioneer who sells without at the time of the sale disclosing the name of his principal, contracts personally.

[12] Ibid at 425.

[13] Ibid at 429–30.

[14] (1847) 4 CB 637.

[15] (1792) Peake 163.

[16] Cf Carter and Harland, above note 3 at 31, fn 58; Slade, 'Auction Sales of Goods Without Reserve' (1952) 68 *LQR* 238; and Gower, 'Auction Sales of Goods Without Reserve' (1952) 68 *LQR* 457, fn 2.

[17] (1792) Peake 163, 163–64.

[18] (1847) 4 CB 637, 644.

In both cases, the contract referred to was the contract of sale. That was also the position in the later case of *Benton v Campbell Parker & Co Ltd*,[19] where Salter J applied to the situation of an auctioneer the principle that:

> Where an agent purports to make a contract for a principal, disclosing the fact that he is acting as an agent, but not naming his principal, the rule is that, unless a contrary intention appears, he makes himself personally liable on the authorized contract. It is presumed that the other party is unwilling to contract solely with an unknown man.

In *Johnson v Boyes*, Cozens-Hardy J went much further and stated that:[20]

> A vendor who offers property for sale by auction on the terms of printed conditions can be made liable to a member of the public who accepts the offer if those conditions be violated.

This would seem to open the possibility that the seller could directly be liable in respect of any collateral contract as to the terms under which a sale was to be held. If that were ever to be the case, it could be argued, it would most likely be when the seller had been named. Where such liability did occur, the seller would doubtless, in turn, have recourse against the auctioneer for breach of the agency contract between them.

But reconciliation of *Warlow* and *Mainprice* on this basis does have its difficulties. The dicta in *Hanson* and *Franklyn* were obiter and they were made in cases where, it seems, no indication had been given to prospective bidders whether the auctioneer was selling as an agent or on his own account. In such situations it is still the case, even today, that the auctioneer is personally liable on the sale as if he or she were the seller. But it appears the reason is not that the auctioneer has failed to name the real seller, but that the inference has been left open that the auctioneer is acting as a principal rather than as an agent.[21] In *Warlow*, the fact of an agency had been asserted by the auctioneer, unless it could be said that the words 'a gentleman' were open, at that time, to the unlikely inference that the auctioneer was himself the person so described. It follows that the Court in that case was prepared to hold the auctioneer liable on the collateral contract in a situation where, on ordinary principles nowadays, it would have been the seller who was liable on the contract of sale, not because he had been named but because the fact of an agency had been expressed. While the two cases, *Hanson* and *Franklyn*, were cited in argument in *Mainprice*, no similar argument had been advanced by counsel in *Warlow*. And while, as indicated, Martin B used the expression 'concealed principal' in *Warlow*, that was not in itself a denial that the auctioneer was acting as an agent. There was no other indication that he saw failure actually to name the seller as being in any way determinative of liability under the collateral contact, whatever the position in respect of the contract of sale might be.

19 [1925] 2 KB 410, 414.
20 [1899] 2 Ch 73, 77.
21 Eg, vol 2, *Halsbury's Laws of England* (4th edn, 1991) 464, para 950.

Whether *Warlow* and *Mainprice* ought to be reconciled on the basis that a named seller will be personally liable under the collateral contact to the exclusion of the auctioneer, but that otherwise the auctioneer will be personally liable to the exclusion of the seller, seems to have received only passing attention in the books. For example, Carter and Harland suggest in a footnote that the contract would possibly be with the seller rather than the auctioneer where the identity of the seller is disclosed.[22] *Benjamin's Sale of Goods* suggests tentatively, and without reference to naming or disclosure, that the undertaking to sell to the highest bidder might be by both auctioneer and seller.[23] In the course of an exchange in the *Law Quarterly Review*, CJ Slade[24] and Professor LCB Gower[25] were agreed that liability on the collateral contract would depend on ordinary principles of agency.[26] Certainly, given what might be considered the artificiality of the collateral contract analysis, a similar or second contract with the seller ought not to be thought altogether impossible. But if the seller were ever to be held so liable, either to the exclusion of the auctioneer or at all, it would (in the absence of indications to the contrary) most likely be in situations where the seller had been named or otherwise held out as a possible principal. Whether the seller might be liable could be of considerable importance if the auctioneer were to be without means and uninsured.

As will shortly become apparent, the questions of the relevance of the seller being named and, to a lesser extent, of possible dual liability, have (inter alia) recently surfaced before the English Court of Appeal in *Barry v Davies (trading as Heathcote Ball & Co)*.[27]

Some Problems with *Warlow*

The just mentioned suggestions apart, the predominant view seems traditionally to have been that the auctioneer alone is liable on the collateral contract, though some commentators have treated even his liability with reserve. For example, the point has been made that, strictly, what was said in *Warlow* about the existence of a collateral contract was only obiter[28] (though in all fairness, given the willingness of the Court to allow amendment of the pleadings, it could have been obiter only in the most technical of senses).[29] Again, it has been doubted whether there could be consideration for any promise by the auctioneer to sell to the highest bidder.[30] It has also been thought inconsistent that the advertisement of an auction could,

22 Above note 3 at 31, fn 58.
23 Above note 1 at para 2-005, 99.
24 Above note 16.
25 Ibid.
26 As to possible joint liability in deceit see Bridge, *The Sale of Goods* (1997) 14.
27 [2000] 1 WLR 1962.
28 Eg, Slade, above note 16 at 239.
29 Cf Gower, above note 16 at fn 1.
30 Eg, Slade, above note 16 at 241.

by the use of the words 'without reserve',[31] be made at the same time as both a statement of intent and the offer of a contract. And why, in such a case, should the auctioneer, having induced potential bidders to attend an auction without reserve, be free to refuse to put up the advertised goods at all, as laid down in *Harris v Nickerson*?[32]

In addition to these perceived difficulties, the statement of principle by Martin B in *Warlow* has also left some other questions unanswered. Why, for example, should the auctioneer's contract to sell to the highest bidder be only with the highest bidder and not with everyone who makes a bid?[33] What should be the position of someone who, like the plaintiff in *Warlow*, ceases to bid on discovering that bids are being taken from the owner (or from others bidding on the latter's behalf) but who finds the goods, the subject of the sale, subsequently knocked down to a third party who, in ignorance of the auctioneer's default, continued to bid? What should be the position of the third party in such a case? Finally, there is the question of damages, which did not have to be addressed by the Court of Exchequer Chamber. How is the value of the goods to be assessed and has the loss suffered by the disappointed bidder been of that value, or only of a chance?

Barry v Davies

The Facts

Since *Warlow* and *Mainprice* there has been no shortage of analogous cases on collateral contracts,[34] and *Warlow* has been cited with approval in different contexts on a number of occasions.[35] But there appear to have been no subsequent reported decisions squarely in point until the recent case of *Barry v Davies (trading as Heathcote Ball & Co)*[36] heard by a two-judge English Court of Appeal (Pill LJ and Sir Murray Stuart-Smith). There, two brand new machines were being sold at auction by customs authorities, in reduction of a VAT liability incurred by the manufacturers. It was not disputed that the sale was without reserve. The price of the new machines from the manufacturers would have been £14,521 each.

[31] Cf Furmston, above note 1 at 33.

[32] (1873) LR 8 QB 286.

[33] Gower, above note 16 at 458.

[34] Eg, *Blackpool and Fylde Aero Club Ltd v Blackpool Borough Council* [1990] 1 WLR 1195; *Harvela Investments Ltd v Royal Trust Co of Canada (CI) Ltd* [1986] AC 207; and *Markholm Construction Co Ltd v Wellington City Council* [1985] 2 NZLR 520.

[35] Eg, *Harris v Nickerson* (1873) LR 8 QB 286; *Ex parte Asiatic Banking Corp* (1867) LR 2 Ch 391, 397; and *Ulbrick v Laidlaw* [1924] VLR 247.

[36] [2000] 1 WLR 1962. Discussed by Meisel, 'What Price Auction Without Reserve?' (2001) 64 *MLR* 468; and Carter, 'Auction "Without Reserve"—*Barry v Davies*' (2001) 17 *JCL* 69. In *AGC Advances Ltd v McWhirter* (1977) 1 BPR 9455 the facts were not too dissimilar but the claim, which failed, was against the vendor in respect of property knocked down to a third party.

The plaintiff's bid of £200 each for the machines was the only one, whereupon the auctioneer withdrew them from sale. He sold them by advertisement a few days later for a total of £1,500. The plaintiff claimed the difference between the value of the machines, said to be £28,000, and the bid of £400. Judgment for that amount was given against the auctioneer in the County Court.

As recounted by Sir Murray Stuart-Smith, the appeal by the auctioneer was based on three main grounds. The first was that to treat notification of a sale without reserve as a promise by the auctioneer was inconsistent with the principles (a) that an auctioneer's requests for bids is not itself an offer and (b) that there being no contract of sale until the hammer fell, any bid could be withdrawn at any time before that point. Moreover, the auctioneer ought to be able to withdraw the lot on grounds such as that an illegal ring was operating or that the vendor had no title to sell. The second ground was that there was no consideration for the auctioneer's promise, since a bid itself was not a promise to do anything. The third and final ground was that, since it was known that the machines were being sold on behalf of Customs, any collateral contract would be with Customs as named principal and not with the auctioneer.

The Named Seller Argument

This last argument was, of course, based on *Mainprice*. Sir Murray Stuart-Smith, who delivered the leading judgment in *Barry*, was not prepared to accept it. On his reading of *Mainprice*, it was true that the Court had distinguished *Warlow* on the basis that in the former the principal was disclosed whereas in the latter he was not.[37] On that reasoning, he said, the Court in *Mainprice* had held the auctioneer to be not liable. It was his Lordship's view, though, that the Court in *Mainprice* had misunderstood the decision in *Warlow*. There had been a separate collateral contract with the auctioneer and there was no reason why the existence of such a contract should turn on whether the principal had been disclosed. It was also apparent in *Warlow* that the auctioneer had been selling as an agent.

This conclusion seems to confirm the dominant view that liability on the collateral contract rests with the auctioneer, even when it is clear that the auctioneer is acting as an agent. It also excludes the possibility that the naming of the seller ought to be determinative of liability. At the same time, it would not necessarily exclude the possibility that the seller might also be liable on the collateral contract, as tentatively suggested in *Benjamin*. Nevertheless, Sir Murray Stuart-Smith later in his judgment went on to say, referring to the collateral contract: 'It is true that there was no such contract between vendor and purchaser'.[38] He gave no reason for this statement and it was in no way necessary for his decision, no claim having been made against the seller.

[37] [2000] 1 WLR 1962, 1966–67.
[38] Ibid at 1968.

The Offer and Acceptance Argument

Counsel's first group of arguments in the *Barry* case (that the holding of the auction did not amount to a promise to sell to the highest bidder, that a request for bids was a mere invitation to treat, and that any bid could be withdrawn up until the fall of the hammer) presuppose that the relevant contract would be a bilateral one, formed by an exchange of promises. That particular premise also has a long history, it having been predicated by counsel for the auctioneer in *Warlow*[39] itself. On that point, the answer given them by the judges remains the answer today, that the contract to sell to the highest bidder is a separate unilateral one, collateral to any bilateral contract of sale between buyer and seller, and that the advertisement or announcement can contain both an invitation to treat in respect of one contract and the offer of another.[40]

In his judgment, Sir Murray Stuart-Smith did not deal individually with each of counsel's points on this issue. He did, however, quote at length from the part of the judgment of Martin B in *Warlow* that identified the contract between the auctioneer and the highest bidder as being what we would now see as one that was unilateral, and collateral to any contract of sale.[41] He also referred to the subsection of the Sale of Goods Act that states that unless the right to do so has been notified, 'it is not lawful for the seller to bid himself or to employ any person to bid at the sale, or for the auctioneer knowingly to take any such bid'.[42] For the auctioneer to withdraw a lot because bids had not reached an appropriate level he saw as tantamount to bidding on behalf of the seller.

The Consideration Argument

Counsel's remaining argument (that there was no consideration for any promise to sell to the highest bidder because the bidder had not promised to do anything, or at the most had made a discretionary promise, which would be an illusory consideration) is again based on the premise that any relevant contract would be bilateral. As an argument, it too goes back some way, having appeared almost 50 years ago in an already mentioned article by CJ Slade in the *Law Quarterly Review*.[43]

After reference to Professor Corbin's view that the mere making of a bid could be a sufficient consideration for the promise to sell without reserve, Slade commented:[44]

39 (1859) 1 El & El 309, 311.
40 Ibid at 316–17.
41 [2000] 1 WLR 1962, 1966.
42 Ibid at 1965. The equivalent subsection of the Sale of Goods Act 1908 (NZ) is s 59(3).
43 Above note 16.
44 Ibid at 241.

> This reasoning cannot at least be accepted in English law. The mere making of a bid is no more consideration for the promise than the effort of saying or even writing the words 'I accept' is consideration to support a gratuitous offer. In reason and in justice there are no grounds for imposing any legal liability on a seller at a point of time before a corresponding liability is imposed on the other contracting party.

In a reply published later in the same volume of the *Law Quarterly Review*,[45] Professor LCB Gower, like Professor Corbin, argued that consideration for a unilateral contract was to be found in the rule that an act done at the request of another, express or implied, is sufficient consideration to support a promise made by that other. What in the case of an auction the particular requested act would be, whether to attend the auction, to bid, or to be the highest bidder, might be a matter of dispute. But on the matter of principle, it is submitted that Professors Corbin and Gower were clearly right. That rule or principle is, by the way, the basis for the argument that, when the contract is a unilateral one, it is only on completion of the required act that consideration for *that* contract can exist and, hence, that a binding contract can come into existence. That in turn goes back to the underlying principle that, deeds and the occasional anomaly apart, no contract can exist at common law without consideration, the necessary consequence being that the consideration has to be present at the point of formation. That is why, for example, a promise to keep an offer of a reward open for acceptance has itself to be the subject of a second (collateral) contract to do so.[46]

But if, as is submitted, the consideration for the promise of a unilateral contract is the performance of the required act, where, it would be asked by someone with Slade's views, is the benefit or detriment in a bid that, without more, is not binding and that can be withdrawn at will at any time before the hammer falls? The answer to that as given by Sir William Anson in his book on contract is that:[47]

> Courts of law will not make bargains for the parties to a suit, and, *if a man gets what he has contracted for*, will not inquire whether it was an equivalent to the promise which he gave in return. The consideration may be a benefit to the promisor, or to a third party, *or may be of no apparent benefit to anybody*, but merely a detriment to the promisee: in any case 'its adequacy is for the parties to consider at the time of making the agreement not for the Court when it is sought to be enforced'.

In other words, if an auctioneer expressly or impliedly stipulates for the highest or any bid as the price of his promise and gets what he asked for, a contract is formed and he is bound by it. The benefit lies in his obtaining the act for which he stipulated and the detriment lies in its being done. It is irrelevant whether or not it has economic worth (provided it otherwise has legal value). Thus, for example, in *Carlill v Carbolic Smoke Ball Co*, Bowen LJ said of the plaintiff:[48]

45 Above note 16 at 458.

46 Cf *Daulia Ltd v Four Millbank Nominees Ltd* [1978] Ch 231. Noted by Harpum and Lloyd Jones [1979] *CLJ* 31.

47 Gwyer (ed) (under the 'guidance' of Sir William Anson, Bart), *Principles of the English Law of Contract* (13th edn, 1912) 97–98 (emphasis added).

48 [1893] 1 QB 256, 272.

> It seems to me that her using the smoke ball was sufficient consideration. I cannot picture to myself the view of the law on which the contrary could be held when you have once found who are the contracting parties. If I say to a person, 'If you use such and such a medicine for a week I will give you £5', and he uses it, there is ample consideration for the promise.

There was no suggestion, at least by that Lord Justice, that for there to be consideration the defendant must make a profit from the sale of the medicine. In a reply to Professor Gower's response to his own earlier article, CJ Slade posed the difficulty of finding a contract where a millionaire promised to give money to a hospital, saying to the secretary, 'If you will please sign this receipt, I will send you a cheque for £10,000 tomorrow'. How could it be said that the secretary's signature would be sufficient consideration to enforce the promise?[49] Always assuming a secretary would be prepared to give a receipt for such a sum in anticipation of payment at a later date, it is submitted that the short answer to the problem posed by Slade is that there would almost always be no contract. The reason would be not want of consideration but want of an intention to contract.

If the emphasis, above, on the act itself being the consideration for the promise of a unilateral contract, whatever its economic significance, seems laboured, the reason for that emphasis is that a very different alternative view has been expressed elsewhere. The alternative view is that consideration is to be found, not in the act itself but in the consequences for the parties of the performance of the act. Thus, in the *Carlill* case, AL Smith LJ found consideration in the inconvenience suffered by the plaintiff from having to use the smoke ball for two weeks and in 'the money gain likely to accrue to the defendants by the enhanced sale of the smoke balls by reason of the plaintiff's user of them'.[50] What makes this significant is that, in *Barry v Davies*,[51] Sir Murray Stuart-Smith also appears to belong to this second school of thought:

> As to consideration, in my judgment there is consideration both in the form of detriment to the bidder, since his bid can be accepted unless and until it is withdrawn, and benefit to the auctioneer as the bidding is driven up. Moreover, attendance at the sale is likely to be increased if it is known that there is no reserve.

That he should have expressed this view in this particular case is perhaps hardly surprising, since it is also the view stated in passages from two text books to which he had just previously referred.[52] In *Barry* it made no difference to the result. But ascription of consideration to the consequences of performance in the case of unilateral contracts (or in the case of executory bilateral contracts, either to actual performance or to the benefits hoped for from performance) does have the

[49] 'Auction Sales of Goods Without Reserve' (1953) 69 *LQR* 21.

[50] [1893] 1 QB 256, 275.

[51] [2000] 1 WLR 1962, 1967.

[52] Vol 1, *Chitty on Contracts* (28th edn, 1999) 94; *Benjamin's Sale of Goods*, above note 1 at 107. The passage in the latter cites only the corresponding passage in *Chitty*, which in turn is in the same terms as those used in relation to the same subject matter in Treitel, above note 1 at 142.

potential to be seriously misleading. Thus, it was the perception that consideration consisted not in the undertaking to perform, but in the hoped for benefit to be derived from performance which led the Court of Appeal to decide as it did in *Williams v Roffey Bros & Nicholls (Contractors) Ltd*.[53] There it was held that, contrary to all previous authority, the practical advantages that might accrue to the promisee from something the promisor was already bound to do, under an existing contract with the promisee could be consideration for additional payment by the promisee. The same sort of reasoning led the High Court of New Zealand,[54] in reliance on that case, to suppose that it was consideration for the offer of a lessee to pay half the current rent and the arrears that, for example, it had enabled the lessor to retain the prospect of a renewed lease at the expiration of the then current term. Clearly, if mere matters of hope and aspiration (or even actual performance in the case of a *bilateral* contract)[55] were really to be accounted the consideration for the formation of a contract, there would be little point in retaining consideration (or the concept of an executory bilateral contract for consideration) as part of the common law.

That aside, Sir Murray Stuart-Smith having found the presence of consideration as he saw it, the Court felt able to follow and confirm the principles stated by Martin B in *Warlow* and to hold that, in failing to knock down the machines to the plaintiff, the auctioneer had been in breach of a unilateral contract with him to sell without reserve.

Damages

The other question the Court had to decide in *Barry* was the quantum of damages payable by the auctioneer. There could be no doubt that what the plaintiff had lost was not the chance of buying the machines but the certainty of purchasing them. Hence, his loss was of their full value. He was, after all, not only the highest bidder but also the only one. The problem was rather what that full value should be. It was argued for the auctioneer that he should pay no more than £1,500, being the amount at which the machines had subsequently been sold, less the £400 bid by the plaintiff. In the County Court below, it had been accepted that the plaintiff's purpose had been to use, and not to trade, the two machines. The machines were brand new, the manufacturer's price was £14,521 and there was no evidence that they could be replaced for less. It was on that basis that judgment had been given for £28,000 less £400, or £27,600.

[53] [1991] QB 1. Discussed in Coote, 'Consideration and Benefit in Fact and Law' (1990) 3 *JCL* 23 reprinted as Chapter 3 of *Assumption*.

[54] *Machirus Properties Ltd v Power Sports World (1987) Ltd* (1999) 4 NZ ConvC 193, 066 (Heron and Gendall JJ). Discussed in Coote, 'Common Forms, Consideration and Contract Doctrine' (1999) 14 *JCL* 116, 122 *et seq.*

[55] As suggested by Treitel, above note 1 at 64–68.

The Court of Appeal agreed with this assessment. Had the plaintiff purchased replacement machines, the price he paid could have been the determinant, but evidence as to that had been excluded at the request of counsel for the auctioneer. In the result, purchase from the manufacturer appeared to constitute the only market. Pill LJ commented that the plaintiff was, perhaps, fortunate in that, in most cases, evidence of second-hand prices would prevent the adoption of the manufacturer's list price.[56] Whether that means he would have treated the brand new goods in the instant case as 'second hand' for that purpose is unclear.

That their Lordships were prepared to uphold a judgment for so comparatively large a sum, when the auctioneer himself had gained only the commission on a sale at £1,500 suggests that there was nothing very sentimental about either their decision or that of the County Court judge below! Had the question asked been for what did the auctioneer assume liability the answer might have been rather different.[57]

Some Questions Still Unresolved

Barry has confirmed the views expressed by Martin B in *Warlow* and has shown that the naming of the seller is not a determinant of whether the auctioneer is liable under the collateral contract to sell to the highest bidder. It also says something about the basis on which damages can be recovered by a successful bidder. But it does leave a few questions that might still be regarded as open.

One such question is whether the *Harris* rule, that an auctioneer is not bound actually to put the advertised goods up for sale, ought properly to apply when the auctioneer has induced potential bidders to attend on such a more than ordinarily attractive basis. Assuming that question to be still open, an auctioneer could be bound to proceed with the auction only if she had a contract to do so. That contract would have to be with all those who had attended since, at the point when the sale failed to proceed, no smaller class would have been identified. Advertisements can, of course, be offers, even to the world at large, as was evidenced by *Carlill v Carbolic Smoke Ball Co*[58] and, in principle, that could extend to an offer to hold an auction. But whether any particular advertisement does constitute an offer is basically a matter of intention to contract. In general, it can be assumed that advertisers would not ordinarily wish to open themselves to the risk of an unlimited number of acceptances from the world at large since that could expose them to an unacceptable degree of liability. The class would potentially be too large. If that could be said to be the reasoning that lies behind the decision in *Harris*, it would apply just as strongly whether a sale were to be with or without reserve.

56 [2001] 1 WLR 1962, 1969.
57 See now Chapter 12 of this volume.
58 [1893] 1 QB 256.

On the other hand, once goods are put up for sale, it might be questioned why any contract to sell to the highest bidder should have to be restricted to that bidder alone rather than be made with all those who do, in fact, make a bid for the relevant lot. They, at least, would make up a class of only limited size. In his *Law Quarterly Review* article,[59] Professor Gower expressed the view that the contract ought to be with all bidders and he found support in the already-cited passage from the judgment in the *Warlow* case where Martin B said:[60]

> We think the auctioneer has contracted that the sale shall be without reserve; and that the contract is broken upon a bid being made by or on behalf of the owner, whether it be during the time when the property is under the hammer, or it be the last bid upon which the article is knocked down; in either case the sale is not 'without reserve', and the contract of the auctioneer is broken.

From this, Professor Gower argued that if it were true that an owner's bid during the course of the auction ('when the property is under the hammer') were to be a breach of contract, it could only be because there were contracts with all the bidders, the reason being that, at that point, the identity of the highest bidder would not yet be known.[61] However, as against that argument, the passage does appear to assume that the property is knocked down and that there is therefore a highest bona fide bidder. It has perhaps become more evident nowadays than it was in 1952, when the article was published, that an acceptance and the resulting contract can have retrospective effect and could therefore apply to the earlier action of one of the parties.[62] Assuming, though, that the argument were correct, it has to be added that Professor Gower raised it, not because it might have practical consequences but because he wished to answer a different point that had been raised by CJ Slade in his own earlier article.[63] Indeed, Professor Gower went on to suggest that any actual claim for breach of the collateral contract would have to be made by the successful bidder alone, since only he would have suffered substantial damage.[64] While the latter might often be true enough, it leaves out of account the possibility that, at the least, the other bidders might pursue claims for nominal damages, the threat of which might have a nuisance value, even if unlikely to come to very much in practice.

On the other hand, it can be argued that if there were indeed contracts with every bidder, it could provide a solution for the problem of a bidder who, like the plaintiff in *Barry*, discovers that bids for or by the seller are being accepted and who ceases to bid, only to find that a third party, unaware of what the seller is doing, makes a higher bid and has the lot knocked down to him. The argument would be that the unsuccessful bidder ought to be able to recover substantial damages not,

[59] Above note 16 at 457–58.
[60] (1859) 1 El & El 309, 317.
[61] Above note 16 at 458.
[62] *Trollope & Colls Ltd v Atomic Power Construction Ltd* [1963] 1 WLR 333, 339.
[63] Above note 16 at 240.
[64] Above note 16 at 458.

of course, for the value of the lot but at least for the loss of a chance to become the successful bidder.[65] As to the successful bidder himself, he would, on discovering the breach of contract, be entitled both at common law[66] and under the Sale of Goods Act[67] to vacate the sale. But that could be small consolation for someone who wished, as well, to retain ownership of the article itself. Arguably the solution for that person could be, while retaining the article, to seek damages for the loss of the chance of obtaining it by the bid of a lesser amount.

Conclusion

As a result of *Barry v Davies*, the principles stated by Martin B in *Warlow v Harrison* have been confirmed and can no longer be challenged as being merely obiter. Moreover, it is now clear that the liability of the auctioneer under a collateral contract to sell to the highest bidder in no way depends on whether or not the seller has been named. It has been confirmed, too, that in situations like that in *Warlow* and *Barry v Davies*, the highest bidder is entitled to recover the real value of the relevant lot and is not restricted to what that lot itself might have realised at a later auction unless, presumably, that person had been the successful bidder at that auction. Other factors relevant to damages would be whether the goods were required for trade or for personal use and, if substitutes had been purchased, the price that had been paid for them.

The possibility that a seller might in some circumstances also be liable on the collateral contract seems to have been negatived by Sir Murray Stuart-Smith, but his comment was obiter and no reasons for it were given. Nor does he appear to have had the benefit of argument on the point. Given the potential importance of such a liability should the auctioneer prove to be insolvent, it may be that the last word on the subject has still to be spoken.

This last question and, doubtless, a few others remain. But given the time it has taken to get this far, it could well be quite some time before they, too, are answered!

[65] Cf *Chaplin v Hicks* [1911] 2 KB 786.
[66] Eg, *Howard v Castle* (1796) 6 TR 642.
[67] Sale of Goods Act 1908, s 59(3).

6

Correspondence with Description in the Law of Sale of Goods

Introduction

Section 13 of the Sale of Goods Act 1893 (UK) provides in part that, in a contract for the sale of goods by description, there is an implied condition that the goods shall correspond with the description. The recent Supply of Goods (Implied Terms) Act 1973 (UK), following the recommendations of the English and Scottish Law Commissions,[1] has left this provision unaltered. But that Act has also, in the case of consumer sales, rendered void terms exempting from all or any of the provisions of section 13 and, in any other case, has required that such terms shall not be enforceable to the extent that it is shown that it would not be fair or reasonable to allow reliance on them.[2]

The law governing the sale of goods is under review in a number of the jurisdictions which adopted the original Sale of Goods Act. Even so, it could well be of continuing importance to know what constitutes correspondence with description and, of course, especially so where the English reform is taken as a guide. That being so, it remains as disconcerting as ever to find on the point two House of Lord decisions, *Arcos Ltd v EA Ronaasen & Son*[3] and *Ashington Piggeries Ltd v Christopher Hill Ltd*,[4] in conflict with each other.

In 1933, the House of Lords held in the former case that goods sold by description could be rejected if they failed (defects de minimis apart) to comply exactly with the description under which they had been sold. It was not sufficient for the seller to deliver something which was the 'commercial equivalent of'[5] or 'substantially like'[6] the goods specified. Now, in the *Ashington Piggeries* case, decided before the Supply of Goods (Implied Terms) Act (UK) was passed, but after the Report of the

[1] *Exemption Clauses, First Report: Amendments to the Sale of Goods Act* 1893 (July 1969) Law Com No 24; Scot Law Com No 12.

[2] s 4, substituting a new s 55, Sale of Goods Act 1893 (UK).

[3] [1933] AC 470.

[4] [1972] AC 441.

[5] [1933] AC 470, 475.

[6] [1933] AC 470, 480.

Law Commissions on which that Act is based, the House has held that goods are sold by description only to the extent that the description 'identifies' the goods or indicates what 'kind' of goods they are.

As at least one commentator has mentioned,[7] a genuine conflict has arisen. If goods can be rejected under section 13 only if they lack the identity (as distinct from the attributes) indicated by a specification, or are not of the same 'kind' as those described, it is difficult to see how the result of *Arcos Ltd v EA Ronaasen & Son* can be justified. The timber delivered in that case was certainly of the 'kind' specified. Even in matters of detail, it was the 'commercial equivalent'. Yet that did not prevent there being a breach of section 13. An even clearer illustration of what is involved in the conflict is provided by the facts of *Re Moore & Co and Landauer & Co.*[8] There, tins of fruit conformed with description in every respect except that some of them were packed in cases of 30 tins instead of 24. The packing made no difference to the market value. Nevertheless, a strong Court of Appeal (Bankes, Scrutton, and Atkin LJJ) held that the tins failed to comply with description and could be rejected.

The present article is an attempt to show how this conflict has come about in England and in so doing, to suggest how it ought to be resolved in jurisdictions where, because decisions of the House of Lords are not of absolutely binding authority, resolution is still possible.

The Ascertainment of the Physical Subject Matter of a Sale

As Salmond J pointed out in his well-known judgment in *Taylor v Combined Buyers*,[9] there are basically two ways in which goods, the subject matter of a sale, can be ascertained.[10] The first method, which typically involves an existing subject matter, is by reference to its position in time and space. Obvious examples are a sale of 'this book in my hand', or 'the mare in the second stall', or 'the cargo loaded on the ss Mary on 1st October last'. This is the process involved in a sale of specific goods, as such. It is a process under which the goods are ascertained by being *identified.*[11] But if, and to the extent that, goods are not capable of being identified

[7] Patient (1971) 34 *MLR* 557, 559. In *Benjamin's Sale of Goods* (1974) para 766, FMB Reynolds recognises the existence of two distinct lines of authority.

[8] [1921] 2 KB 519.

[9] [1924] NZLR 627, 636. See also *Ashington Piggeries Ltd v Christopher Hill Ltd* [1972] AC 441, 503 per Lord Diplock.

[10] This topic is treated at greater length, with references to other views, in Coote, *Exception Clauses* (1964) 37 *et seq.*

[11] Cf *Smith's Leading Cases* (13th edn, 1929) vol 2, 78. Arguably future goods might also be 'identified' in this sense as, eg, in 'the next season's crop from this field' or 'this mare's next foal': *Benjamin's Sale of Goods* above note 7 at para 106.

in this sense, the only other way they can be ascertained is by *defining* them; by setting out, in the abstract, the characteristics they shall possess.[12] Examples are the sale of 'a new Singer 8 hp motor car' or 'a book the same as the one in my hand'. This is the process involved in the sale of goods by description.

Once this distinction is accepted, an important consequence is seen to follow. If a sale is by identification only, that is, is a sale of specific goods solely as such, the buyer receives what he has bought, whatever the quality or condition of the goods may turn out to be. He can reject them only if the contract contains some express or implied stipulation enabling him to do so. On the other hand, if goods are sold purely by definition, that is, by prescribing the characteristics they are to possess, then, as Salmond J went on to point out in *Taylor v Combined Buyers*,[13] every element of the description, whether it relates to number, quality, kind, state, quantity, condition, or other attribute, is in theory equally part of the definition. In consequence, the subsequent delivery of goods which in any respect whatever fail to conform to the definition would be the delivery of goods other than those contracted for and the buyer should be free to reject them. This would mean in the examples given that, prima facie, the car delivered would have to possess all the characteristic attributes of 'a new Singer 8 hp motor car',[14] and the book would have to be in all significant respects like the one in my hand.[15]

Already, then, we have two radically different types of sale. Under the one, every descriptive word could potentially be the basis for rejection. Under the other, it would not be necessary that any descriptive word have this effect. For these very reasons, the one might be thought potentially too favourable to the buyer and the other too favourable to the seller. And indeed, out of this distinction and its disadvantages to one party or the other, two quite different groups of authority have emerged, one appearing to enjoin strict compliance with the whole specification and the other seeming to allow a much looser standard.[16] It is proposed to look at each in turn.

The Strict Approach

The strict view of compliance with description has two aspects. The whole of the description must be complied with, and compliance must be exact.

[12] Cf *Australian Knitting Mills Ltd v Grant* (1933) 50 CLR 387, 417 per Dixon J. Cf *David Jones Ltd v Willis* (1934) 52 CLR 110, 125.

[13] [1924] NZLR. 627, 636. Cf *Heyworth v Hutchinson* (1867) LR 2 QB 447, 451 per Blackburn J.

[14] Cf *Taylor v Combined Buyers* [1924] NZLR 627, 631–32; *Wilson v Rickett, Cockerell & Co Ltd* [1954] 1 QB 598, 603, 608.

[15] Cf *Champanhac & Co Ltd* v *Waller & Co Ltd* [1948] 2 All ER 724, 725; *Mody v Gregson* (1868) LR 4 Exch 49, 53–54.

[16] Cf *Benjamin's Sale of Goods*, above note 7 at para 766; Fridman, *Sale of Goods* (1966) 151 *et seq*.

One of the best known statements of the need for strict compliance is that of Lord Blackburn in *Bowes v Shand*,[17] where he said: 'If the description of the article tendered is different in any respect it is not the article bargained for and the other party is not bound to take it'. *Arcos Ltd v EA Ronaasen & Son*,[18] where the House rejected any notion of 'substantial' compliance with description or 'commercial equivalence' is an application of this approach.

As to the other aspect, if the whole of the definition has to be adhered to, it could be expected that a range of attributes would be treated as definitive which went well beyond the setting of any mere genus for the goods sold.[19] This has in fact happened. In the reported cases, things like quantity,[20] dimensions,[21] quality,[22] shippers' or other mark,[23] mode of packing,[24] place of origin,[25] and even date[26] and mode[27] of shipment have all been treated as part of the description by which goods have been sold. However, if, for the reasons already given, logic both allows and requires that on a sale purely by description, the whole of the contract description should be complied with, it seems likely that a substantial impetus to the adoption of this position in practice has been provided by the use of exception clauses which exclude liability for defects in quality. It was established early on that, on a sale by description, an exclusion of liability for faults and defects had no application to any description by which the goods might have been sold.[28] A similar limitation has been placed on exceptions couched in general words, 'no rejection' clauses being the most common.[29] Just as, in contracts for the carriage of goods by sea, the similarly special status of the warranty of seaworthiness encouraged the

[17] (1877) 2 App Cas 455, 480. See also *Manchester Liners Ltd v Rea Ltd* [1922] AC 74, 80 per Lord Dunedin. (In that case the description was merely '500 tons South Wales coal'.)

[18] [1933] AC 470.

[19] Cf *Green v Arcos Ltd* (1931) 39 Ll L Rep 229, 231 per Greer LJ.

[20] Ibid. Compliance must be even more strict where a sale is financed by letter of credit: *Moralice (London) v Man* [1954] 2 Lloyd's Rep 526.

[21] *Arcos Ltd v EA Ronaasen & Son* [1933] AC 470; *Rapalli v KL Take Ltd* [1958] 2 Lloyd's Rep 469.

[22] *Re North Western Rubber Co Ltd and Hüttenbach & Co* [1908] 2 KB 907; *Wimble, Sons & Co v Lillico & Son (London)* (1922) 38 TLR 296; *Champanhac & Co Ltd v Waller & Co Ltd* [1948] 2 All ER 724, 725; *Glass's Fruit Markets v Southwell & Son* [1969] 2 Lloyd's Rep 398; *Toepfer v Continental Grain Co* [1973] 1 Lloyd's Rep 289.

[23] *'Exportles' v Allen* [1938] 3 All ER 375; *Scaliaris v E Ofverberg & Co* (1920) 37 TLR 307.

[24] *Re Moore and Landauer* [1921] 2 KB 519; *Manbre Saccharine v Corn Products* [1919] 1 KB 198.

[25] *Jones v Clarke* (1858) 2 H & N 725; 27 LJ Ex 165; *Wieler v Schilizzi* (1856) 17 CB 619; 139 ER 1219; *Peters & Co v Planner* (1895) 11 TLR 169.

[26] *Bowes v Shand* (1877) 2 App Cas 455; *J Aron & Co (Inc) v Comptoir Wegimont* [1921] 3 KB 435; *Montague L Meyer Ltd v Osakeyhtio Carelia Timber Co Ltd* (1930) 36 Com Cas 17; cf *Fletcher v Bowsher* (1819) 2 Stark 561; 171 ER 736 (date of manufacture). Cf *Miller v Industrial Acceptance Corporation* [1956] Tas LR 125 (year of manufacture of truck).

[27] *Montague L Meyer Ltd v Travaru A/B H Cornelius of Gamleby* (1930) 46 TLR 553; *White Sea Timber Trust Ltd v WW North Ltd* (1933) 49 TLR 142.

[28] *Shepherd v Kain* (1822) 5 B & Ald 240; 106 ER 1180; *Barr v Gibson* (1838) 3 M & W 390; 150 ER 1196.

[29] Eg, *Vigers Bros v Sanderson Bros* [1901] 1 QB 608; *Green* v *Arcos Ltd* (1931) 39 Ll L Rep 229; *Montague L Meyer Ltd v Travaru A/B H. Cornelius of Gamleby* (1930) 46 TLR 535; *Champanhac & Co Ltd v Waller & Co Ltd* [1948] 2 All ER 724; *Minister of Materials v Steel Bros & Co Ltd* [1952] 1 All ER 522.

courts to characterise a very wide range of faults as unseaworthiness,[30] so, in sales of goods, there was an incentive to characterise defects as a non-compliance with description in order to evade the effect of exception clauses.[31]

There is, then, a good deal of authority both for treating as description a very wide range of what might be thought of as 'attributes', and also for requiring strict compliance with the description so arrived at.

The Non-Strict Approach

Just as there are two aspects to strict compliance, so there are two aspects to the rival line of authority. But here it is particularly important to keep them separate. The first is concerned with descriptions which are minimal or rudimentary. Under the other, the courts appear to have countenanced something less than full compliance with whatever description has been used.

The Minimal Description

Minimal descriptions first appeared in connection with sales of specific goods. The legal position of a seller of specific goods before the Sale of Goods Act 1983 (UK) was a little confused. On the one hand, there is authority that before the Act no warranty of quality would be implied.[32] On the other, sellers evidently thought it worth their while to exclude liability for faults and defects.[33] It was accepted quite early on, however, that a seller could be bound by any description by which he had sold specific goods[34] and, moreover, that this description bound him, notwithstanding that the goods had been sold with all faults.[35] And because the sellers of specific goods could be bound by description, exception clauses were also used which excluded 'errors of description'.[36]

The fact that the goods were specific and so could be ascertained merely by identification in the sense already defined made it unnecessary to the existence of the contract to find any contractual description at all. If anything, the presence of exception clauses would have tended to confirm that the goods had been sold as specific goods simpliciter.[37] In practice, though, despite the fact that the sale was of

[30] See Carver, *Carriage by Sea* (12th edn, 1971) 105 *et seq.*

[31] Cf Fridman, *Sale of Goods*, above note 16 at 152–53.

[32] *Barr v Gibson* (1838) 3 M & W 390; 150 ER 1196; *Parsons v Sexton* (1847) 4 CB 899; 136 ER 763; *Robertson v Amazon Tug and Lighterage Co* (1881) 7 QBD 598, 606.

[33] Eg, *Shepherd v Kain* (1822) 5 B & Ald 240; 106 ER 1180; *Taylor v Bullen* (1850) 5 Ex 779; 155 ER 341.

[34] *Shepherd v Kain*, ibid; *Taylor v Bullen*, ibid.

[35] *Shepherd v Kain* (1822) 5 B & Ald 240; 106 ER 1180.

[36] *Taylor v Bullen* (1850) 5 Ex 779; 155 ER 341.

[37] Ibid at 784 per Pollock CB

specific goods and despite the presence of exception clauses, the courts tended to discover some measure of description *by which* the goods had been sold, in order to give some degree of protection to the buyer.[38] It is in this context that reference is found in nineteenth-century cases to descriptions of goods such as 'barque'[39] *or* 'copper fastened'[40] in the case of a ship, or as 'spring wheat' in the case of seed,[41] or even as 'pigs' in the case of animals sold at auction.[42] A similar development occurred in relation to land sales.[43] The description of trades which might be carried out on leasehold premises was held not to fall within an exception of 'errors of description',[44] as was a failure to pass title.[45]

Elementary description, then, had a natural place in contracts for the sale of specific goods, particularly where 'errors of description' had been excepted. In theory at least, they would seem to be less obviously appropriate in cases where future goods were being sold. In such cases, the description being the definition of the goods, the more elementary the description the wider the range of goods potentially covered by the sale and, hence, the less certain the contract.[46] And in practice there do seem to have been relatively fewer reported cases where future goods have been sold with an exception of errors of description.[47]

Non-Full Compliance

It was suggested earlier that the requirement on a sale by definition that goods comply with every aspect of the description could be regarded as too favourable to the buyer. Predictably, the response of sellers was the use of exception clauses. But in addition, it seems that at one time arbitrators evolved a principle of substantial compliance with description. This was something against which Scrutton LJ protested in several reported cases in the 1920s.[48] It was rejected finally by the

[38] Cf *Benjamin's Sale of Goods*, above note 7 at para 768.

[39] *Taylor v Bullen* (1850) 5 Ex 779; 155 ER 341.

[40] *Shepherd v Kain* (1822) 5 B & Ald 240; 106 ER 1180.

[41] *Shelton v Livius* (1832) 2 Cr & J 411; 149 ER 175.

[42] *Ward v Hobbs* (1878) 4 App Cas 13. Further examples are those of 'Skirvings swedes' in *Allan v Lake* (1852) 18 QB 560; 118 ER 212 and 'Calcutta linseed' in *Wieler v Schilizzi* (1856) 17 CB 619; 139 ER 1219. Cf *Couchman v Hill* [1947] 1 KB 554.

[43] See Farrand, *Contract and Conveyance* (2nd edn, 1973) 53–55.

[44] *Flight v Booth* (1834) 1 Bing NC 370; 131 ER 1160.

[45] *Jacobs v Revell* [1900] 2 Ch 858. Yet another context in which a limited description could be found was that of insurance. See also *Duthie v Hilton* (1868) LR 4 CP 138 (cement); and *Asfar & Co v Blundell* [1896] 1 QB 123. And cf 'essential difference' in cases of mistake: *Nicholson and Venn v Smith Marriott* (1947) 177 LT 189; and the 'perishing' of goods under ss 6 and 7 Sale of Goods Act 1893 (UK); *Horn v Minister of Food* [1948] 2 All ER 1036.

[46] Cf Macleod, *Sale and Hire Purchase* (1971) 71; Unger [1957] *Bus LR* 30, 35.

[47] Such clauses have been used, for example, in sales of seed: *Reynolds v Wrench* (1888) 23 LJNC 27; *Howcroft v Laycock* (1898) 14 TLR 460; *Howcroft and Watkins v Perkins* (1900) 16 TLR 217.

[48] *Re Moore and Landauer* [1921] 2 KB 519, 524; *Montague L Meyer Ltd v Osakeyhtio Carelia Timber Co Ltd* (1930) 36 Com Cas 17, 19; *Green v Arcos Ltd* (1931) 39 Ll L Rep 229, 231; *EA Ronaasen & Son v Arcos Ltd* (1932) 43 Ll L Rep 1, 4–6.

House of Lords in *Arcos Ltd v EA Ronaasen & Son*.[49] Nevertheless, traces of this approach remain and find expression in a concept of goods being 'commercially' within description, which has been accepted by the English courts over the last 20 years or so.[50]

But a very much more important form of non-full compliance is the 'difference in kind' principle which evolved during the 'fundamental breach' period between 1953 and 1966. Under this principle, a seller was in 'fundamental breach' of his contract if he delivered goods 'different in kind' from those contracted for. This was a breach which no exception clause could exclude. Its corollary was that if exception clauses had been used, the seller need comply with description only to the extent that he must deliver goods of the 'kind' described. The concept was first stated by Devlin J in *Smeaton Hanscomb & Co Ltd v Sassoon I Setty, Son & Co*[51] a case where a contract for the sale of timber contained a time limitation on claims. Notwithstanding that there had been a substantial failure to comply with specification, the learned judge held the buyers' claim barred by the exception clause, on the ground that the timber delivered was at least 'round mahogany logs'. The concept was subsequently developed to comprehend the delivery of a motor car which was unroadworthy as delivered.[52]

The 'difference in kind' fundamental breach can be criticised on several grounds, not the least being that it could unnecessarily reduce the rights of a buyer, as it is submitted it did in the *Smeaton Hanscomb* case. On earlier authority, exception clauses in general terms (as was the time limitation clause in that case) did not ordinarily apply to failure to comply with the description by which goods had been sold. Moreover, to require in any circumstances no more than that the goods should be of the 'kind' contracted for was prima facie inconsistent with *Arcos Ltd v EA Ronaasen & Son*,[53] which required delivery of precisely the goods contracted for.

The notion of a partial compliance with description and, hence, the inconsistency with *Arcos Ltd v EA Ronaasen & Son* arose because of the view of the function of exception clauses held by the proponents of 'fundamental breach'. For them, exception clauses had no bearing on the description by which goods had been sold, but operated as mere defences to breach of contract.[54] A failure to comply with description was a breach of contract, to which the exception clause operated as a defence. On this view, if exception clauses were to be contained, it was necessary to

49 [1933] AC 470.

50 Eg, *Steels and Busks v Blecker Bik & Co* [1956] 1 Lloyd's Rep 228; *Glass's Fruit Markets v Southwell & Son* [1969] 2 Lloyd's Rep 398, 404; *Ashington Piggeries Ltd v Christopher Hill Ltd* [1972] AC 441, 489 per Lord Wilberforce.

51 [1953] 2 All ER 1471. Cf *The Council of the City of Sydney v West* (1965) 114 CLR 481.

52 *Karsales (Harrow) Ltd v Wallis* [1956] 1 WLR 936; *Charterhouse Credit Co Ltd v Tolly* [1963] 2 QB 683 (CA); *Astley Industrial Trust Ltd v Grimley* [1963] 1 WLR 584; *Yeoman Credit Ltd v Apps* [1962] 2 QB 508 (CA).

53 [1933] AC 470.

54 *Smeaton Hanscomb & Co Ltd v Sassoon I Setty, Son & Co* [1953] 2 All ER 1471, 1473; *Karsales (Harrow) Ltd v Wallis* [1956] 1 WLR 936, 940.

identify a species of breach more 'fundamental' than breach of warranty or breach of condition. The 'difference in kind' test was one result. An exception clause could excuse a failure to comply with description, that is, an ordinary breach of section 13, but not a failure to deliver goods of the 'kind' contracted for.[55]

But, as the late Professor JL Montrose pointed out years ago,[56] the real function of exception clauses directed to the description of goods is to help determine whether the goods are sold by description in the first place and, if so, the extent of the description *by which* they are sold. Once matters covered by the exception clauses have been subtracted, those aspects of the description which remain apply in full force and the buyer can reject goods which in any respect whatever fail to comply with that residue. On this view there is no inconsistency with *Arcos Ltd v EA Ronaasen & Son*. The goods delivered must be those contracted for, and not merely goods of the same 'kind'.

Two factors have tended to keep alive the fundamental breach 'difference in kind' idea. The first is the fact that, as Lord Wilberforce pointed out in the *Suisse Atlantique* case,[57] the expression 'fundamental breach' has been used to cover two quite different meanings. One, which it acquired in the period between 1953 and 1966, is the type of breach more 'fundamental' than breach of condition which, it was supposed during that period, no exception clause could exclude. The other is the kind of breach which is the basis for discharge for breach, which of course includes breach of condition. So long as discharge for breach continues to be called 'fundamental breach', there is a risk of confusion between the two and, in particular, the risk that a breach will be thought not to be a discharging one unless it is also a 'fundamental breach' in the 1953 to 1966 sense.[58] The risk exists, therefore, that 'difference in kind' which before the *Suisse Atlantique* case was thought to be the measure of what was unexcludable, should come to be thought of thereafter as the measure of what constitutes a discharging breach, including a breach of condition.[59]

The other factor is the continuing problem, in sales of specific goods or in contracts containing exception clauses, of deciding by what residual or elementary description goods have been sold. It is to this problem that we now turn.

[55] *Smeaton Hanscomb & Co Ltd v Sassoon I Setty, Son & Co*, ibid at 1473; cf *Chitty on Contracts* (23rd edn, 1968) vol 2, para 1516; Reynolds (1963) 79 *LQR* 534, 542.

[56] (1937) 15 *CBR* 760. See also Unger [1957] *Bus LR*, above note 46; Coote, *Exception Clauses* (1964) Ch 3, esp 40–45; *Benjamin's Sale of Goods*, above note 7 at para 938.

[57] *Suisse Atlantique Société & Armement Maritime SA v NV Rotterdamsche Kolen Centrale* [1967] AC 361, 431.

[58] In the *Suisse Atlantique* case, ibid, at 372, counsel for the appellants submitted that 'Fundamental breach is exactly equivalent to repudiation by breach'. Cf *H and E Van Der Sterren v Cibernetics (Holdings) Pty Ltd* (1970) 44 ALJR 157.

[59] Fundamental breach, and failure to comply with s 13 of the Sale of Goods Act 1893 are treated as being the same in *Astley Industrial Trust Ltd v Grimley* [1963] 2 All ER 33, and by: *Chalmer's Sale of Goods* (16th edn, 1971) 91; Guest, *The Law of Hire Purchase* (1966) para 268; Goode, *Hire Purchase Law and Practice* (2nd edn, 1970) 218; Diamond, *Introduction to Hire Purchase Law* (2nd edn, 1971) 57–58.

Tests for Elementary or Reduced Descriptions

In theory, every contract is to be interpreted in the light of its own terms, and of the circumstances which surrounded its making. The interpretation of one contract is ordinarily not binding in respect of another.[60] Accordingly, in the case of a sale of goods solely by description, the words of description ought to be given their full effect, except in respect of matters covered by any exception clauses appearing in the contract. However, while interpretation ought, accordingly, to be of that kind, in practice both practitioners and judges tend to prefer 'objective' or 'stereotyped' criteria. It is an aspect of the quest for certainty in a case law system.

A well-known attempt to devise an objective test of description under section 13 on a sale of specific goods was made by Bailhache J in *Harrison v Knowles & Foster*.[61] The case involved the sale of two ships with an exception of 'errors of description'. Their deadweight capacity was 360 tons, instead of the 460 tons stated in the written particulars. Bailhache J held the sellers not liable on the ground that they were protected by the exception clause. The steps in his reasoning were:

1. An exception of 'errors of description' does not apply to conditions of the contract.
2. On the sale of a specific existing chattel, a statement as to some quality of the chattel is a warranty, and not a condition unless the absence of the quality makes the thing sold different in kind from the thing described in the contract.
3. The difference of 100 tons deadweight was a matter of degree, not of kind and was therefore a matter of warranty.
4. It being a matter of warranty, the mis-description of the deadweight capacity was covered by the exception clause.

It is of course true that an exception of 'errors of description' does not apply to conditions, to the extent that any description not affected by the exception applies in full force and therefore operates as a condition, but Bailhache J was, with respect, begging the question at issue when he suggested that the exception did not apply to the descriptive words to the extent that they constituted a condition. However, the significance of his judgment was that it purported to provide an objective test or stereotype (restricted, be it emphasised, to the sale of specific existing goods) by which to determine how much of a specification comprised description by which goods had been sold, especially in contracts containing exception clauses. His test

[60] There is an exception where words which have been the subject of litigation are used thereafter in commercial contracts.

[61] [1917] 2 KB 606, affd [1918] 1 KB 608, where the Court of Appeal indicated it would otherwise have required further argument on the point. For criticisms of the test, see *Benjamin's Sale of Goods*, above note 7 at para 774; Macleod, *Sale and Hire Purchase*, above note 46 at 75.

was approved by Salmond J, again in respect of specific goods only, in *Taylor v Combined Buyers*.[62]

There is some authority, then, for fixing on the genus as the measure of description by which goods have been sold in those contexts (namely, sales of specific goods, or where exceptions, particularly of 'errors of description', have been used) where a reduced or rudimentary description has to be identified. The similarity of this to the 'difference in kind' test of fundamental breach is obvious. On the other hand, to adopt an 'objective' test is, in theory, contrary to the ordinary principles of interpretation.[63]

The *Ashington Piggeries* Case

We are now, perhaps, in a better position to understand what happened in *Ashington Piggeries Ltd v Christopher Hill Ltd*.[64]

Two contracts were involved in that case. Under the first, the plaintiffs had contracted to supply the defendants, who were mink breeders, with feeding stuff compounded in accordance with a formula which had been drawn up by the defendants in consultation with the plaintiffs. The formula included a proportion of 'herring meal' and this expression was the only relevant 'description'. The second contract, which was between the plaintiffs and a Norwegian third party, was for the supply of Norwegian herring meal under a rather more detailed specification. The second contract contained an exception clause, while the first one did not.

In the initial stages, the mix supplied by the plaintiffs to the defendants was perfectly satisfactory. But once the plaintiffs began to include in the mix Norwegian herring meal supplied by the third party, it proved fatal to mink. The reason was that sodium nitrate, a preservative present in some of the Norwegian meal, set off a reaction which produced dimethylnitrosamine (DMNA) which was highly toxic to mink. An initial question under each contract was whether the goods supplied corresponded with description under section 13 of the Sale of Goods Act (UK).

The First Contract

The problem under the first contract was whether herring meal contaminated with DMNA complied with the description of 'herring meal'. All their Lordships except Lord Dilhorne held that it did so comply. However, with respect, it is submitted that the conclusion reached by Lord Dilhorne is the one which might have been expected on earlier authority. This was a sale by description of future goods,

62 [1924] NZLR 627, 639. Cf *Couchman v Hill* [1947] 1 KB 554, 559.

63 Cf Patient, above note 7 at 559.

64 [1972] AC 441.

so that the words 'herring meal' defined the goods to be supplied. The buyer ought to have been entitled to receive goods which possessed the attributes implied by the expression 'herring meal', and which did not possess additional attributes not normally incidental to such meal. As was said by Milmo J at first instance, 'herring meal does not normally contain a poison'.[65] Unless the expression 'herring meal' implied the presence of DMNA, the description had not been complied with.

But whether this result is accepted or not, of much greater importance is the reasoning by which the House reached the conclusion it did. Their Lordships proceeded on the basis that compliance with description was a matter only of 'identification'.[66] So long as the goods were of the 'kind' described they must be accepted.[67] Words prescribing quality might be part of a description, but only so far as they were necessary to identify the goods.[68] Even Lord Dilhorne accepted this test[69] and, though he reached a different result, it is easy to see how the rest of their Lordships were able to decide that the meal possessed the identity of herring meal, notwithstanding that it was contaminated. For them, it seems, contamination would not transform goods into a different class unless foreign substances had been introduced which comprised a substantial proportion of the whole.[70]

The crucial part of the reasoning is, of course, the matter of identification. As has already been shown, identification of already existing goods is a concrete process, but goods not yet in existence have to be defined. To have recourse to 'identification' at this point is to leave the concrete process of identification behind, and to introduce into the process of definition abstract distinctions between 'identity' and 'attributes'. The introduction of these distinctions was something Lord Wilberforce (with respect, correctly) protested against,[71] though his solution was to fall back on the 'broader, more common sense, test of a mercantile character' (in which respect, incidentally, he may have been coming rather close to the 'commercial equivalence' rejected by the House in *Arcos Ltd v EA Ronaasen & Son*).[72]

In the past, recourse has been had to the difference between identity and attributes when it has been necessary to arrive at a rudimentary description, either on a sale of specific goods, or in cases where exceptions, particularly of errors of description, have been used. But under the first contract in the *Ashington Piggeries* case, the sale was not of specific goods, nor was there present an exception clause of any kind. It was a straightforward sale of future goods by description, and there was no factor present which could have prevented the description being applied in full force. Why, then, the recourse to 'identification' and 'difference in kind'?

65 [1968] 1 Lloyd's Rep 457, 481.
66 [1972] AC 441, 466, 467, 470, 473, 475, 486, 489, 503–04.
67 Ibid at 484, 486, 503–04, 511.
68 Ibid at 470, 475, 486, 503.
69 Ibid at 486.
70 Ibid at 472–73, 489.
71 Ibid at 489.
72 [1933] AC 470.

In adopting the identification test, their Lordships appear to have accepted the submissions of counsel for the plaintiff and for the third party. It appears from the summary in the Law Reports that counsel argued that section 13 related to identity, while quality was dealt with in sections 14 and 15.[73] It also appears that counsel for the defendants did not seriously challenge this analysis. However, the cases reported as being cited in support of the identity analysis dealt with the sale of existing goods, or involved exception clauses, or both, and two of them, *Varley v Whipp*[74] and *MacPherson Train & Co Ltd v Howard Ross & Co Ltd*,[75] may be regarded as, if anything, authorities the other way. In the former, the description by which a specific reaper had been sold was held to include its being a self-binder, at Upton, nearly new and as having been used to cut only about 50 or 60 acres. In the latter case, a reference to goods as 'due London approximately 8th June' was held to be part of the contract description. In fact, that case is a nice illustration of the proper significance of 'identification' in sale of goods cases. It had to be decided whether the reference to due date merely identified the goods, in which case they must be accepted notwithstanding non-conformity, or was description by which they had been sold, in which case non-conformity would justify refusal to accept.

Since the cases cited did not support a general 'identity' test for ascertaining future goods, why did counsel for the three parties, and their Lordships, all so easily accept it? Of course, the answer has to be a matter of deduction. But, clearly, the effects of exception clauses in the cases relied on, and the distinction between existing and future goods, appear to have been overlooked. Moreover, it also seems not unlikely that in the minds of those concerned, non-compliance with description under section 13, a matter of 'fundamental breach' in the sense of discharge for breach, was identified with the 'difference in kind' type of 'fundamental breach' which was said to be unexcludable in *Smeaton Hanscomb & Co Ltd v Sassoon I Setty, Son & Co*[76] and *Karsales v Wallis*.[77] Yet, as has already been explained, the two types of 'fundamental breach' are quite different, as the *Smeaton Hanscomb* case itself illustrates. In that case, Devlin J was at pains to show that 'fundamental breach' in the sense of a 'difference in kind' was something narrower than a breach of condition, which is what non-compliance with section 13 amounts to.[78]

To treat section 13 as requiring only that goods delivered be of the same 'kind' or 'identity' as those described is in effect to take a test devised to shelter buyers

[73] [1972] AC 441, 450, 459.

[74] [1900] 1 QB 513.

[75] [1955] 1 WLR 640. The other cases relied on by counsel were *Ward v Hobbs* (1878) 4 App Cas 13 (sale of pigs by auction, with all faults); *WN Lindsay & Co Ltd v European Grain & Shipping Agency Ltd* [1963] 1 Lloyd's Rep 437 (no rejection permitted for want of quality); *Pacific Trading Co v Wiener* (1923) 14 Ll L Rep 51 (apparently, provision for allowance for defects).

[76] [1953] 2 All ER 1471.

[77] [1956] 1 WLR 936.

[78] [1953] 2 All ER 1471, 1473. See also *Yeoman Credit Ltd v Apps* [1962] 2 QB 508, 520 per Holroyd Pearce LJ.

from the effect of exception clauses, and use it to diminish the rights given to buyers by the Sale of Goods Act.

The Second Contract

Like the first contract, the contract between the plaintiffs and the Norwegian third party was for the sale of future goods. But it differed in that it contained an exception clause, the object of which was to prevent rejection for faults and defects, or if the goods were damaged or inferior. Moreover, to the description 'Norwegian herring meal' were appended the words 'fair average quality of the season' and 'expected to analyse not less than 70 per cent protein, not more than 12 per cent fat and not more than 4 per cent salt'. Alongside this clause was the marginal note 'quantity and description'. The contract also contained a clause providing for an allowance for any excess of fat and salt up to 1 per cent of the whole in each case, at which point the buyer would be entitled to reject.

On general principles, the words 'fair average quality of the season'[79] and the expected analysis provision[80] ought, had they stood alone, to have been treated as part of the description by which the meal had been sold, because they helped to define the goods which were to be delivered, but under this second contract there were, again on general principles, two reasons for restricting the contractual description. One was typographical.[81] The words 'Norwegian herring meal' were, alone, set out in capitals. This was hardly decisive and might be said to have been offset by the marginal reference to 'quantity and description'. The other and much stronger reason was the exception clause. If the goods were to be taken with all faults and defects, damaged or inferior, this could only be at the expense of the 'fair average quality' provision. Lord Hodson did in fact refer to both these reasons.[82] On general principles, then, the Norwegian herring meal was not sold by description to the extent that it had faults, defects, or was damaged or inferior. Whether the meal delivered complied with description would turn on whether Norwegian herring meal as specified would contain DMNA and if not, whether the presence of DMNA constituted a fault or defect or rendered the meal delivered damaged or inferior.

In the event, of course, the majority of their Lordships, applying their identity test, concluded that the contaminated meal was 'Norwegian herring meal', and therefore complied with description. Their reason for applying this test, as has already been explained, went back to an across-the-board understanding of what constituted compliance with description. However, in the context of the second

[79] *Re North Western Rubber Co Ltd and Hüttenbach & Co* [1908] 2 KB 907.

[80] *Wimble, Sons & Co v Lillico & Son (London)* (1922) 38 TLR 296.

[81] Cf *Montague L Meyer Ltd v Kivisto* (1929) 35 Ll L Rep 265 (with which contrast *White Sea Timber Trust Ltd v WW North Ltd* (1933) 49 TLR 142). Cf *WN Lindsay & Co Ltd v European Grain & Shipping Agency Ltd* [1963] 1 Lloyd's Rep 437.

[82] [1972] AC 441, 470. See also at 511 per Lord Diplock.

contract, their reference to 'identity' might also be justified as the application of an objective test or a stereotype to the problem of finding the residually binding description in a contract containing exception clauses.

Conclusion

If the foregoing analysis has been correct, compliance with the description *by which* goods have been sold ought always to be strict, but the extent of the contract description may vary widely, depending on whether the goods are specific or future, on whether they are sold purely by description or partly by description and partly as specific, and on whether exception clauses have or have not been used. The relevance of 'difference in kind' is as a stereotype in cases where it appears that goods have been sold by something less than the full description used. Whether that test is a proper one is open to argument.

In the past, exception clauses have been used to indicate that goods have been sold by a reduced description, or with no contractual description at all. The question arises whether a reform which purported to prevent the exclusion of section 13 would prevent their serving this function. The amendment by the Supply of Goods (Implied Terms) Act 1973 (UK) of section 55 of the Sale of Goods Act 1893 (UK) is a case in point. That section now avoids in the case of consumer sales, and subjects to a fairness test in other cases, terms which exempt from or restrict the requirement of section 13 that goods sold by description shall correspond with the description. If it is correct that section 13 requires correspondence only with the description *by which* goods have been sold, it is at least arguable that exception clauses which were directed not to correspondence with description, but to the delimitation of the description itself would not be caught by the amended section 55. Whether it is realistic to expect such a distinction to be drawn by the courts is, of course, another matter.

However, if, as seems not unlikely, exception clauses which limit the description by which goods had been sold are taken to have been outlawed in consumer sales by the Supply of Goods (Implied Terms) Act 1973 (UK), the decision in *Ashington Piggeries v Christopher Hill*[83] seems somewhat ironic. For it means that at a time when the United Kingdom legislature was on the point of proscribing the use of exception clauses in consumer sales, the House of Lords, in respect of section 13, guaranteed to sellers advantages which until then they would have had to use exception clauses to achieve.

[83] [1972] AC 441.

7

Deviation and the Ordinary Law*

Introduction

Francis Reynolds has been a wonderful friend to the Auckland Law School, its staff, and its students, and our good wishes for his retirement are warmly felt.

I first met him at a function at Oxford in 1970, at a time when he was soon to make his first visit to Auckland and I was engaged in writing a piece for the *Cambridge Law Journal* on exception clauses and discharge for breach, in response to *Harbutt's 'Plasticine'*.[1] As I recall it, he brought the conversation round to the chapter on Deviation in *Exception Clauses*,[2] and asked (in the nicest possible way) to know how I could possibly justify disposing of the *US Shipping Board*[3] case in a mere footnote.[4]

The chapter to which he referred was one part of a lengthy attack on the doctrine of fundamental breach, then (1964) in the ascendant. It began with the assertion that deviation and quasi-deviation belonged to a single genus and were confined to bailment. It argued that, so far as *Hain v Tate & Lyle*[5] had ascribed the incidents of deviation to discharge for breach, it was inconsistent with the more recent House of Lords decision in *Heyman v Darwins Ltd*.[6] It suggested that, where there was a contract, the non-application of exception and limitation clauses could be attributed to their having no reference to the altered risks incurred through a deviation. But, since not all bailments were contracts and the non-application of exculpatory clauses was not the only incident to be accounted for, the wider explanation offered was that deviation and quasi-deviation were what happened when a bailee stepped outside any limitations attaching to his rights of possession.

* I am much indebted to Francis Dawson for the discussions we have had about dependent and independent covenants. It should be noted that this piece is concerned only with the carriage and bailment of goods and is in no way concerned with the rather different law covering the carriage of passengers.

[1] *Harbutt's 'Plasticine' Ltd v Wayne Tank & Pump Co Ltd* [1990] 1 QB 477.

[2] *Exception Clauses* (1964) Ch 6.

[3] *US Shipping Board v Bunge & Born* (1924) 134 LT 303.

[4] *Exception Clauses*, 82.

[5] *Hain Steamship Co Ltd v Tate & Lyle Ltd* (1936) 41 Com Cas 350.

[6] [1942] AC 356. See also *Exception Clauses*, Ch 5, especially 75–76.

By so doing, he became a mere detainer, and lost the benefits of the bailment relationship. Neither of those explanations required or depended in any way upon a discharge for breach.

The point Francis Reynolds was making was that the *US Shipping Board* case, in which the House of Lords took it for granted that deviation was a breach which literally terminated a contract of carriage and, for that reason, prevented reliance on its demurrage provisions, was directly contrary to the thesis of the chapter. I might have replied (had I not been too over awed to do so!) that the chapter had gone on to say that 'it would no doubt be unrealistic to expect any such rethinking of the law to take place', in which case 'deviation must be expected to remain an anomalous type of breach'.[7] Still, I took the admonition to heart and in the finished article[8] was careful to emphasise, not so much that cases like *US Shipping Board* and *Hain v Tate & Lyle* were wrong, but that, being inconsistent with the ordinary law of discharge for breach, they had to be regarded as '*sui generis*'. As it happened, that description was taken up by *Cheshire and Fifoot* in their next two editions[9] and (who knows?) it may have been from there that it found its way into the speech of Lord Wilberforce in *Photo Production v Securicor.*[10] If so, it shows what consequences may flow from even the most casual encounter of the Reynolds kind!

Of course, since *Exception Clauses* and the article were written, the House of Lords in *Photo Production* has come down on the side of the *Heyman v Darwins* version of discharge for breach. It has rejected any notion of a substantive doctrine of fundamental breach so that, for the most part, the effect of an exception clause now depends on its interpretation. Even the rights-to-possession theory has gained some support and can now be found in the leading textbook on bailment.[11] It might be asked, therefore, what there could be left to say on the subject. Upon re-reading Professor Reynolds' splendid 1990 Butterworth Lecture,[12] I confess to having wondered that myself. On reflection though, there do seem to be a few problems remaining.

The main incidents of deviation by a carrier by water before *Photo Production* were that his obligation to follow the contract route had the status of a promissory condition[13] and that, on a deliberate and unjustified departure from his

[7] *Exception Clauses*, 95–96.

[8] 'The Effect of Discharge by Breach on Exception Clauses' [1970] *CLJ* 221, 238 reprinted as Chapter 8 Part I in this volume.

[9] See their *The Law of Contract*, 8th edn (London, 1972) 140; (9th edn, 1976) 165.

[10] *Photo Production Ltd v Securicor Transport Ltd* [1980] AC 827.

[11] NE Palmer, *Bailment*, 2nd edn (Sydney, 1991) 1539, and esp 835, 990, 1270, 1271. See also CD Mills, 'The Future of Deviation in the Law of the Carriage of Goods' [1983] *LMCLQ* 587, 588 and Christopher Cashmore, 'The Legal Nature of the Doctrine of Deviation' [1989] *JBL* 492. Contrast Charles Debattista, 'Fundamental Breach and Deviation in the Carriage of Goods by Sea' [1989] *JBL* 22, 32, who sees it as merely a matter of history.

[12] FMB Reynolds, 'The Implementation of Private Law Conventions in English Law' in *Butterworth Lectures 1990–1991* (London, 1992) 29–53 (hereafter 'Butterworth Lecture').

[13] Eg, *Hain v Tate & Lyle* (1936) 41 Com Cas 350, 354.

route,[14] he lost the protection of any contractual limitation and exception clauses, as well as of the common law exceptions.[15] He became strictly liable for any loss of or damage to his cargo which he could not show would have happened anyway.[16] This result followed whether the loss or damage had occurred during, after,[17] or even before the deviation.[18] In the same way, he also lost the protection of other provisions of the contract inserted for his benefit such as demurrage and freight clauses.[19] On the other hand, these disadvantages were prevented or reversed should the goods owner elect to waive the deviation.[20] Many of these incidents, mutatis mutandis, followed quasi-deviations in other types of bailment.[21]

What has concerned commentators since *Photo Production* has been how far these various incidents have been altered or abolished as a result of that decision. Did the abolition of the doctrine of fundamental breach mean the demise of deviation and quasi-deviation as well? What are the implications of the preference shown for the *Heyman v Darwins* version of discharge for breach? What should happen, nowadays, if the contract is discharged for breach in mid-voyage? Anyway, ought the obligation to follow the contract route still to be characterised as a promissory condition? And how should cargoes carried on deck in breach of contract now be treated?

The Doctrine of Fundamental Breach

Fundamental breach and breach of a fundamental term were conceived of by their proponents as two aspects of a single, unified principle, of which the various streams of authority thought to support it were simply examples.[22] It might be tempting, therefore, to conclude that, when the fundamental breach doctrine received its *quietus* in *Photo Production*,[23] deviation, as one of its manifestations, necessarily died too. But by the same reasoning, a similar fate would in that case also have befallen such other purported manifestations as 'congeries of defects' and the condition as to title in sale of goods, 'difference in kind', total failure of consideration, and the warranty of seaworthiness. That has not so far been suggested, for

[14] Eg, *Kish v Taylor* [1912] AC 604, 617. At common law, deviation is justified to save life or the vessel itself: *The Teutonia* (1872) LR 4 PC 171. Under Article IV, rule 4 of the Hague rules, deviations to save life or property or which are otherwise 'reasonable' are permitted.

[15] *James Morrison v Shaw Saville and Albion Co* [1916] 2 KB 783.

[16] *Davis v Garrett* (1830) 6 Bing 716; 130 ER 1456.

[17] *Joseph Thorley Ltd v Orchis Steamship Co Ltd* [1907] 1 KB 660.

[18] *International Guano En Superphosphaatwerken v Robert MacAndrew & Co* [1909] 2 KB 360.

[19] *Hain v Tate & Lyle* (1936) 41 Com Cas 350.

[20] Ibid.

[21] Quasi-deviation is dealt with in more detail in the text, below, following note 96.

[22] Eg, *Smeaton Hanscombe & Co Ltd* v *Sassoon I Setty & Co (No 1)* [1953] 1 WLR 1468, 1470 per Devlin, J its real originator.

[23] [1980] AC 827.

the very good reason that the respective streams of authority were not manifestations of a single principle at all but quite disparate, each having its separate origins, incidents, and justifications.[24]

What the House of Lords actually held in *Photo Production*, effectively for the second time,[25] was that there was no substantive doctrine of fundamental breach at common law which overrode contractual terms clearly expressed to apply in the events which had occurred.[26] Whether those terms applied depended on their proper interpretation.[27] As already mentioned, their Lordships also preferred the version of discharge for breach expressed in *Heyman v Darwins* to that in *Hain v Tate & Lyle*, so far as the latter presupposed a literal termination of the contract from the commencement of the deviation, unless the breach were waived.[28]

That being so, it can no longer be maintained that the special incidents of deviation can be explained by reference to discharge for breach as it is now understood. Accordingly, if the incidents which resulted *exclusively* from earlier concepts of discharge for breach are to remain, it has to be on grounds of authority rather than of principle. Lord Wilberforce was careful to say in *Photo Production*[29] that the body of authority on deviation might be '*sui generis* with special rules derived from historical and commercial reasons'. However, deviation was not in issue in that case and, moreover, his reservation was only tentative.

As we shall see, there are good reasons for arguing that several of the special features of deviation have survived. But it would be a pity if those which depend solely on discredited perceptions of discharge for breach were to be amongst them. In *The Antares*,[30] Lloyd LJ has expressed the view that deviation ought now to be assimilated into the ordinary law of contract. If by that he meant that, where relevant, the ordinary law of discharge for breach should now be applied, it is easy to agree with him. Whether the assimilation should be taken to have gone beyond that is largely the subject of this essay.

Discharge for Breach

The Position Prior to Termination

If the ordinary rules governing discharge for breach do now apply to deviation and quasi-deviation, several consequences are clear enough. Thus, with a few exceptions, contracts of carriage and bailment remain in full force and effect, despite the

[24] I tried to demonstrate this in *Exception Clauses*, esp Chs 3–8.

[25] The first time was in *Suisse Atlantique Société d'Armement Maritime SA v NV Rotterdamsche Kolen Centrale* [1967] 1 AC 361.

[26] *Photo Production* [1980] AC 827, 842, 847.

[27] Ibid at 842–43.

[28] Ibid at 844, 845, 450.

[29] Ibid at 845.

[30] *Kenya Railways v Antares Co Pte Ltd (The Antares) (Nos 1 and 2)* [1982] 1 Lloyd's Rep 424, 420.

commencement of a deviation. They continue to do so unless and until the injured party has elected a 'termination' and has notified the carrier or bailee accordingly. If no such election is communicated and the goods are delivered and accepted, the carrier or bailee is able to rely on the terms of the contract, such as those governing freight and demurrage. Should the goods have been damaged, liability turns in the first instance on whether it is covered by any exception or limitation clauses.[31] However, liability may also in part depend on whether, since *Photo Production*, it is to be confined to loss or damage actually proved to have been caused by the deviation, or whether the deviating party remains liable, as before, for loss or damage which he cannot show affirmatively would have occurred even if there had been no deviation. It will be necessary to return to that question.[32]

In the meantime, an area of continuing uncertainty is the law to be applied when a cargo owner, having become aware of a deviation, notifies his election to discharge the contract while the voyage is still in progress. That raises several problems, not least of which is whether the obligation to pursue the ordinary route should any longer properly be characterised as a condition, any breach of which gives a right to terminate even after a voyage has begun. That apart, and assuming a termination, what regime should govern the relations of the parties for the rest of the voyage? And, if the goods should finally be delivered, should the carrier be entitled to his freight or (if not) to payment on any other basis?

Discharge for Breach in Mid-Voyage

It is now well established that when a contract is discharged for breach it does not for that reason cease to exist, either *ab initio* or *in futuro*.[33] What happens, according to the House of Lords in *LEP Air Services Ltd v Rollowswin Investments Ltd*,[34] is that, upon discharge, neither party is obliged or entitled to perform it further. The contract itself governs anything that happened before the discharge and remains in being for the purpose of settling the rights and liabilities of the parties which accrued to that point. It follows that, in the case of a ship in mid-voyage, the contract cannot govern events occurring after it has been discharged unless some sort of new arrangement comes into existence. That rather inconvenient consequence was just as apparent under the law as it was before *Photo Production*.

To fill the gap, one resort was for the courts to hold that, upon a discharge for deviation, the carrier became subject from the commencement of the deviation (or even from the start of the voyage) to the 'insurer's' liability of a common carrier at common law. This carried the benefit of the common law exceptions of the acts of God and of the Queen's enemies, and inherent vice in the goods

[31] All of these incidents follow from the adoption of the *Heyman v Darwins* model of discharge for breach in the *Photo Production* case.

[32] See text below, following note 95.

[33] Again, this follows from the *Heyman v Darwins* model.

[34] [1973] AC 331, esp 345–46, 350. There is a much earlier statement to similar effect by Lord Sumner in *Hirji Mulji v Cheong Yue Steamship Co Ltd* [1926] AC 497, 509–10.

carried, but not the benefit of any of the terms of the contract.[35] As a solution, it was of relatively little value to the carrier because of the onus on him at common law of showing that the loss or damage would have occurred anyway,[36] a burden extremely difficult (though perhaps not altogether impossible)[37] to meet except in the case of inherent vice.

Nor, as a solution, is it without its difficulties conceptually. Thus, it assumes that a carrier's repudiation is directed solely to his contract of carriage and has no reference to his status at common law. Moreover, the notion that a common carrier can operate as such without a contract, express or implied, is itself not easy to envisage. So it is perhaps not surprising that in *Hain v Tate & Lyle*[38] the House of Lords should have left open the possibility that upon a discharge for breach an implied contract might replace the original one. Their Lordships also appear to have favoured the view that, if the cargo were delivered, the carrier would be entitled to a quantum meruit. This, too, seems a little strange since, if there were an implied contract it would have been expected to provide for not a quantum meruit, but the payment of the contract freight itself, for, as Lord Wright emphasised in the *Hain* case,[39] contract freight had always historically been regarded as payable on delivery of the cargo, despite any intermediate deviation. On ordinary principles, the existence of so long-standing a practice would be the obvious indication of what the relevant implied term should be. Even if the obligation as such to pay freight under the contract of affreightment were to be regarded as extinguished by a discharge for breach, the law relating to deviation clearly had allowed the continued existence of an equivalent obligation, whatever its theoretical source might be. As we shall see shortly, this history of the claim for freight may have an even wider significance.

Condition or Innominate Term?

The Change Proposed

The problem of what to do after a termination in mid-voyage stemmed, ultimately, from what seems to have been an assumption by the Court of Appeal in the 1907

[35] All these consequences would have followed from Pickford, J's having held, in *Internationale Guano* [1909] 2 KB 360, 365, that the defendants had to be treated after the deviation as common carriers who could not rely on the terms of the contract. See also *F Kanematsu & Co Ltd v The Ship Shelzada* (1957) 96 CLR 477; Baughen, *Shipping Law* (London, 1988) 89; Tan, *The Law in Singapore on Carriage of Goods by Sea*, 2nd edn (Singapore, 1994) 123; Davies and Dickey, *Shipping Law*, 2nd edn (Sydney, 1995) 274; Wilson, *Carriage of Goods by Sea*, 3rd edn (London, 1998) 23; Debattista, above note 11 at 24.

[36] Eg *Morrison v Shaw Saville* [1916] 2 KB 783.

[37] Cf *Paterson Steamships Ltd v Robin Hood Mills Ltd (The Thordoc)* (1937) 58 Ll L Rep 33 (PC).

[38] (1936) 41 Com Cas 350, 358, 367, 368, 370. Cf *Thorley v Orchis* [1907] 1 KB 660, 667.

[39] (1936) 41 Com Cas 350, 368.

case of *Thorley v Orchis*[40] and those which followed it, including *Hain v Tate & Lyle* itself, that the incidents of deviation were to be explained by reference to discharge for breach. In consequence, the undertaking to follow the contract route had to be accorded the status of a condition, any breach of which would give a right to terminate, as was done, effectively, by Lord Atkin and Lord Wright in the *Hain* case.[41] It is that characterisation which, in turn, makes it still possible to discharge the contract for deviation halfway through a voyage.

Deviation has often been said to be a breach of a particularly serious kind or of a particularly important undertaking.[42] That might once have been true for reasons of insurance, but cover for deviation has long since been available.[43] In practice, the seriousness of departures from a contract route (as distinct from their potential legal consequences) can vary widely, much as is the case with unseaworthiness. For its part, the warranty of seaworthiness has, since the *Hong Kong Fir* case,[44] been classed not as a condition but as an innominate term, somewhere between a condition and a warranty. Simon Baughen[45] has suggested that deviation ought similarly to be reclassified. Since the main justification for treating the obligation not to deviate as a condition (ie, that the incidents of deviation were the result of discharge for breach) has gone, that suggestion can now more readily be considered on its merits. More than that, it is believed that a change of that kind can be supported by reference to the earlier law and especially to the history of the claim for freight.

The Claim for Freight

An appropriate starting point is *Cole v Shallet*,[46] decided in the Court of Common Pleas late in the seventeenth century. To a claim for freight by the master of a ship, the defendant merchant pleaded 'divers deviations by which the goods were spoiled'. There was also a claim for demurrage to which the defendant pleaded the neglect of the mariners. On both claims, judgment was given for the master on the ground that 'the covenants are mutual and reciprocal, whereupon each hath his action against the other and cannot plead the breach of one covenant in bar of the other'. The obligation to pay freight was thus treated by the Court as falling

[40] [1907] 1 KB 660. We return to this question in the text, below, following note 72.

[41] (1936) 41 Com Cas 350, 354, 362–63.

[42] Eg, *Hain v Tate & Lyle* (1936) 41 Com Cas 350, 354, 363, 371; *Thorley v Orchis* [1907] 1 KB 660, 669; *Cunard Steamship Co v Buerger* [1926] AC 1, 8; *Rio Tinto Co Ltd v The Seed Shipping Co Ltd* (1926) 24 Ll L Rep 316, 320; Palmer, above note 11 at 578, 989, 1535; Cashmore, above note 11 at 496.

[43] See, eg, TE Scrutton KC in *Thorley v Orchis* [1907] 1 KB 660, 633; *Hain v Tate & Lyle* (1936) 41 Com Cas 350, 355; *State Trading Corporation of India Ltd v Golodetz Ltd* (*The Sara D*) [1989] 2 Lloyd's Rep 277, 288.

[44] *Hong Kong Fir Shipping Co Ltd v Kawasaki Kisen Kaisha Ltd* [1962] 2 QB 26.

[45] Baughen, 'Does Deviation Still Matter?' [1991] *LMCLQ* 70, 84. Francis Reynolds, in his Butterworth Lecture, above note 12 at 46, also leaves open the possibility.

[46] (1693) 3 Lev 41; 83 ER 567.

within the first of the types of covenant subsequently identified by Lord Mansfield in *Kingston v Preston*.[47] Those of the first kind, he said, were:

> Such as are called mutual and independent, where either party may recover damages from the other, for the injury he may have received by a breach of the covenants in his favour, and where it is no excuse for the defendant to allege a breach of the covenants on the part of the plaintiff.

Lord Mansfield contrasted that type of covenant with those which, in his words, were,

> conditions and dependent, in which the performance of one depends on the prior performance of another and therefore, till this prior covenant is performed, the other party is not liable to an action on his covenant.[48]

What distinguished these two kinds of covenant from each other was that, again in the words of Lord Mansfield, this time in *Boone v Eyre*,[49]

> where mutual covenants go to the whole of the consideration on both sides they are mutual conditions; but where the covenants go only as to a part, and where recompense can be had in damages, it is a different thing.

An argument based on a dependent covenant type of analysis was addressed to the court in the later case of *Bornmann v Tooke*,[50] where again a captain who had deviated was suing for his freight. For the defendant it was claimed that the obligation to sail on the first favourable wind by the direct route was a condition precedent to freight becoming due. Lord Ellenborough would have none of this and held for the plaintiff, leaving the defendant to his cross action. On the condition precedent point, his comment was:[51]

> To hold that any short delay in setting sail or trifling departure from the direct course of the voyage would entirely destroy the plaintiff's right to be remunerated for transporting the cargo would indeed be going *inter apices facti*.

An elaboration of Lord Ellenborough's reasoning appeared at the beginning of his judgment in *Davidson v Gwynn*[52] two years later:

> The sailing with the first convoy is not a condition precedent: the object of the contract was the performance of the voyage, and here it has been performed. The principle laid down in *Boone v Eyre* has been recognised in all the subsequent cases, that unless the non-performance alleged in breach of the contract goes to the whole root and consideration of it, the covenant broken is not to be considered as a condition precedent, but as a distinct covenant, for the breach of which the party injured may be compensated in damages.

[47] (1773) 2 Doug 689; 99 ER 436. For a detailed discussion of this subject, see SJ Stoljar, 'Dependent and Independent Promises' (1957) 2 *Syd LR* 217.

[48] (1773) 2 Doug 689, 690–91.

[49] (1779) 1 Hy Bl 273n; 126 ER 160.

[50] (1808) 1 Camp 377; 170 ER 991.

[51] (1808) 1 Camp 377, 378–79.

[52] (1810) 12 East 381, 389; 104 ER 149.

The perception that a claim for remuneration was not to be reduced, and that the injured party was to be left to his cross action, was not confined to contracts of carriage but extended to other contracts of service. In some contexts this proved to be too inconvenient and in 1806 the Court of King's Bench in *Basten v Butter*[53] allowed what was, in effect, a kind of set-off in a claim for work and materials. That change was made easier by the claim having been for a quantum meruit, but there was a suggestion that the same result might also apply to a claim for a fixed price. By the middle of the nineteenth century, Parke B was able to say, in *Mondel v Steel*,[54] that this new practice had since been generally followed. As a justification for the original rule as it had existed before *Basten v Butter*, he referred to cases where,

> the law appears to have construed the contract as not importing that the performance of every portion of the work should be a condition precedent to the payment of the stipulated price, otherwise the least deviation would have deprived the plaintiff of the whole price.[55]

However, having said that the new practice was so convenient that it was generally followed, he went on to make the point that it had not been applied in all cases. Amongst the exceptions, he mentioned actions for freight, citing *Shiels v Davies*.[56] Freight is still an exception, as was reaffirmed by the House of Lords as recently as 1977 in *Aries Tanker Corp v Total Transport Ltd*.[57] In other words, the promise to pay freight remains to this day an independent covenant of the seventeenth century kind.

That raises the question whether, in *Cole v Shallet* and *Bornmann v Tooke*, it was solely because the contract had been executed that the obligation to pay freight was treated as an independent covenant and, hence, as not being conditional on the absence of a deviation. Lord Ellenborough referred to *Boone v Eyre*, in which, according to one report,[58] Ashhurst J pointed to a difference between executed and executory contracts. It might be argued, therefore, that the obligation to follow the contract route could still be a condition precedent in any context other than a claim for freight. One test for that would be to look to the way in which the courts treated claims for loss or damage suffered after the commencement of a deviation or quasi-deviation. And here it has to be significant that it was not until a hundred years after *Bornmann v Tooke* that a claim of that kind was held to turn on its being a condition precedent that the contract route be followed. Moreover, Lord Ellenborough himself made the point in a third case, *Havelock v Geddes*,[59] that whether undertakings, generally, were conditions precedent could vary, depending on the stage performance had reached.

[53] (1806) 7 East 479; 103 ER 185.
[54] (1841) 8 M & W 870; 151 ER 1288.
[55] (1841) 8 M & W 870, 870–71.
[56] (1841) 4 Camp 119; 171 ER 39 (claim for freight following damage due to bad stowage).
[57] [1977] 1 WLR 185.
[58] (1779) 2 Black, W 1312, 1314n; 96 ER 767. See also Stoljar, above note 47 at 244, and *Graves v Legg* (1854) 9 Ex 709, 716–17; 156 ER 304.
[59] (1809) 10 East 555, 564; 103 ER 886.

These early cases amply explain at least the origins of the practice which, according to Lord Wright in *Hain v Tate & Lyle*,[60] had persisted until that time of paying the contract freight for goods delivered, despite an intermediate deviation. They also suggest the need for a reconsideration of *Thorley v Orchis*[61] not only because it appears to have altered the status of the obligation to follow the contract route, but also because it led to the notion that, despite all previous practice, deviation fell outside the ordinary rules governing the payment of freight.

Thorley v Orchis Reconsidered

The *Thorley* case was one where, after a ship had deviated on its way to its port of destination, goods which were being unloaded were damaged through the negligence of stevedores employed by the shipowners. The bill of lading exceptions were expressed to cover such negligence. For the defendant shipowners, TE Scrutton KC[62] argued on the analogy of the warranty of seaworthiness that, though the obligation not to deviate was a condition precedent while the contract was executory, once it had been executed by the goods being carried to their destination, it turned into what he called 'a warranty in the stricter sense' (what came to be called a warranty ex post facto), sounding only in damages.

While Scrutton's arguments reflected developments in the law of discharge for breach which had taken place during the nineteenth century, there is a sense in which he might be said to have sold the pass by, in effect, conceding that the obligation not to deviate was a condition precedent. In hindsight, we now know that the warranty of seaworthiness, which he took as his analogy, is itself not a condition. He may have been influenced to some extent by the comment of Lord Esher MR in *Leduc v Ward*[63] that the obligation was 'a most important part of the contract'. More immediately, there was a suggestion in the 1900 decision of the Court of Appeal in *Balian and Sons v Joly, Victoria and Co Ltd*[64] that 'the whole bill of lading [might be] gone', though the report in the *Times Law Reports* is so brief that the reasoning in that case might more probably have been based on bailment or the interpretation of the contract than on discharge for breach. Scrutton could well have been right, though, to characterise as obiter the suggestion that the bill of lading had gone. By contrast, counsel for the goods owners, JA Hamilton KC, based his argument[65] squarely on the decision in that case and was able to persuade the

[60] (1936) 41 Com Cas 350, 368.

[61] [1907] 1 KB 660.

[62] Ibid at 662. His argument was analogous, eg, to the division in the Sale of Goods Act 1893 between conditions and warranties.

[63] (1888) 20 QBD 475, 481.

[64] (1900) 6 TLR 345.

[65] [1907] 1 KB 660, 663–64.

court that it was both conclusive and binding. Delivering the leading judgment, Collins MR said of it:[66]

> The principle underlying those judgments seems to be that the undertaking not to deviate has the effect of a condition, or a warranty in the sense in which the word is used in speaking of the warranty of seaworthiness, and, if that condition is not complied with, the failure to comply with it displaces the contract. It goes to the root of the contract, and its performance is a condition precedent to the right of the shipowner to put the contract in suit.

That last sentence is expressed very much in the language of a dependent covenant analysis and carries the inference that deviation is a breach which goes to the whole consideration for the contract. It also, consistently with that sort of analysis, postulates a consequent release of the goods owner from the contract without the need for him to give any notification to the other side. That such notification was unnecessary was apparently the received view at the time.[67]

A logical consequence of this approach is that the right to the contract freight would have been lost. Yet the long-standing practice of paying freight on delivery must still have been in the minds of the judges, though, clearly, not the reasons for it. Significantly, in *Balian v Joly*,[68] Lord Esher MR had allowed that both the right to freight and the lien for freight might remain. For his part, in *Thorley v Orchis*[69] Collins MR went on to say:

> It may be, no doubt, that, although that condition is broken, the circumstances are such as to give rise to an implied obligation on the part of the cargo owner to pay the shipowner the freight, and, it may be, to perform other stipulations which may be implied under the circumstances from the fact of the carriage of the cargo to its destination; but that is quite consistent with the effect of the deviation being to displace the special contract expressed in the bill of lading.

Fletcher Moulton LJ also spoke in terms of a claim as a common carrier for the agreed freight.[70] He thought that was 'the most favourable position the shipowner could claim' but added, 'I do not say that in all circumstances he would be entitled as of right to be treated even as favourably as this'. The full implications of the supposed disappearance of the contract were finally accepted by the House of Lords in *Hain v Tate & Lyle*,[71] where, as we have seen,[72] it was said that entitlement, if any, was not to the agreed freight but to a quantum meruit.

[66] Ibid at 667.

[67] It was reasoned that the innocent party was released, not because the contract had ceased to exist, but because a condition precedent to the wrongdoer's being able to sue had failed. See Morison, *Rescission of Contracts* (1916) 69; Francis Dawson, 'Metaphors and Anticipatory Breach of Contract' [1981] *CLJ* 83, 87–89.

[68] (1900) 6 TLR 345.

[69] [1907] 1 KB 660, 667.

[70] Ibid at 669.

[71] (1936) 41 Com Cas 350.

[72] Text, above at note 38.

For present purposes, the significance of all this lies not so much in the claim for freight, as such, as in the light shed on the changing perceptions of deviation. We have seen that for a very long time the obligation to follow the contract route was not treated as having in all circumstances the status of a condition precedent. It has to be asked, therefore, why there should have been such a reversal of that view at the beginning of the twentieth century. If deviation did not always go to the whole consideration before then, why should it have been supposed that it did so thereafter? Almost certainly, the explanation lies in a misunderstanding, particularly in *Thorley v Orchis*, of the reasons for the well-established and very serious effects of deviation, especially on exception and limitation clauses. The fact that those effects are automatic, from the commencement of the deviation, without the need for any intervention by the goods owner, makes it impossible, nowadays, to accept a discharge for breach explanation. What made it credible at the time was a then still current perception of discharge for breach as turning on dependency, without the need for any act of 'acceptance of repudiation'. There is no evidence in the reports that, in *Thorley* and the subsequent cases, serious regard was paid to the prior question whether the obligation not to deviate really did go to the whole consideration. Rather, the impression left is that it was classified as a condition precedent more because of the established consequences of deviation than by reference to the intention of the parties.[73]

If we now accept that discharge for breach cannot properly explain all the incidents of deviation, it is submitted that we ought also to be free once more to conclude, as was once the case, that deviation does not automatically go to the whole consideration. And, if that is accepted, the way should be open to a recharacterisation of the obligation to follow the contract route such as that suggested by Mr Baughen and left open by Professor Reynolds. It might be tempting to suppose that a change of that kind would be unlikely to occur, but unexpected things have happened in this field before and could happen again.

Interpretation and Construction

If the incidents of deviation solely attributable to discharge for breach are eliminated, that still leaves the forms of strict liability which existed before *Thorley v Orchis*. In particular, under the law as it then was, exception and limitation clauses ceased to apply as from the start of the deviation unless the deviator could show that the loss or damage would have happened anyway.[74] The same applied to the

[73] See esp [1907] 1 KB 660, 666–67. Though Collins MR purported to base his judgment on *Balian v Joly* (1900) 6 TLR 345, there was no attempt made in that case to classify the undertaking to follow the contract route.

[74] *Davis v Garrett* (1830) 6 Bing 716.

common law exceptions.[75] In neither case was any contract between the parties necessarily brought to an end.[76]

So long as discharge for breach were thought to be the explanation for the incidents of deviation, it would have seemed plausible to infer that, if the cargo owner did elect to continue the voyage after a deviation, the carrier would be protected by his exceptions in respect of events occurring before as well as after the election.[77] But it is one thing to waive a right to terminate a contract for breach of condition. It is quite another to waive causes of action which, because they arose while the exception clauses did not apply, have accrued since the deviation began. That would ordinarily need fresh consideration.[78] Likewise, unless it could be shown that the hazards of the voyage experienced since the election would have been encountered anyway,[79] there would need to be a variation before the exception clauses could apply to them.

In bailments where a contract exists, a sufficient explanation for the non-application of exception and limitation clauses can be found in their interpretation or construction. Thus, if goods are required[80] to be carried along a particular route or on a particular vessel,[81] on a passenger express rather than a freight train,[82] or be stored in a particular place,[83] or in, say, a cold store rather than an unrefrigerated one,[84] it can be inferred that the exception and limitation clauses were intended to apply only to loss or damage suffered within those parameters.[85] Arguably, that was all that was meant originally by the 'four corners' rule,[86] which, unless it were confined in some such way could, as Professor Reynolds has pointed out,[87] prevent reliance on exception clauses wherever there was any 'bad' departure from an agreed performance. An alternative approach to interpretation is to enquire whether the exculpatory clauses were intended to apply only to the *risks*

[75] *Parker v James* (1814) 4 Camp 112; 171 ER 37.

[76] This follows from the then continuing existence of the right to the contract freight. Cf *The Good Luck* [1992] 1 AC 233, 263; *Reliance Car Facilities Ltd v Roding Motors* [1952] 2 QB 851.

[77] Eg, *Hain v Tate & Lyle* (1936) 41 Com Cas 350, 363 per Lord Wright; 372 per Lord Maugham.

[78] Eg, *Atlantic Shipping Co v Dreyfus* [1922] 2 AC 250, 261–62 per Lord Sumner.

[79] Eg, because the vessel would have been in the same place at the same time had it strictly followed the contract route.

[80] *Sleat v Fagg* (1822) 5 B & Ald 342; 106 ER 1113.

[81] Cf *Tobin v Murison* (1845) 5 Moore 110, 129; 13 ER 431.

[82] *Gunyon v South Eastern and Chatham Railway Companies' Managing Committee* [1915] 2 KB 370.

[83] *Harris v Great Western Railway Co* (1876) 1 QBD 515, 534; *Lilley v Doubleday* (1881) 7 QBD 510; *Roberts v McDougall* (1887) 3 TLR 666.

[84] Cf *Tor Line AB v Alltrans Group of Canada Ltd* [1984] 1 WLR 48 (height of deck less than specified).

[85] See also *The Cap Palos* [1921] P 458, 470–71; *London and North Western Railway Co v Neilson* [1922] 1 KB 192, CA 197, 204; [1922] 2 AC 263, HL, 273.

[86] *Gibaud v Great Eastern Railway Co* [1921] 2 KB 426; *Alderslade v Hendon Laundry Ltd* [1945] KB 189. I reviewed this line of authority in some detail in *Exception Clauses*, Ch 7.

[87] Butterworth Lecture, above note 12 at 33.

that would be encountered on the contract voyage at the contracted site, or on the contracted conveyance, and so on.[88]

However, while the interpretation approach can explain the automatic non-application of exculpatory clauses as from the very start of the deviation, it cannot explain the 'insurer's' liability, which descends on bailees who deviate, even where there is no contract. Nor does it explain why the deviator should carry the special burden of showing that any loss or damage happening after the start of the deviation would have occurred anyway.

In *Exception Clauses*,[89] I suggested that a good many of the incidents of deviation could be explained by reference to a 'principle' which Lord Wright expounded in *AS Rendall v Arcos Ltd*[90] in these terms:

> The essence of the principle is that damage has been sustained under conditions involving danger other than and therefore different from the conditions which would have operated if the contract had been fulfilled; for the consequences of such conditions the defendant is held liable. The principle thus applies whenever the breach of contract has the consequence of exposing the subject-matter to conditions of risk different from those which would have operated if the contract had not been broken … The defendant must show (if he can) that there must have been the same damage if the contract had not been broken … the mere fact that the risk is changed will be enough to shift the onus on to the defendant.

That dictum now seems to me to be more a description than a principle, in which case it is hardly surprising that it should reflect so many of the features of deviation and quasi-deviation. What it does not do, though, is identify the kinds of breach which attract the so-called principle. Negligence[91] and unseaworthiness[92] increase or alter the risks of an adventure but they are not deviations. Nor is delay, by itself.[93] And the dictum takes no account of non-contractual bailments. It was mainly for those reasons that in *Exception Clauses*[94] I looked for an explanation within bailment itself.

Bailment

Whatever else it might be, a contract for the carriage of goods is a bailment of those goods, as the Privy Council confirmed not long ago in *The Pioneer Container*.[95]

[88] Eg, *Scaramanga & Co v Stamp* (1880) 5 CPD 295, 299 per Cockburn CJ; *A/S Rendal v Arcos Ltd* (1937) 43 Com Cas 1, 15 per Lord Wright; *Suisse Atlantique v NV Rotterdamsche Kolen Centrale* [1967] 1 AC 361, 412 per Lord Hodson. Interpretation and construction can, of course, have the result that at least some of the incidents associated with deviation in bailment contracts can apply to deviations by carriers of passengers.

[89] *Exception Clauses*, 87–88.

[90] (1937) 43 Com Cas 1, 15.

[91] *Smackman v General Steam Navigation Co Ltd* (1908) 13 Com Cas 196.

[92] *The Europa* [1908] P 84; *Kish v Taylor* [1912] AC 604.

[93] *The British Monarch* [1949] AC 196. Delay may, of course, be caused by a deviation: *Mallet v Great Eastern Railway Co Ltd* [1899] 1 QB 309.

[94] *Exception Clauses*, 84–95.

[95] [1994] 2 AC 324.

It will therefore exhibit the features of a bailment except to the extent those features have been added to or modified by custom or the agreement of the parties.

The modern law of deviation in contracts of carriage by sea is commonly thought to have had its beginning in 1830 in *Davis v Garrett*,[96] though, as we have seen, the term 'deviation' itself was used much earlier.[97] And deviation had also for a long time been a ground for vacating a contract of insurance.[98] This last fact has been thought by some commentators and judges to be the explanation for the very serious effects of deviation on contracts of carriage.[99] It is doubtless on the same premise that it has also been suggested that quasi-deviation in other kinds of bailment is a later development, derived by analogy from deviation properly so-called.[100] That may well have been true of incidents solely attributable to the discharge for breach approach adopted in *Thorley v Orchis*.[101] But the essential characteristic of deviation and quasi-deviation, namely the strict liability of a bailee who commits a breach of a particular sort of obligation, can be traced back to Roman law and was well established in English law long before 1830 and *Davis v Garrett*.

In his classic account of bailment in *Coggs v Bernard*,[102] Holt CJ referred to several breaches of the quasi-deviation type. Under the heading of '*Commodatum* or lending gratis', he instanced the case of a bailee who had been lent a horse to go westwards, or for a month. If the bailee should go northwards, or keep the horse above a month, and an accident should happen to the horse on the northern journey, or after the expiry of the month, the bailee would be chargeable

> because he has made use of the horse contrary to the trust he was lent to him under, and it may be that if the horse had been used no otherwise than he was lent, that accident would not have befallen him.[103]

That can be compared with *commodatum* in Roman times, under which, if goods were borrowed for a specific use and were used in some other way, the borrower was liable for any loss or damage regardless of fault. In the same way, under Roman law the use of goods loaned gratuitously for safe custody (*depositum*) also imported absolute liability.[104] Where Holt CJ may have differed slightly was in the seeming inference from his dictum that liability would be avoided if the accident would have befallen the horse anyway.

[96] (1830) 6 Bing 716.

[97] Text, above at notes 47–51.

[98] Eg, *Green v Young* (1702) 2 Salk 444; ER 358; *Lavabre v Wilson* (1779) 1 Doug 284, 291; 99 ER 185.

[99] Eg, *Hain v Tate & Lyle* (1936) 41 Com Cas 350, 354 per Lord Atkin, 363 per Lord Wright; *The Sara D* (1989) 2 Lloyd's Rep 277, 287 per Lloyd LJ; Baughen, above note 45 at 71, 83; Tan, above note 35 at 121; Wilson, above note 35 at 22; Mills, above note 11 at 587.

[100] Mills, above note 11 at 587. Cf Palmer, above note 11 at 835; *Van Dorne v North American Van Lines (Canada) Ltd* [1979] 2 WWR 385, 385–86.

[101] [1907] 1 KB 660.

[102] (1703) 2 Ld Raym 909; 92 ER 107. He based himself largely on Bracton, who in turn had drawn on Roman law.

[103] (1703) 2 Ld Raym 909, 915.

[104] RW Leage, *Roman Private Law*, 3rd edn by AM Prichard (London, 1961) 325; JAC Thomas, *The Institutes of Justinian* (Oxford, 1975) 204, 205.

Later in his judgment, under the heading of *vadium* or pawn, Holt CJ indicated that if the pawnee were to use the goods for his own purposes he would do so 'at his peril'. Similar rules, he said, would apply to goods found.[105] He also referred to common carriers, though in this case, without any reference to the special consequences of breaches of the deviation kind. Perhaps this was because, at a period before the use of exception clauses became widespread, he was able to say that the carrier was 'bound to answer for the goods at all events … [other than] acts of God and of the enemies of the King'.[106]

In his *Essay on the Law of Bailments*,[107] Jones said that a borrower would be absolutely liable who went to a different destination from the one specified or who left the ordinary road and chose to go instead through thickets where robbers lurked. A hirer would also be liable for loss by robbery if he travelled by an unusual road.[108] So too, he said, all bailees were responsible for losses by casualty or violence who refused after lawful demand to return bailed goods.[109] There was a similar liability for use different from that agreed and for unauthorised use of goods deposited or pawned.[110] Significantly, Jones allowed two exceptions to the absolute liability of a defaulting borrower: that the same accident would have befallen the bailed goods in any event; and that the loss or damage had been due to the bailor's default.[111] While it is true that none of these accounts of the law of bailment refers to an effect on exception clauses, that is hardly surprising, given the periods at which they were written or to which they referred.

Examples of quasi-deviation in English law prior to *Davis v Garrett* are not confined to Holt CJ's account or to the early textbooks. Thus, in 1615, in *Isaack v Clark*,[112] it was said that:

> If a man delivers to another a horse to ride to York, if he rides him on to Carlisle an action [in trespass] well lyeth, the reason is, because he by his wrongful act hath now destroyed the privity of the first bailment by doing contrary to it.

The effect on a warehouseman of keeping bailed goods other than on specified premises was in issue in the 1818 case of *Sidaways v Todd*,[113] as was carriage in other than the stipulated form of conveyance in *Garnett v Willan and Jones*[114] in 1821 and in *Sleat v Fagg*[115] the following year. In *Davis v Garrett*[116] itself, a case

105 (1703) 2 Ld Raym 909, 917.
106 Ibid at 917–18.
107 (London, 1781) 68, 69.
108 Ibid at 88.
109 Ibid at 70, 72.
110 Ibid at 121.
111 Ibid at 70.
112 (1615) 2 Bulst 306, 309; 80 ER 1143. Cf *Bringloe v Morrice* (1676) 1 Mod Rep 210; 86 ER 834.
113 (1818) 2 Stark 400, 402; 171 ER 685.
114 (1821) 5 B & Ald 53; 106 ER 1113.
115 (1822) 5 B & Ald 342.
116 (1830) 6 Bing 716.

involving the carriage by sea of a cargo of lime which had been destroyed in the course of a deviation, the argument for the plaintiffs included the following:[117]

> The exception of perils of the sea and navigation, &c applies only to perils incurred in the direct and usual course; and of perils encountered out of that course the Defendant must take on himself the responsibility. So, upon policies of insurance, if a loss happen during a deviation it is not a loss within the meaning of the policy, and the underwriter is exonerated. So if a party direct a horse to be led by a given road, and the conductor chooses to proceed by a different track, he will be responsible for any injury the horse may sustain.

The main argument for the defence was that it could not be averred with certainty that the deviation was even the remote cause of the loss. The barge carrying the lime, it was said, might, and probably would, have encountered the same storm if she had proceeded in a direct course. Tindall CJ's response to that argument was that, if it were to prevail, deviation would never, or only under very peculiar circumstances, entitle the plaintiff to recover. One example he gave was of a parcel forwarded by the wrong conveyance, in which case, he said, the defendant would undoubtedly be liable.[118] He then continued:[119]

> But we think the real answer to the objection is, that no wrong-doer can be allowed to apportion or qualify his own wrong; and that as a loss has actually happened whilst his wrongful act was in operation and force, and which is attributable to his wrongful act, he cannot set up as an answer to the action the bare possibility of a loss if his wrongful act had never been done. It might admit of a different construction if he could shew, not only that the same loss might have happened, but that it must have happened if the act complained of had not been done; but there is no evidence to that extent in the present case.

The fact that the argument of counsel for the plaintiff included a reference to contracts of insurance may help to explain why the special incidents of deviation have been thought to derive from the effects such breaches had on marine policies. But Tindall CJ did not himself mention any such reason. Indeed, his dictum has been taken to suggest that, initially, deviation might even have been simply the matter of a special onus of proof.[120] As to that, it needs to be remembered that the Chief Justice was responding to a particular line of argument. But he had also had drawn to his attention, and himself had referred to, established instances of quasi-deviation in bailment. That being so, it seems, with respect, not unlikely that in referring to the question of onus he was simply applying what he supposed was the explanation for an already existing incident of bailment.

Perhaps the most famous statement of quasi-deviation in bailment as the law stood at the end of the nineteenth century was that of Grove J in *Lilley v Doubleday*,[121]

[117] Ibid at 719.
[118] Ibid at 723.
[119] Ibid at 724.
[120] Reynolds, Butterworth Lecture, above note 12 at 30–32. Though see *Harris v Great Western Railway Co* (1876) 1 QBD 515, 534 per Blackburn J.
[121] (1881) 7 QBD 510, 511.

a case where goods had been kept at a place other than the one contracted for. He said this:

> The defendant was entrusted with the goods for a particular purpose and to keep them in a particular place. He took them to another, and must be responsible for what took place there. The only exception I see to this general rule is where the destruction of the goods must take place as inevitably at one place as at the other. If a bailee elects to deal with the property entrusted to him in a way not authorised by the bailor, he takes upon himself the risks of so doing, except where the risk is independent of his acts and inherent in the property itself.

That statement makes no reference to exception and limitation clauses, but it seems from the report that there were no such clauses in the contract.

Whether or not deviation and quasi-deviation originated in bailment will no doubt continue to be a matter of argument. What is indisputable is that the carriage of goods does still involve bailments. Breaches of the deviation type in bailment had incidents which were established and defined long before the Court of Appeal attributed them to discharge for breach in *Thorley v Orchis*.[122] Hopefully, *Photo Production*[123] has eliminated the incidents which followed uniquely from that misattribution. But it would be a strange result if that case had also, by a side wind, put paid entirely to deviation and quasi-deviation as such.

A Test for Deviatory Breaches

Assuming quasi-deviation remains part of the law of bailment and that the parties have no clearly expressed agreement to the contrary, a bailee who commits a deviatory breach will continue, as before, to be strictly liable for loss of or damage to the bailed goods which he is unable to show would have been suffered anyway. However, the fact that these consequences are so special makes it the more important that deviations and quasi-deviations be distinguishable from other breaches of contract since they might otherwise invite a revival of the fundamental breach doctrine, a concern which Professor Reynolds has articulated.[124]

In *Exception Clauses*,[125] I suggested that, if the examples given by Holt CJ and the early text writers were brought together, the picture that emerged was of breaches by a bailee which involved:

a. Retention of bailed goods after the bailee's authority to do so has expired.
b. The presence of bailed goods in a place or on a conveyance other than that authorised.

[122] [1907] 1 KB 660.
[123] *Photo Production v Securior* [1980] AC 827.
[124] Butterworth Lecture, above note 12 at 47.
[125] *Exception Clauses*, 91.

c. The use of bailed goods for a purpose, in a manner, to an extent, or by a person, other than the one authorised.

Very few, if any, later cases of deviation and quasi-deviation fall outside this pattern nor, it is believed, are the categories arbitrary. Hence my suggestion,[126] adverted to at the beginning of this essay, that deviation is what happens when a bailee exceeds limitations placed upon his rights to possession. When that happens, he loses those rights, and the protection of the bailment relationship, and becomes a mere detainer.[127] That does not by itself mean that any contract between the parties has been discharged for breach,[128] but it does mean that the immediate right to possession has reverted to the bailor.[129] Put another way, a bailee's rights to possession are conditional upon limitations placed upon them even though the contract itself may not be so conditioned. Accordingly, what is distinctive about deviations is not that they are, necessarily, 'bad' breaches, either morally or in terms of the scale of the loss or damage which may result. Rather, they are breaches of a particular type of obligation.

If that is so, it goes a long way to explaining why deviation and quasi-deviation have always, to some degree, involved the presence of goods in the wrong place at the wrong time (location, location!) contrary to an express or implied requirement by the bailor. That, in turn provides a test for distinguishing deviation from other kinds of breach, though there may sometimes be an overlap. One example would be delay, which might be treated as a deviation where it resulted effectively, in a different voyage.[130] Another could be unseaworthiness if, say, a frozen cargo were stowed, in breach of contract, on an unrefrigerated vessel. That would be a quasi-deviation but the vessel, itself, would also be unfit to receive the cargo.

Deck Cargo

On the 'wrong place–wrong time' test, the carriage of cargo on deck contrary to an undertaking not to do so is classic quasi-deviation. Yet whether it is or should be so characterised has become a matter of controversy.[131]

[126] Ibid at 91–93.

[127] Cf *Hain Steamship Co Ltd v Tate & Lyle Ltd* (1934) 39 Com Cas 259, 284–85 per Greer LJ; *London and North Western Railway Co Ltd v Neilson* [1922] 2 AC 263, 269, per Lord Buckmaster.

[128] *Reliance Car Facilities Ltd v Roding Motors* [1952] 2 QB 851; *J Evans & Son (Portsmouth) Ltd v Andrea Mezario Ltd* [1976] 1 WLR 1078, 1084 per Roskill LJ.

[129] Cf *Gordon v Harper* (1796) 7 TR 9, 12; 101 ER 828; *Bryant v Wardell* (1848) 2 Ex 479; 154 ER 580; *R v Poyer* (1851) 7 Ex 152, 159–60; 155 ER 895.

[130] *Brandt v Liverpool Brazil and River Plate Steam Navigation Co* [1924] 1 KB 575, 601.

[131] Those against include Reynolds, Butterworth Lecture, above note 12 at 47–50; BJ Davenport (1989) 105 *LQR* 521; Yates (ed), *Contracts for the Carriage of Goods by Land Sea and Air* (London, 1993) 1–392. See also *Tasman Express v Case, The Canterbury Express* (1992) 111 FLR 108, 111 (NSWCA). On the other hand, according to Tetley, *Marine Cargo Claims*, 3rd edn (Montreal, 1988) 656–57 the courts of the world have usually held that unauthorised deck cargo is not covered by the exceptions in the Hague Rules or in the contract of carriage.

Of course, if a ship goes down and its whole cargo is lost, it may not matter very much to an owner of goods where they were stowed. Short of that, it seems obvious enough that stowage on deck substantially alters and increases the risks of loss or damage. As one writer has said, it is potentially a far more serious departure than a mere geographical deviation.[132] Tetley[133] makes the point that, in the case of containers on deck, it may even affect the stability of the vessel. Short of that, goods on deck are rather more likely to be washed overboard, to shift in a storm, and to suffer water damage than would be the case if they were stowed below deck. So, Lord Wright's test of altered risks is met whether it is founded on interpretation or exists as a separate principle.[134] As Hirst J said of a package limitation clause in *The Chanda*,[135] a case involving wrongful stowage on deck:

> [I]t can hardly have been intended to protect the shipowner who, as a result of the breach, exposed the cargo in question to such palpable risk of damage. Otherwise the main purpose of the shipowners' obligation to stow below deck would be seriously undermined.

At the least, the parties would need to use very clear words if their intentions were different.

Perhaps not surprisingly, unauthorised deck cargo is accorded special treatment in the Hamburg Rules.[136] In relation to the earlier Hague Rules, such unauthorised carriage would anyway have been classed as a deviation because of the decision of the House of Lords to that effect in *Royal Exchange Shipping Co Ltd v Dixon*[137] and on that basis would, after *Stag Line Ltd v Foscolo Mango & Co Ltd*,[138] have fallen outside the Rules in cases where the unauthorised carriage was unreasonable.[139] The Hague–Visby Rules do not expressly purport to alter that characterisation but the definition of goods in Article 1(c) excludes cargo stated in the contract to be carried on deck. That exclusion was reversed by the Carriage of Goods by Sea Act 1971, section 1(7). Like other forms of deviation, unauthorised deck carriage is, under those Rules, subject to the time bar in Article III, rule 6[140] though, according to one New Zealand judge, not to the package limitation.[141]

There appear to be two main arguments why wrongful deck carriage should not be classed as a deviation. One is linked to *Photo Production* and the demise of fundamental breach. The other is based on appeals to policy and convenience. The

[132] Baughen, above note 45 at 93.

[133] Tetley, above note 131 at 656.

[134] Text, above at note 90.

[135] [1989] 2 Lloyd's Rep 494, 505. And see *J Evans & Son (Portsmouth) Ltd v Andrea Mezario Ltd* [1976] 1 WLR 1078, 1084 per Roskill LJ, to similar effect.

[136] Article 9, under which carriage on deck contrary to agreement would fall outside the protection of the Rules.

[137] (1887) 12 App Cas 11.

[138] [1932] AC 328.

[139] *The Chanda* [1989] 2 Lloyd's Rep 494; *Svenska Traktor Aktiebolaget v Maritime Agencies (Southampton) Ltd* [1953] 2 Lloyd's Rep 124, 129–30; *St Simeon Navigation Inc v A Couturier & Fils Ltee* (1974) 44 DLR (3d) 478, 480 (SCC).

[140] *The Antares* [1987] 1 Lloyd's Rep 424.

[141] *Nelson Pine Industries Ltd v Seatrans New Zealand Ltd (The Pembroke)* [1995] 2 Lloyd's Rep 290 (NZHC).

leading judicial expression of the former view is that of Lloyd LJ in *The Antares*,[142] where machinery had wrongfully been stored on deck and had been seriously damaged. It was argued for the cargo owner that at common law stowage in that manner was a fundamental breach which displaced the exception clauses in the bill of lading, including in this case the time bar in Article III, rule 6 of the Hague–Visby Rules. Neither Steyn J at first instance[143] nor the Court of Appeal had much difficulty in holding that since, under the Carriage of Goods by Sea Act 1971, the Hague–Visby Rules had the force of statute law and the time limit was expressed to apply 'in any event' to 'all liability whatsoever', the carrier was entitled to be protected by it. On that basis, the exact characterisation of wrongful carriage on deck was hardly relevant. To some extent, therefore, what was said about deviation as a fundamental breach might be regarded as unnecessary to the decision.

Referring to the argument based on fundamental breach, Lloyd LJ commented:[144]

> The doctrine of fundamental breach on which [counsel] relies, that is to say the doctrine that a breach of contract may be so fundamental as to displace exception clauses altogether, no longer exists.

He cited *Suisse Atlantique* and *Photo Production* and then went on to refer to a submission that the deviation cases might have survived the demise of fundamental breach and with them, by analogy, the rules relating to carriage on deck. He referred to Lord Wilberforce's contrasting dicta in *Suisse Atlantique*[145] and *Photo Production*[146] and concluded:[147]

> Whatever may be the position with regard to deviation cases strictly so-called, (I would myself favour the view that they should now be assimilated into the ordinary law of contract) I can see no reason for regarding the unauthorised loading of deck cargo as a special case. The sole question therefore is whether on its true construction art III r 6 applies.

If Lloyd LJ could see no reason for regarding unauthorised loading of deck cargo as a special case, it may be that the matter had not been fully canvassed before him. There is nothing in the published reports of *The Antares*, at first instance or in the Court of Appeal, to indicate that the specifically bailment aspects of deviation and quasi-deviation were drawn to the attention of the Court or were considered by the judges. Nor was anything said about those aspects by their Lordships sitting in the *Photo Production* case.

The policy considerations against treating wrongful deck carriage as a quasi-deviation were canvassed by Mr BJ Davenport in a note[148] on the decisions of Hirst J in *The Chanda*[149] and the *Captain Gregos No 1*.[150] Those cases, and the note

142 [1987] 1 Lloyd's Rep 424.
143 [1986] 2 Lloyd's Rep 633.
144 [1987] 1 Lloyd's Rep 424, 429.
145 [1967] 1 AC 361, 424.
146 [1980] AC 827, 845.
147 [1987] 1 Lloyd's Rep 424, 430.
148 'Limits on the Hague Rules' (1989) 105 *LQR* 521.
149 [1989] 2 Lloyd's Rep 494.
150 [1989] 2 Lloyd's Rep 633.

itself, are concerned mainly with the application of the Hague and Hague–Visby Rules respectively but they both also address wider issues. In the note, reference is made to the conclusion of Hirst J in *The Chanda* that an exception clause in that case did not apply because it was intended to do so only if the goods were stowed under deck. The note continues:[151]

> [T]he supposed intention of the parties does seem to lead to somewhat perverse results. Thus, they must evidently have intended that the shipowners could have limited their liability if the [article carried] had been stowed under deck but so inadequately lashed down that it broke loose in a storm and had to be written off. Likewise, they presumably intended that the shipowners could limit their liability if the ship was so badly maintained that she sank, carrying the [article carried] to the ocean floor. The extent which the almost geographical basis underlying *Lilley v Doubleday*[152] and *Gibaud*[153] is sound today requires detailed analysis. Although any contract must be carefully construed in order to decide how far the parties intended it to apply in unexpected circumstances, the supposed intention of the parties must be derived from more than a mixture of legal concepts of uncertain status and a healthy dislike of any clause limiting the damages recoverable for a gross breach of contract to an almost nominal sum.

The learned writer returns to these seeming inconsistencies at the end of his note. Nor is he alone in not wanting unauthorised deck carriage treated as a type of deviation. In his Butterworth Lecture,[154] Professor Reynolds describes such carriage as 'simply another example of a very bad breach' and he goes on to observe:

> Quite apart from the general difficulties of deviation, wrongful deck stowage has attained a significance beyond what is appropriate. Other breaches as to stowage, and other breaches in general (such as furnishing an unseaworthy ship) may be just as serious.

I am not competent to assess the practical implications of what Mr Davenport and Professor Reynolds are saying. All I can do is suggest, very tentatively, that those who come to make decisions in this area have regard to such considerations as following:

— Wrongful deck carriage is a classic form of quasi-deviation.
— It seems to be generally agreed that the risks of carriage on deck differ from those of carriage below deck and are in a number of respects greater.
— Quasi-deviation has a very long history in a wide range of bailment relationships.
— The common law system of decision by analogy would mean that judicial abolition of quasi-deviation in one kind of bailment would have a similar effect in others.
— Quasi-deviation is not merely another form of bad breach. Rather, it is the breach of a particular kind of obligation in bailments.

151 Above note 148 at 522.
152 (1881) 7 QBD 510.
153 [1921] 2 KB 426.
154 Above note 12 at 50.

- If the relationship of quasi-deviation to rights of possession is accepted, it can more readily be distinguished from other kinds of breach.
- Neither explicitly, nor by inference, did the decision of the House of Lords in *Photo Production* necessarily involve any reversal of the law of bailment as it existed before *Thorley v Orchis*.

Conclusion

By ascribing the effects of deviation to discharge for breach in *Thorley v Orchis*, the Court of Appeal opened the way to a series of distortions the removal of which, fortunately, has now been made possible by the House of Lord in the *Photo Production* case. But it does not follow that deviation and quasi-deviation have thereby ceased to have special effects. Some of these may turn on the interpretation of exception and limitation clauses. Others, though, are very long-established incidents of a continuing law of bailment, the relevance of which may not yet have been fully appreciated.[155]

[155] Since this essay was written Professor M Dockray has published 'Deviation: Doctrine all at Sea?' [2000] *LMCLQ* 76, an interesting and valuable contextual study of some of the leading cases.

8

PART I: The Effect of Discharge by Breach on Exception Clauses

Introduction

It was perhaps never very likely that the proponents of fundamental breach would allow their doctrine to die just because of some obiter dicta on the subject from the House of Lords.[1] In that respect, therefore, the recent decision of the Court of Appeal in *Harbutt's 'Plasticine' Ltd v Wayne Tank & Pump Co Ltd*[2] need cause no surprise. What had happened in that case, essentially, was that the defendants had agreed to manufacture some equipment and to install it in the plaintiffs' factory under a contract, clause 15 of which limited the defendants' liability to the amount of the contract price (£2,330). A small and easily corrected defect in the equipment caused a fire which destroyed the factory and resulted in a loss to the plaintiffs of some £150,000. The Court of Appeal held (Lord Denning MR *dubitante*) that on its true construction clause 15 covered the loss in the events which had occurred. The whole Court nevertheless joined in holding that the destruction of the factory and consequent discharge by breach of the contract had the effect of making clause 15 inapplicable. Judgment was given for the full amount of the loss.

What is surprising about *Harbutt's* case, at least to a contract lawyer, is its finding that a contractor can be impressed with a liability even though he has adopted the correct formula for excluding it. That, surely, is rather odd; and one may be forgiven for suspecting that somehow or somewhere, something has gone wrong. The purpose of this article is to investigate whether that suspicion is well founded. The Court of Appeal justified their decision by reference to discharge of the contract for breach, and it is accordingly with that aspect of the law that we will chiefly be concerned.

[1] *Suisse Atlantique Société d'Armement Maritime SA v NV Rotterdamsche Kolen Centrale* [1967] 1 AC 361.

[2] [1970] 1 QB 447; [1970] 2 WLR 198 (CA).

The Ordinary Law of Discharge by Breach

For some time now, the common law has recognised that the conduct or non-performance of one party to a contract may be such that, in justice, the other party ought to be allowed to recover damages without himself having first to perform his own side of the bargain.[3] That is the question with which discharge by breach is concerned, and it has two aspects: the conditions under which the remedy arises, and the incidents of the remedy when it applies. Unfortunately, in both cases there is some degree of uncertainty. Writing in 1916, Morison said the situation was an 'embarrassment' to every practising lawyer.[4] If the position is any better today it is mainly because, since then, trends and tendencies have had longer to develop.

The Conditions of the Remedy

The conditions for discharge by breach exist at common law when one party to a contract has by the default of the other been denied, in a sufficiently serious degree, the substance of what he bargained for.[5] Two methods have been used for fixing the appropriate measure of seriousness: reference to the character of the term broken or not performed, and reference to the quality or scale of the breach.[6] Examples of the first approach are the divisions of contractual terms into dependent and independent covenants, conditions precedent and concurrent, and conditions and warranties. Examples of the second are the concepts of failure of consideration, self-induced frustration, and repudiation.

Experience has shown that neither of these two approaches is sufficient by itself. Thus, the dependent–independent covenant test had to be modified by the introduction of a test of substantial performance.[7] The question whether a term were a condition precedent tended at times to be decided ex post facto by reference to the scale of the breach.[8] For much of the first half of the twentieth century, the condition–warranty test was thought of as exclusive.[9] In practice, it too was modified by the device of characterising the term broken by reference to the importance of the breach rather than by reference to the intention of the parties at the time

[3] Williams' notes on *Pordage v Cole* (1669) 1 Wms Saund 319, from which most modern discussion starts, date from the end of the 18th century.

[4] Morison, *Rescission of Contracts* (1916). The passage occurs in the Preface.

[5] Cf *Hong Kong Fir Shipping Co Ltd v Kawasaki Kisen Kalsha* [1962] 2 QB 26, 66 (CA) per Diplock LJ.

[6] A third approach, the nature of the event which results from the breach, was suggested by Diplock LJ in the *Hong Kong Fir* case, ibid at 66 *et seq*, but his point there was to demonstrate the similarity for some purposes of discharge by breach to frustration. As he pointed out (at 69–70), the character of an event as one giving rise to discharge is to be determined by reference to the term in some cases and to the breach in others.

[7] *Boone v Eyre* (1779) 1 Hy Bl 273.

[8] Contrast *Poussard v Spiers* (1876) 1 QBD 410 with *Bettini v Gye* (1876) 1 QBD 183.

[9] See the *Hong Kong Fir* case [1962] 2 QB 26, 69 per Diplock LJ. It is interesting to find Lord Devlin still favours the view that breach of the type which gives rise to discharge is always the breach of a condition or fundamental term: 'The Treatment of Breach of Contract' [1966] *CLJ* 192, esp 200, 202, 204.

they entered into the contract.[10] Another device was to allow the existence of a class of conditions, only the more extensive breaches of which could give rise to a discharge.[11] The significance of the *Hong Kong Fir* case[12] when it appeared was not that it evolved a new category of term or that it divided warranties into two classes. It was that it reaffirmed what seemed to have been forgotten, that the nature of the term broken and the scale of the breach can, each of them, be relevant to the question whether a discharge by breach is justified.[13]

Equally, the *Hong Kong Fir* case did not establish that discharge by breach can occur only on a breach of condition or on the frustration by delay of a commercial adventure.[14] All the following approaches (and it is not claimed that the list is exhaustive) still retain some degree of life:

— Breach of condition[15]
— Failure of condition precedent[16]
— Non-performance of a dependent covenant[17]
— Breach of a fundamental term[18]
— Repudiation[19]
— Anticipatory breach[20]
— Failure of consideration[21]
— Self-induced frustration[22]
— Self-induced impossibility[23]
— Fundamental breach.[24]

[10] *Harrison v Knowles & Foster* [1917] 2 KB 606, 610 per Bailhache J; *Taylor v Combined Buyers* [1924] NZLR 627, 630–40 per Salmond J.

[11] *Tramways Advertising Pty Ltd v Luna Park (NSW) Ltd* (1938) 38 SR(NSW) 632, 641–42 (FC) per Jordan CJ (reversed on other grounds *sub nom Luna Park (NSW) Ltd v Tramways Advertising Pty Ltd* (1938) 61 CLR 286).

[12] [1962] 2 QB 26 (CA).

[13] Cf *The Mihalis Angelos* [1971] 1 QB 164, 193; [1970] 3 All ER 125, 128–29 (CA) per Lord Denning MR.

[14] The judgment of Diplock LJ might appear to suggest that frustration and discharge by breach always arise from the same events, the difference between the two being in the presence or absence of fault ([1962] 2 QB 26, 68, 69).

[15] *Hong Kong Fir* [1962] 2 QB 26 (CA); Cheshire and Fifoot, *The Law of Contract* (7th edn, 1969) 127 *et seq*; *Chitty on Contracts* (23rd edn, 1968) vol I, 279 *et seq*; Treitel, *The Law of Contract* (2nd edn, 1966) 571 *et seq*.

[16] *Halsbury's Laws of England*, vol 8 (Simonds ed) 205; Chitty, ibid at 633; *Sutton and Shannon on Contracts* (5th edn, 1956) 286–87; Salmond and Williams, *The Law of Contracts* (1945) 534–36.

[17] Chitty, above note 15 at 631–32; *Anson's Law of Contract* (23rd edn, 1969) 491–92; Sutton and Shannon, ibid at 291.

[18] Devlin, above note 9; *Suisse Atlantique* [1967] 1 AC 361 (HL).

[19] Cheshire and Fifoot, above note 15 at 531–33; Chitty, above note 15 at 626–27.

[20] Cheshire and Fifoot, above note 15 at 530–31; Chitty, above note 15 at 625–26; Treitel, above note 15 at 600–03.

[21] Glanville Williams, *Law Reform (Frustrated Contracts) Act, 1943* (1944) 2 *et seq*; *Exception Clauses*, 65 and cases there cited.

[22] *Hong Kong Fir* [1962] 2 QB 26 (CA); Chitty, above note 15 at 631.

[23] Salmond and Williams, above note 16 at 543; Anson, above note 17 at 488–89; Sutton and Shannon, above note 16 at 315.

[24] *Suisse Atlantique* [1967] 1 AC 361 (HL).

While these approaches are all of them directed to the same object, it would be a mistake to regard them as identical. Thus, breach of a condition is the breach of a term so fundamental that any default gives a right to elect a discharge.[25] Fundamental terms, it was at one time suggested, are more fundamental even than that.[26] Repudiation denotes words or conduct evincing an intention not to perform.[27] That intention may be deliberate, or it may be forced upon the defaulter by his inability to perform, despite his best endeavours. Failure of consideration may embrace anything from a relatively slight breach of an entire contract to a gross breach which leaves the injured party with substantially nothing of what he bargained for.[28] Self-induced impossibility occurs when further performance passes beyond the powers of the parties, as for example when a master aborts a contract of affreightment by scuttling his ship and cargo.[29] On the other hand, self-induced frustration can occur when performance of a kind may still be possible but would be commercially different from what was contracted for.[30]

The two avenues of approach to discharge by breach, by way of the term broken and by way of the breach itself, are occasionally given the labels of fundamental term and fundamental breach.[31] Those words, however, acquired overtones before the *Suisse Atlantique* case which since then are no longer justified. Moreover, they tend to obscure the fact that there are more than two approaches to the problem. On both these grounds, it is submitted, their use in this way is undesirable.

The Incidents of Discharge by Breach

A description of the incidents of discharge by breach presents rather more difficulty though, fortunately, strong trends have become apparent in the law.

The initial problem is whether discharge by breach operates automatically when a sufficient breach occurs, or whether it is in the election of the innocent party. Outside the field of anticipatory breach, there is very little indication in the nineteenth-century cases of any need for an election and, as late as 1916, Morison felt able to argue that discharge was automatic on breach of condition or on failure of consideration.[32] Since then, however, the trend has been very strongly towards assimilating discharge by breach to anticipatory breach by requiring an election by the innocent party and a communication of that election to the wrongdoer.[33] The reason usually given is that to allow a wrongdoer unilaterally to terminate

[25] *Wallis v Pratt* [1911] AC 394 (HL); *Hong Kong Fir* [1962] 2 QB 26 (CA).

[26] *Smeaton Hanscomb & Co Ltd v Sassoon I Setty, Son & Co* [1953] 2 All ER 1471, 1473.

[27] Cheshire and Fifoot, above note 15 at 531; *Heyman v Darwins* [1942] AC 356 (HL).

[28] Glanville Williams, above note 21 at 2 *et seq.*

[29] Salmond and Williams, above note 16 at 560.

[30] As in the *Hong Kong Fir* case [1962] 2 QB 26 (CA).

[31] *Suisse Atlantique* [1967] 1 AC 361 (HL).

[32] Morison, *Rescission of Contracts*, above note 4 at 18.

[33] *Heyman v Darwins Ltd* [1942] AC 356 (HL); *Mason v Clouet* [1924] AC 980 (HL); *Thorpe v Fasey* [1949] Ch 649. This is the view found in current English textbooks on Contract.

the contract would be to allow him to profit by his wrongdoing.[34] This argument depends on the hypothesis that the effect of discharge by breach is a termination of the contract, a point which will be dealt with separately. In practical terms, however, it does seem good sense to allow the injured party a choice in cases where the possibility of an acceptable degree of performance or substituted performance remains.

On the other hand, it would not be hard to imagine cases where it would be otiose to require an election because further performance would literally have become impossible.[35] The scuttling of a ship and cargo has already been instanced. The destruction of both factory and equipment in the *Harbutt's 'Plasticine'* case[36] is another example and the Court of Appeal was no doubt correct in dispensing, as they did, with the need for an election in that case. On the other hand, it is doubtful whether, as dicta in that case seem to suggest, mere frustration as distinct from impossibility would be enough. If it were, there would be practical difficulties for both parties on the facts of cases like that of the *Hong Kong Fir*.[37]

The other requirement under this head, that the election must be communicated to be effective,[38] is again good sense, in that it would undoubtedly be unfair to the party in breach to leave him uncertain whether or not a discharge had taken place. Here again, the law seems to allow for some degree of flexibility and it looks as though the requirement of communication will be dispensed with in cases where the wrongdoer has deliberately made communication impossible.[39]

The next problem is whether or not discharge by breach results in a termination of the contract. Many observers may find it surprising that this should be regarded as a problem at all.[40] What makes it so is that termination of the contract is not in any way necessary to what discharge by breach seeks to achieve, which is to release the injured party from any further obligation to perform his part and to enable him, nevertheless, to recover damages from the other side. The only termination that that involves is of the injured party's obligations and of the wrongdoer's power to perform,[41] except by way of reduction of damages.[42] Moreover, it is commonly insisted that the contract survives for purposes of recovery of damages by the injured party[43] and, as an aspect of that, arbitration clauses normally continue to apply.[44] What, it is submitted, discharge by breach really does is not so much

[34] *Heyman v Darwins* [1942] AC 356, 373 (HL).

[35] *Joseph Constantine Ltd v Imperial Smelting Corporation* [1942] AC 154, 191 (HL) per Lord Wright; Salmond and Williams, above note 16 at 559–60.

[36] [1970] 1 QB 447; [1970] 2 WLR 198 (CA).

[37] *Hong Kong Fir* [1962] 2 QB 26 (CA).

[38] *Berners v Fleming* [1925] Ch 264 (CA).

[39] *Car & Universal Finance Co Ltd v Caldwell* [1965] 1 QB 525 (CA); though see *Macleod v Kerr*, 1965 SC 253 *contra*.

[40] It seems, for example, to have been taken for granted that there was a literal rescission (at least as to the future) both in the *Suisse Atlantique* case and in the *Harbutt's 'Plasticine'* case.

[41] *Heyman v Darwins* [1942] AC 356, 367, 372–74, 399–400 (HL); *Williston on Contracts* (3rd edn, 1957) vol 11, §§ 1305, 1306; and see *Corbin on Contracts* (1951) vol 4, § 982.

[42] *Bastin v Bidwell* (1881) 18 Ch D 238, 252.

[43] Chitty, above note 15 at 624; Sutton and Shannon, above note 16 at 298; Salmond and Williams, above note 16 at 562; Anson, above note 17 at 157, 482; *Bines v Sankey* [1958] NZLR 886.

[44] *Heyman v Darwins* [1942] AC 356 (HL).

to 'terminate' as to 'truncate'. Its function is, notionally at least, to take the parties direct from the point of termination to the point where completion is due.[45] In doing so, it gives the injured party an immediate right of action. It deprives the wrongdoer of any rights or advantages which might have accrued to him during that interval, and by removing any further possibility of completion, prevents his enforcing the obligations of the party injured, including for example those arising under covenants in restraint of trade.[46]

Nevertheless, despite protests in the House of Lords that the contract does not terminate,[47] and despite the evidence for its survival after discharge, it has to be admitted that many would say a literal termination does occur. On this theory such things as demurrage clauses,[48] exception clauses,[49] and covenants in restraint of trade are rescinded beyond recall, while other parts of the contract including arbitration clauses, somehow manage to retain after rescission the same effect they would have had without it.

If, however, it is accepted that discharge by breach does effect an actual termination of the contract, the next question is the point from which that termination operates. Theoretically, there are several possibilities; in particular, the point at which the contract is entered into, the moment of breach, the moment of election, and the moment of communication of election. The first of these, termination *ab initio*, does in fact exist as a remedy under the name of rescission[50] but it is to be distinguished from discharge by breach, more especially because it involves a surrender by the injured party of his rights to recover damages.[51] The real choice lies between the moment of breach on the one hand and the election, or its communication, on the other.

In those cases where the breach renders an election otiose, termination and breach are no doubt simultaneous. On the other hand, in cases where an election is required, termination would have to be retrospective if it were to date back to the breach. The question has practical consequences only where the wrongdoer after breach continues to perform and this may explain why it has been so little discussed in the cases. Nevertheless, there does seem to be wide agreement that discharge by breach is prospective rather than retrospective in its effect.[52] This in

45 Cf *The Mihalis Angelos* [1970] 1 All E.R. 673, 684 per Mocatta J (reversed [1971] 1 QB 164 (CA)).

46 *General Bill Posting Co Ltd v Atkinson* [1909] AC 118 (HL).

47 *Viz* in *Heyman v Darwins* [1942] AC 356, 367, 372–74, 399–400 (HL), above note 41.

48 *Suisse Atlantique* [1967] 1 AC 361 (HL).

49 *Harbutt's 'Plasticine'* [1970] 1 QB 447; [1970] 2 WLR 198 (CA).

50 *Smith's Leading Cases* (13th edn, 1929) 46–47. Though it holds that rescission *ab initio* is not necessary to recovery in quasi contract; *Fibrosa Spolka Akcyjna v Fairbairn Lawson Combe Barbour, Ltd* [1943] AC 32 (HL) does not exclude the possibility of a rescission in the full sense.

51 *De Bernardy v Harding* (1853) 3 Exch 822.

52 Cheshire and Fifoot, above note 15 at 531, 533; Salmond and Williams, above note 16 at 565; *Yeoman Credit Ltd v Apps* [1962] 2 QB 508 (CA); *Hirji Mulji v Cheong Yue Steamship Co Ltd* [1926] AC 497, 510 (JC); *Heyman v Darwins* [1942] AC 356, 366, 374, 379, 381, 383, 397–98, 399 (HL); *Fibrosa Spolka Akcyjna v Fairbairn Lawson Combe Barbour, Ltd* [1943] AC 32, 65; *Boston Deep Sea Co v Ansell* (1888) 39 Ch D 339, 352, 360, 365; *Healy v SA Francaise Rubastic* [1917] 1 KB 946. Australian dicta to the same effect are listed in *Exception Clauses*, 74, fn 36.

fact is what would be expected, consistently with the idea of discharge by breach as a decision by an injured party thenceforth no longer to be bound to perform his side of the bargain. And though there is apparently no case on the point, it would seem fair to assume that, in those cases where communication of the election is required, termination will date from the communication. The consequence of all this would be that the contract would govern the dealings of the parties down to the moment of termination, but would have no application to what took place thereafter.

There is a distinction essential to any understanding of the effect of discharge by breach on exception clauses, which needs to be made at once. It is between exception clauses directed to the very breach upon which the claim to discharge is based and clauses directed to other breaches or obligations. On facts like those of *Harbutt's 'Plasticine'*, it is the difference between an exception clause purporting to govern the destruction of the premises by fire and, say, a clause dealing with other matters such as compliance with specification, liability for theft, or vandalism and so on. To claim that on discharge for a breach not itself the subject of an exception clause, the wrongdoer lost the benefit of his exception clauses, would be one thing. To say that a contract could be discharged despite an exception clause covering the very point, and that the discharge would in turn cause the clause to become inapplicable, could be quite another.

A further point that has to be made, however apologetically, is that the effect of discharge by breach may depend very materially on what the function of an exception clause is conceived to be. If exception clauses have a bearing on the obligations of the parties the answer is one thing; if they have nothing to do with obligation, but operate merely as procedural obstacles to suit, it might well be another. The jurisprudential arguments for the former view have been canvassed at length elsewhere[53] and it is not proposed to burden the reader of this article with a restatement of them here. What the theory says, though, is that exception clauses have a substantive effect in any of several different ways. Thus, an exclusion of an implied-by-law term prevents the implication of that term into the contract. When a contractor follows one of his promises by an exception clause saying he will not be liable in certain circumstances for failure to perform it, what he is really doing is to qualify his promise. And this is so whether he excludes his liability altogether, or merely limits it to a given amount or imposes a time limit on claims against him. What he says in effect is 'I undertake this liability, as limited by my exception clauses'. And he says this as he enters into his contract. Accordingly, this is the measure of his obligations from the start,[54] so that at no stage can it ever be possible to decide what he has undertaken by referring to his promises alone, without taking into account the qualifications he has placed upon them.

[53] *Exception Clauses*, esp Ch 1 and the Appendix. Chapter 1 is reproduced in *Assumption* as Chapter 6.

[54] *Grein v Imperial Airways Ltd* [1937] 1 KB 50, 88 (CA). Compare *Heyman v Darwins* [1942] AC 356, 368 (HL) (submission to arbitration). And see *The Council of the City of Sydney v West* (1965) 114 CLR 481, 495–96 per Kitto J. See also *Firestone Tyre & Rubber Co v Vokins* [1951] 1 Lloyd's Rep 32, 39.

While this theory has attracted a measure of judicial support since 1964,[55] it is still far from gaining universal acceptance. The excuse for resurrecting it here is that the *Harbutt's 'Plasticine'* case[56] demonstrates as clearly as may be the extraordinary consequences which can be made to flow from the adherence to the rival approach. While it will be argued that even on that approach, *Harbutt's 'Plasticine'* was wrongly decided, the 'exceptions-as-qualifications' theory offers a much more direct path to that result. It is proposed first to consider the effect of discharge by breach on exception clauses on the assumption that such clauses qualify obligations and then to return to the other approach.

Exception Clauses as Substantive

On the assumption that exception clauses have a qualifying effect on obligation, certain of them at least can have a crucial relevance to the first question with which discharge by breach is concerned, which is whether the conditions for the remedy exist. Some clauses go to the very question whether the term broken or the breach alleged is of a kind upon which discharge can be founded. A clause which, for example, prevented the implication of any condition as to title under section 12 of the Sale of Goods Act 1893 would have the effect that failure to pass title could not be the breach of condition of the contract. Similarly, a limitation of the right to reject goods could (though not necessarily would)[57] have the effect of reducing what would otherwise be a condition to the status of a warranty. Less obviously, an exclusion of all liability for breach of what would otherwise be a promissory condition could have the effect of preventing the promise operating as a ground for discharge by *breach*, even though it might not stop failure to perform operating as the failure of a contingency under the contract. These, presumably, were the types of clause Lord Wilberforce had in mind when, in the *Suisse Atlantique* case, he said:

> An act which, apart from the exception clause, might be a breach sufficiently serious to justify refusal of further performance, may be reduced in effect, or made not a breach at all, by the terms of the clause.[58]

Clearly, discharge by breach can have no effect on exception clauses of this kind if the 'breach' upon which the claim to discharge is founded falls within the scope of

[55] *Viz*, from Lord Wilberforce in the *Suisse Atlantique* case [1967] 1 AC 361, 431; Diplock LJ in *Hardwick Game Farm v Suffolk Agricultural Poultry Producers Assn* [1966] 1 WLR 287, 339 *et seq* (CA) and see also his judgment in *C Czarnikow Ltd v Koufos* [1966] 1 Lloyd's Rep 595, 607; Kitto J in *The Council of the City of Sydney v West* (1965) 114 CLR 481, 495–96 and Windeyer J in *Thomas National Transport (Melbourne) Pty Ltd v May & Baker (Australia) Pty Ltd* (1966) 115 CLR 353, 385–86. In *Torquay Hotel Co Ltd v Cousins* [1969] 2 Ch 106, Lord Denning accepted that the effect of an exception clause was to prevent there being a breach of contract. See also Sellers LJ in the *Hardwick Game Farm* case [1966] 1 WLR 287, 309 and Winn LJ in *Gillette Industries Ltd v WH Martin Ltd* [1966] 1 Lloyd's Rep 57, 68.

[56] *Harbutt's 'Plasticine'* [1970] 1 QB 447; [1970] 2 WLR 198 (CA).

[57] Jenkins, 'The Essence of the Contract' [1969] *CLJ* 251, 253.

[58] *Suisse Atlantique* [1967] 1 AC 361, 431 (HL). On the other hand, the contrary view is implicit in the judgment of Lord Denning MR in *Farnworth Finance Facilities v Attryde* [1970] 1 WLR 1053 (CA).

the clause. The reason is that the conditions for discharge by breach are prevented by the exception clause from ever arising. Whether such exception clauses would be effected by a discharge founded on some other breach *not* covered by them would depend upon the effect of a valid discharge by breach on exception clauses generally, and the solution here turns to some degree on the view taken of the ordinary incidents of discharge by breach.

In the first place, if the effect of discharge by breach is not a termination of the contract but, as has been claimed in the House of Lords,[59] a termination only of certain obligations and rights, the position is quite straightforward. Upon the discharge, the injured party acquires an immediate right to recover damages from the wrongdoer for his breach and the contract remains alive for that purpose. It then becomes a matter for the court to determine what the obligations of the wrongdoer are and the recoverable damages flowing from such breach of those obligations as he has committed. The measure of those obligations is not to be found merely by reference to the contractor's promises in isolation from the qualifications he placed upon them. The promises and the exceptions must be looked at together, and this is as true of partial qualifications as it is of total exclusions. This being so, discharge by breach as such would have no effect whatever on exception clauses. Whether the wrongdoer would be impressed with liability would depend solely upon the interpretation of the contract, upon whether the acts complained of fell within the contractor's promises and outside the qualifications or limitations he had placed on those promises.

The other possible view of discharge by breach is that it literally terminates the contract, albeit only *in futuro*. Since displacement is only as to the future, it would follow that the exception clauses would apply in full force until the moment of termination. Again the result is that, at least until that point, whatever breaches occur happen subject to the exception clauses and it is only acts committed after termination which would be unprotected. The result in the *Harbutt's 'Plasticine'* case[60] would be that at the point of time when the factory was destroyed by fire, the obligations of the contractor were limited to payment of not more than £2,330. That was what the parties agreed when they entered into the contract, and it was still their contract at the point when the loss occurred.[61]

There is another way of reaching the same result, even assuming that the effect of discharge by breach is a literal termination of the contract. Even on that assumption, the contract remains alive for the purpose of recovery by the injured party. This must mean that the contract remains alive for the purpose of assessing the wrongdoer's liabilities and these in turn depend upon his obligations. Once again, the exception clauses are just as essential a part of the definition of those obligations as are his positive promises. It would be extraordinarily difficult to justify the survival of the one without the other.

[59] *Heyman v Darwins* [1942] AC 356 (HL). See above, note 40.

[60] *Harbutt's 'Plasticine'* [1970] 1 QB 447; [1970] 2 WLR 198 (CA).

[61] See above, note 54.

The result of all this is that there is nothing magical about discharge by breach; nothing in it to justify any disregard of the terms of the contract. The determinant of whether an exception clause protects a party to a contract remains in every case whether or not the clause properly bears such an interpretation.

Exception Clauses as Procedural

While it is submitted that the exception clauses-as-qualifications theory offers a solution to the difficulties raised by *Harbutt's 'Plasticine'* it would be a pity if the case against that decision were seen to rest solely on a particular and possibly over subtle academic argument. Even on the other approach, *Harbutt's 'Plasticine'* raises doubts.

The finding in that case, that discharge by breach prevents reliance on a clause which directly covers the events which occurred, could be justified on four possible grounds. One would be that, as a matter of substantive law, exception clauses can have no application to breaches of the type which ordinarily justify termination. This of course is the 'fundamental breach' principle which the House of Lords rejected in the *Suisse Atlantique*[62] case. The second ground can be disposed of as quickly. It would be that as a matter of construction the exception clauses were subject to a condition that they would not apply in the event of what, apart from them, would be a repudiatory breach. This was the sort of approach the House of Lords rejected in *Hain v Tate & Lyle*[63] when they held that there was no warrant for a finding that the exception clause in that contract was alone subject to a 'no-deviation' condition. In any event, it was not the construction adopted by the Court of Appeal in the *Harbutt's 'Plasticine'* case.

The other two possibilities depend upon what happens to the contract on a discharge by breach. One is that, on a discharge, the exception clause terminates retrospectively to a point before the breach occurs. This of course runs counter to the predominant view that discharge by breach operates only *in futuro*. More than this, Lord Denning himself, in the course of his judgment, accepted that the discharge operated 'for the future'.[64]

The last possibility and, though it was never declared in the judgments, undoubtedly the one on which the Court of Appeal based their reasoning, is that the exception clause had no relevance or effect before termination occurred and that, after that point, it could not take effect because the contract of which it was part had been rescinded. Superficially, perhaps, that approach looks attractive enough. On any analysis, though, it tends to break down. For one thing, it assumes that when the parties exclude or limit liability for breach, the liability referred to is one declared and imposed at the point of *adjudication*. But a much more natural

[62] *Suisse Atlantique* [1967] 1 AC 361.
[63] [1936] 2 All ER 597, 601, 608, 614–15 (HL).
[64] *Harbutt's 'Plasticine'* [1970] 1 QB 447, 466; [1970] 2 WLR 198, 210 (CA).

interpretation is that the liability concerned is liability for breach of contract and that, of course, accrues at the moment of breach.[65] At that particular moment, on any view of the effect of discharge by breach, the contract (including the exception clause) is still in existence. Again, the approach carries the surely uncomfortable consequence that, despite assertions in the *Suisse Atlantique* case that liability for fundamental breach can be excluded,[66] that rule would have no effect unless the injured party after breach elected that it should.

Just as difficult is the fact that it involves in effect the partial rescission of the contract. Here again, it is not just that the House of Lords has rejected any suggestion that the injured party has a right to both approbate and reprobate, to affirm some parts of the contract and terminate others.[67] The Court of Appeal would no doubt claim that the contract as a whole had been terminated. The fact remains that, somehow, the contract does survive for the purpose of fixing the wrongdoer's responsibility and for assessing the damages recoverable by the injured party. Even if exception clauses were not qualifications attached by the wrongdoer to his undertakings and were mere procedural obstacles to recovery, they would still be relevant to the purposes for which the contract survives. Thus, if a party to a sale of goods is charged that he has not given title, it must be germane, even as only a procedural defence, that the contract expressly provides that no undertaking as to title is given or is to be implied. Equally, if the contract is to be referred to in order to assess damages payable for its breach, it is surely relevant that the parties have agreed that damages should be limited to a stated amount. Even assuming that discharge brings about a total termination of the contract, there needs to be some explanation of why only some of the relevant parts of it take part in the subsequent revival. There is, for example, no self-evident justice in the suggestion that liquidated damages clauses lack this capacity for revival, with the result that injured parties lose the benefit of them if they elect a discharge.[68] A partial explanation which might conceivably be advanced would be that on termination the wrongdoer loses the capacity to compel performance by the injured party. The answer to that is that on any view of the nature of exception clauses they are not promises or obligations which can be enforced or performed. Indeed, they have nothing whatever to do with the injured party's promises or obligations.

At the risk of overemphasising the point, it needs to be repeated that the real test of the applicability of an exception clause, on discharge by breach or at any other time, is quite simply whether on its proper construction the clause covers what has occurred.[69] On the facts of the *Harbutt's 'Plasticine'* case, this means that the

[65] *Bosma v Larsen* [1966] 1 Lloyd's Rep 22.

[66] At 392 per Viscount Dilhorne; 399, 405 per Lord Reid; 410 per Lord Hodson; 427 per Lord Upjohn.

[67] *Hain Steamship Co Ltd v Tate & Lyle Ltd* [1936] 2 All ER 597 (HL); *Heyman v Darwins* [1942] AC 356 (HL); *Suisse Atlantique* [1967] 1 AC 361, 398 per Lord Reid.

[68] Cf the *Suisse Atlantique case* [1967] 1 AC 361, 405 per Lord Reid.

[69] This ultimately was the emphasis in *Heyman v Darwins* [1942] AC 356 (HL) in relation to arbitration clauses.

liability of the contractor would have been limited to £2,330, always provided that the exception clause did in fact, on its proper construction, cover the events which had occurred. In the *Suisse Atlantique* case,[70] the House of Lords went a long way towards reaching this sort of conclusion. It is at least conceivable that they would have gone the whole way had it not been for two factors: the agreement of counsel appearing before them that discharge by breach makes an exception clause cease to apply;[71] and the line of cases on deviation and quasi-deviation on which, it seems certain, counsel's agreement was based.[72]

The Effect of the Deviation Cases

In the strict sense, deviation is what occurs when a carrier of goods, without lawful excuse, departs from the contract route.[73] But the incidents of deviation are found in connection with other types of bailment, in which context they are usually referred to as 'quasi-deviation'.[74] These incidents occur whenever a bailee, without lawful excuse, disregards limitations upon his authority as bailee, as for example when he holds goods in a place,[75] for a purpose,[76] or at a time[77] when he has no mandate to do so. When that happens, he automatically becomes an insurer against loss or damage to the goods and in so doing loses the protection not only of his contractual exceptions, but even of the common law exceptions of Act of God and of the Queen's enemies.[78] His only available defence is to show that the loss or damage would have occurred anyway.[79] The explanation for these phenomena springs from the nature of bailment itself. When a bailee's authority to hold the bailed goods has been limited in particular ways and he then fails to observe those limitations, he ceases to hold the goods within the ambit of the bailment and is reduced to the status of a mere detainor. As such, he loses the benefits of the bailment relationship and thereafter has to carry the risk of loss or damage to the goods.[80] An alternative partial explanation is that when a bailee, by altering the nature of an adventure, alters its risks, he automatically loses the protection of his exception clauses because they are directed only to the risks which attend the

[70] *Suisse Atlantique* [1967] 1 AC 361.

[71] Ibid at 419 per Lord Upjohn. A similar concession was apparently made by counsel for the defendants in *Harbutt's 'Plasticine'* [1970] 1 QB 447; [1970] 2 WLR 198 (CA).

[72] *Suisse Atlantique* [1967] 1 AC 361, 372, where counsel for the appellants submitted that fundamental breach and repudiation by breach were the same 'animal' as deviation.

[73] Carver, *Carriage by Sea* (11th edn, 1963) vol 2, 593.

[74] There is a full discussion of deviation and quasi deviation and their effect upon exception clauses in *Exception Clauses*, Ch 6.

[75] *Lilley v Doubleday* (1881) 7 QBD 510.

[76] Story, *The Law of Bailments* (1839) 160.

[77] *Coggs v Bernard* (1703) 2 Ld Raym 909, 915, 917; *Shaw v Symmons* [1917] 1 KB 799.

[78] *Ellis v Turner* (1800) 8 TR 531; *Davis v Garrett* (1830) 6 Bing 716; *Lilley v Doubleday* (1881) 7 QBD 510.

[79] *Davis v Garrett*, ibid; *James Morrison v Shaw Saville and Albion Co* [1916] 2 KB 783 (CA).

[80] This explanation is discussed more fully in *Exception Clauses*, 89–93.

bailment itself.[81] But whichever way they are to be explained, the important points are that deviation and quasi-deviation are peculiar to bailment,[82] and that they are unique in bringing about an automatic non-application of the exception clauses as from the moment the deviation commences, without the need for an election to that effect by the injured party.[83] It is these features which have caused difficulty in relation to discharge by breach.

As might be expected, the origins of these phenomena in the law of bailment were lost sight of as the nineteenth century advanced and by 1890 the courts had begun to seek explanations in the law of discharge by breach.[84] At that time, the requirement that the injured party elect a discharge had not fully emerged, so that the absence of any such election in typical deviation cases was not seen as an embarrassment. For a similar reason, the fact that, on a deviation, the exception clauses cease to apply from the moment the deviation commences was not seen to raise any problem either. But because the non-applicability of the exception clause was thought to depend on a rescission for breach, and because there is no warrant for a selective or partial discharge, it was concluded that the contract as a whole, and not just the exception clause, was rescinded from that moment.[85] This in turn caused embarrassment over the question of freight in cases where goods had been delivered in good time at their port of destination, notwithstanding an intermediate deviation. If the contract terminated, it seemed, freight ceased to be recoverable, even though, in commercial circles, it had always been regarded as payable in such cases.[86] The courts had to turn round and invent devices which would have been quite unnecessary under the ordinary rules of discharge by breach.[87] Under those rules, in the absence of any earlier election by the injured party, a timeous delivery of the goods would have been a substantial performance and no question of discharge by breach would have arisen.

Once the need for an election became established under the ordinary law of discharge by breach, further distortions were found to be necessary in the deviation cases. The question of election was one of the problems the House of Lords had to contend with in *Hain v Tate & Lyle* in 1936. The solution they adopted was to hold that termination of the contract operated automatically from the moment of breach, unless the injured party chose to affirm it. This can be contrasted with the ordinary rule that, on a discharge by breach, the contract remains in being unless and until the injured party elects to terminate it. There were other distortions

[81] *Rendall v Arcos Ltd* (1937) 43 Com Cas 1, 15 (HL) per Lord Wright, delivering the opinion of the House. And see also the *Suisse Atlantique* case [1967] 1 AC 361, 434 per Lord Wilberforce.

[82] They do not occur when a carrier of passengers departs from the contract route, *Hobbs v LSW Railway Co* (1875) LR 10 QB 11. See also *McMahon v Field* (1881) 7 QBD 59 for another act which would have been deviation, had there been a bailment.

[83] The possible uniqueness of deviation is recognised in Chitty, above note 15 at 333 and Anson, above note 17 at 157. See also *The Albion* [1953] 1 WLR 1026 (CA).

[84] *Balian and Sons v Joly, Victoria and Co Ltd* (1890) 6 TLR 345 (CA); *Joseph Thorley Ltd v Orchis Steamship Co Ltd* [1907] 1 KB 660; *Morrison v Shaw Saville* [1916] 2 KB 783 (CA).

[85] [1936] 2 All ER 597 (HL).

[86] Ibid at 612.

[87] These devices are discussed in Goff and Jones, *The Law of Restitution* (1966) 354–55.

forthcoming. It was assumed by the House in the *Hain* case that it was termination of the contract which prevented the exceptions applying. A corollary to this was that, if the contract were affirmed, the exception would protect the wrongdoer. In truth, though, affirmation by itself can never have that effect.[88] Exception clauses can only take effect if they are drawn widely enough to do so. Prima facie, exception clauses in contracts of affreightment are not to be interpreted as applying to the risks of a deviation. They could be made to apply on affirmation only if the contract were varied to that effect, whether by an agreed alteration to the contract route or by an alteration to the exception clause itself. No doubt, on the facts of *Hain v Tate & Lyle*,[89] it would be easy enough to imply such a variation, but in principle there is no reason why the owner of goods which have been damaged during a deviation should, by subsequent affirmation, be denied the right to recover his loss. These two beliefs, that it is termination which denies the wrongdoer the protection of his exceptions, and that affirmation of the contract gives him back that benefit, eventually caused trouble during the heyday of the fundamental breach theory. In *Charterhouse Credit Co Ltd v Tolly*,[90] the hirer of a vehicle under a hire-purchase agreement had affirmed his contract, notwithstanding that the owner had committed a fundamental breach. This affirmation, it was thought, would prevent the hirer's recovering damages because it meant that the exception clauses now protected the wrongdoer. The apparent problem would never have arisen had the enquiry been directed to the question whether the exception clause, on its proper construction, covered the breach complained of. The court would have decided that the exceptions did not cover delivery of an unroadworthy car.[91]

There is one solecism, though, from which the deviation cases seem to have remained free. Nowhere has it been held that discharge by breach for deviation prevents reliance upon a liberty clause directed to the question of deviation itself.

In general, however, the unfortunate impression left by the deviation cases is that discharge by breach and deviation are one and the same thing. That being so, discharge by breach appears to become something which literally rescinds a contract from the moment breach commences, unless the injured party subsequently elects to affirm. And it is this which gives plausibility to the view that neither exception clauses nor agreed damages clauses survive a repudiatory breach, notwithstanding the contradiction that the rest of the contract remains available for the purpose of assessing damages and notwithstanding, also, protests from the House of Lords, both that no termination of the contract does occur, and that selective rescission of one part of the contract without the others is not an option open to the injured party. It is this, as much as anything, which sustains the myth that exception clauses are somehow different in function from the rest of the contract and that, on

[88] Cf Anson, above note 17 at 156; *Suisse Atlantique* [1967] 1 AC 361, 399, 413 (HL).

[89] [1936] 2 All ER 597 (HL).

[90] [1963] 2 QB 683 (CA).

[91] Similar difficulties were experienced in *John Carter v Hanson Haulage* [1965] 2 QB 495 (CA) and by Windeyer J in *Thomas National Transport (Melbourne) Pty Ltd v May & Baker (Australia) Pty Ltd* (1966) 115 CLR 353.

discharge by breach, the obligations of the wrongdoer can be defined and enforced without reference to any qualifications the contract may have placed upon them.

It was deviation which, in turn, led to and sustained the concept of a fundamental breach the effect of which was to disqualify a wrongdoer from relying on his exception clauses, however widely drawn.[92] In the earliest stages in the development of that doctrine, it was recognised in some degree that the fundamental (deviation) type of breach must be different from breach of a condition (the ordinary discharge by breach) since, manifestly, promissory conditions could successfully be excluded. Hence the characterisation of the new breach as 'fundamental' and as something narrower than breach of condition.[93] Inevitably, though, the existence of the cases identifying deviation with discharge by breach meant that sooner or later the distinction would be lost. Deviation equals fundamental breach; discharge by breach equals deviation.[94] The circle was finally completed when, in the *Suisse Atlantique* case, the House of Lords categorised 'fundamental terms' and 'fundamental breach' as shorthand expressions for the circumstances giving rise to discharge by breach.[95]

In sum, what bedevils the common law of discharge by breach, it is submitted, is this existence, parallel to each other, of two mutually inconsistent streams of authority, discharge by breach proper and deviation. That would be a difficult enough position by itself but it is made worse by the fact that, between them, the two streams have spawned a spurious third. It is a situation in which one might not be surprised to find a near flood of cases, comments, and articles in which judges and academics resorted to one refinement after another in a vain attempt to reconcile the irreconcilable.

Conclusion

The way out of all this difficulty is not a particularly hard one to find. The chief step of course would be to recognise that deviation and quasi-deviation are *sui generis* and to be kept distinct from discharge by breach. The second necessary step would be to allow the substantive doctrine of fundamental breach to remain where the *Suisse Atlantique* case left it, decently interred. The third step would be to complete the process begun by the House of Lords in that case and move

[92] The origin of the doctrine can be traced through *Chandris v Isbrandtsen Moller* [1951] 1 KB 240 and *Alexander v Railway Executive* [1951] 2 KB 882 (in both of which Devlin J referred back to *Hain v Tate & Lyle* [1936] 2 All ER 597 (HL) and to *Smeaton Hanscombe v Sassoon I Setty* [1953] 2 All ER 1471 where it emerged as a distinct new doctrine). In *The Albion* [1953] 1 WLR 1026 (CA) the Court of Appeal tried to confine it to deviation and quasi deviation.

[93] *Smeaton Hanscomb v Sassoon I Setty* [1953] 2 All ER 1471, 1473.

[94] See above, note 72.

[95] *Suisse Atlantique* [1967] 1 AC 361. Fundamental terms were described as those underlying the whole contract, so that any breach would give rise to a right to elect termination of the contract (see 422 per Lord Upjohn). Five kinds of fundamental breach were identified *viz* (i) performance totally

directly to the acceptance of a universal rule that the effect of exception clauses depends on their proper interpretation, and on that alone (questions of fraud, illegality and the like, apart).[96]

No doubt, some would object that to do all this would be to reduce the courts to a state of impotence. Such a result, it is submitted, need not follow at all. There is already in existence an impressive array of interpretative devices for containing exception clauses, and they are open to still further development. It is worth remembering what some of them are.

a. Every exception clause is to be interpreted, in case of ambiguity, *contra proferentem*.[97]
b. Only in the clearest circumstances will general words of exclusion be interpreted to cover important terms or liability for serious breaches.[98] The more important the term or the breach, the clearer those circumstances must be.[99]
c. Exception clauses are to be interpreted consistently with the main objects of the contract and, under this head, the literal meaning can be modified substantially.[100]
d. In case of genuine inconsistency with the positive parts of the contract, exception clauses can be modified or ignored altogether on grounds of repugnancy.[101]
e. Exception clauses have no application to acts falling beyond the contemplated ambit of the contract.[102]
f. General words of exclusion have no application to negligence, unless negligence is the only liability to which they could apply.[103]
g. In bailment contracts, exception clauses have no application once the bailor exceeds any limitation on his authority.[104]

different from that contemplated by the contract (at 393 per Viscount Dilhorne, 397 per Lord Reid, 409 per Lord Hodson, 431 per Lord Wilberforce); (ii) breach entitling the injured party to terminate (at 397–98 per Lord Reid, 410 per Lord Hodson, 418, 422 per Lord Upjohn, 431 per Lord Wilberforce); (iii) repudiatory conduct evidencing an intention by the wrongdoer no longer to be bound (at 394 per Viscount Dilhorne, 397–98 per Lord Reid); (iv) breach going to the root of the contract (at 397 per Lord Reid, 409 per Lord Hodson, 418 per Lord Upjohn, 431 per Lord Wilberforce; (v) breach amounting to self-induced frustration or impossibility (at 409 per Lord Hodson). These are, all of them, readily identifiable examples of the circumstances under which discharge by breach can occur.

[96] Compare the decision of the High Court of Australia in *The Council of the City of Sydney v West* (1965) 114 CLR 481. And is there, one wonders, any significance in the fact that since the *Harbutt's 'Plasticine'* case, Lord Denning has, in *Farnworth Finance Facilities v Attryde* [1970] 1 WLR 1053 (CA) at least partially returned to a construction approach?

[97] One striking example is *Webster v Higgin* [1948] 2 All ER 127 (CA).

[98] See *Exception Clauses*, 114 and cases there cited at fn 75.

[99] *Suisse Atlantique* [1967] 1 AC 361, 432 (HL) per Lord Wilberforce.

[100] *Glynn v Margetson* [1893] AC 351 (HL); *Sze Hai Tong Bank v Rambler Cycle Co* [1959] AC 576 (JC); *Anglo Continental Holidays v Typaldos Lines* [1967] 2 Lloyd's Rep 61 (CA).

[101] *Suzuki v Benyon* (1926) 42 TLR 269, 271 (HL); *Forbes v Git* [1922] 1 AC 256, 259 (JC) and see *Exception Clauses*, 5, 98.

[102] *Gibaud v Great Eastern Railway Co* [1921] 2 KB 426 (CA); *Alderslade v Hendon Laundry Ltd* [1945] KB 189 (CA).

[103] *Rutter v Palmer* [1922] 2 KB 87 (CA); *Canada SS Lines v The King* [1952] AC 192 (JC).

[104] This is the deviation rule discussed above.

There is scope for other rules to be developed, consistently with the general *corpus* of the law. Possibilities include the following:

a. A suggestion by Kitto J that the courts extend to exception clauses the rule that a release should ordinarily be limited to those things which were specifically in the contemplation of the parties at the time the release was given.[105]
b. A suggestion from another Australian judge, Bright J, that the presumption of an intention to do justice, used in the interpretation of statutes, be adapted to exception clauses.[106]
c. There is already a presumption that commercial parties intend their agreements to have contractual effect.[107] On the existing authorities, this could well be extended to a presumption that particular promises within contracts are also intended to have enforceable contractual content.[108]
d. There is the rule, long propounded, but overlooked during the fundamental breach era, that the onus is upon the proferens so to word his exceptions as to make them clear to the class of persons to whom they are addressed.[109] This must give at least some scope for consumer protection.

Properly applied and developed, rules of interpretation such as these would achieve virtually all that fundamental breach could have done and more besides. Importantly, they would make for considerably more flexibility, allowing, for example, differences to be drawn between consumer transactions on the one hand and commercial ones on the other, or between transactions commonly or not commonly the subject of insurance cover. In this way, the law would be enabled to come to the aid of the 'little' man without incurring the risk of being the destroyer of commercial bargains. All of this could be achieved without distortion of the law of contract as a whole. The reproach against fundamental breach is not just that it was a concept arbitrary in its application[110] and distorting in its influence. Ironically enough, it also served to divert attention from other and, it is submitted, more effective ways of achieving the objects it was intended to serve.

The pursuit of elegance for its own sake would be an object unworthy of any system of law. On the other hand, that doctrinal coherence has its advantages no law teacher and, one suspects, few legal practitioners would deny. The common law of discharge by breach, it is submitted, is one field where a return to first principles would be not unjustified.

[105] *Miller v Australian Oil Refining Ltd* (1968) 117 CLR 288, 293–94 and see also his judgment in *Davis v Commissioner for Main Roads* (1968) 117 CLR 529, 533–34.

[106] (1967) 41 *ALJ* 261, 263.

[107] *Hillas v Arcos* (1932) 147 LT 503 (HL); *Suisse Atlantique* [1967] 1 AC 361, 432 per Lord Wilberforce, and see also 427 per Lord Upjohn.

[108] *Stuart v B & A Steam Navigation Co* (1875) 2 Asp MC 497, 501; *Wallis v Pratt* [1910] 2 KB 1003, 1016 (CA); *Firestone Tyre & Rubber Co v Vokins* [1951] 1 Lloyd's Rep 32, 39.

[109] *Waikato v NZ Shipping Co* [1899] 1 QB 56, 58; *Elderslie v Borthwick* [1905] AC 93 (HL); *Weiner v Wilsons* (1910) 15 Com Cas 294, 300, 301; *Philippson v Imperial Airways* [1939] 1 All ER 761 (HL) 779.

[110] This was the criticism levelled against fundamental breach by Lord Reid in the *Suisse Atlantique* case [1967] 1 AC 361, 406.

8

PART II: Discharge for Breach and Exception Clauses Since *Harbutt's 'Plasticine'*

Introduction

It is, of course, well known that in *Harbutt's 'Plasticine' Ltd v Wayne Tank and Pump Co Ltd*[1] the Court of Appeal (Lord Denning MR, Widgery and Cross LJJ) held that an exception clause which, on its proper construction, covered the events which had occurred nevertheless failed to protect the proferens. What may be less widely appreciated is the full potential application of that decision. The reasoning is simple enough, but it was not completely articulated in *Harbutt's 'Plasticine'* itself. There are three steps:

1. The effect of a discharge for breach is the termination, *in futuro*, of the contract,[2] unless the injured party elects to affirm.[3]
2. Termination prevents the exception clauses taking effect because, by the stage when they become relevant (ie, at the point of adjudication) they, with the rest of the contract, have ceased to exist.[4]
3. Whether a breach is a discharging one or not is to be determined without reference to the exception clauses. This can be explained partly because, on termination, the exception clauses cease to exist; partly because the function of exception clauses is to act as mere defences so that they have no effect to qualify the obligations of the parties; and partly because (and most explicitly) in dealing with exception clauses 'the thing to do is to look at the contract

[1] [1970] 1 QB 447.

[2] *Harbutt's 'Plasticine' Ltd v Wayne Tank and Pump Co Ltd* [1970] 1 QB 447, 465, 466, 470, 475.

[3] Ibid at 464–65, 475; *Farnworth Finance Facilities v Attryde* [1970] 2 All ER 774, 778.

[4] *Harbutt's 'Plasticine'* [1970] 1 QB 447, 465, 466, 470; *Suisse Atlantique Société d'Armement Maritime SA v NV Rotterdamsche Kolen Centrale* [1967] 1 AC 361, 425 per Lord Upjohn. It is because the exception clauses are regarded as being relevant only after breach that they can be treated as having ceased to apply, in spite of the fact that the rest of the contract remains relevant to the assessment of damages.

> apart from the exempting clauses to see what are the obligations imposed on the party'.[5]

It follows from these premises that unless the injured party elects to affirm, no exception clause can have any effect on a term or breach which (ignoring the exception clause) would give a right to discharge for breach. A fortiori, discharge for frustration would cause the same result.[6] On a termination, the wrongdoer would lose the whole benefit of his exception clauses, even to the extent that they might be directed to terms or breaches less than 'fundamental'. It follows, further, that as well as fundamental terms and fundamental breaches, in the pre-*Suisse Atlantique*[7] sense, conditions and breaches of condition would also be unexcludable, apart from the election of the injured party to affirm.[8] Together, then, the three propositions achieve not just a substantial reinstatement of the pre-*Suisse Atlantique* fundamental breach theory, but in effect a significant extension of it.

The purpose of the present article is not to rehearse the criticisms made at the time of the reasoning in *Harbutt's 'Plasticine'*.[9] Instead it is proposed to look at what has happened since that decision to the premises stated above, to try to evaluate two attempts which have been made to limit or distinguish the decision, to deal briefly with a recent attempt to explain and justify it, and finally, to look at two recent cases in which the *Harbutt's 'Plasticine'* approach has been followed. For these purposes it is important to realise that the full *Harbutt's 'Plasticine'* effect depends on the interrelation of all three premises. If discharge for breach does not extinguish the contract, exception clauses (with the rest of the contract) will continue to be applicable at least to matters occurring before the discharge. If exception clauses come into operation not at adjudication, but when the contract is formed, no subsequent termination can deprive them of the effect they have already had. And, if exception clauses are not mere defences, but qualify

[5] *Karsales (Harrow) Ltd v Wallis* [1956] 1 WLR 936, 940 per Denning LJ; *Farnworth Finance Facilities v Attryde* [1970] 2 All ER 774, 777 per Lord Denning MR; Cf *Arrow Transfer v Royal Bank of Canada* (1971) 19 DLR (3d) 420, 432 (affd (1972) 27 DLR (3d) 81). Because the clause in *Harbutt's 'Plasticine'* merely limited the quantum of damages, this particular question could not arise in that case.

[6] *Harbutt's 'Plasticine'* [1970] 1 QB 447, 465 per Lord Denning MR; Weir [1970] *CLJ* 189.

[7] *Suisse Atlantique Société d'Armement Maritime SA v NV Rotterdamsche Kolen Centrale* [1967] 1 AC 361.

[8] Cf Treitel (1966) 29 *MLR* 546, 548–49. The use of the expression 'fundamental breach' in *Harbutt's 'Plasticine'* tends to obscure this result. That a 'fundamental breach', in the 1953–66 sense of a breach which no exception clause could exclude, was more fundamental than a merely discharging breach is obvious when it is remembered that before 1953 there was ample authority that conditions of the contract could be excluded, as Devlin J himself fully recognised in *Smeaton Hanscomb v Sassoon I Setty, Son & Co* [1953] 1 WLR 1468, 1470. That the distinction has not been fully understood is illustrated, it is submitted, by the treatment accorded s 13 of the Sale of Goods Act 1893 by the House of Lords in *Ashington Piggeries Ltd v Christopher Hill Ltd* [1972] AC 441; Coote (1976) 50 *ALJ* 17 reprinted as Chapter 6 in this volume.

[9] Coote [1970] *CLJ* 221 reprinted as Chapter 8 Part I in this volume; Legh-Jones and Pickering (1970) 86 *LQR* 513; (1971) 87 *LQR* 515; Weir, above note 6; Baker (1970) 33 *MLR* 441; *Benjamin's Sale of Goods* (1974) 440–44 (FMB Reynolds); Goode, *Hire Purchase Law and Practice* (2nd edn, 1970) 199–200; *Sutton and Shannon on Contracts* (7th edn, 1970) 117–18.

obligation, they may potentially be relevant to the question whether the events which have occurred can give rise to a discharge.

Termination of the Contract

Since *Harbutt's 'Plasticine'* was decided, the terminating effect of a discharge for breach has been discussed in two well-known cases.

The first was *The Mihalis Angelos*[10] in which the Court of Appeal (Lord Denning MR, Edmund Davies and Megaw LJJ) had to decide whether a right of termination given to the 'wrongdoer' by the contract, but which he could have exercised only after the contract had been discharged for anticipatory breach, could be taken into account in assessing damages. The court was unanimous that, though the contract had come to an end on the acceptance of the repudiation, damages were to be assessed on the basis that the wrongdoer would inevitably have taken advantage of the subsequent right to terminate the contract. According to Edmund Davies LJ, the true test was:

> 'What would the position of the parties have been if the defendant had *not* wrongly announced his refusal to fulfil his part of the contract when the time for the performance arrived?' One must look at the contract as a whole, and if it is clear that the innocent party has lost nothing, he should recover no more than nominal damages.[11]

For his part, Megaw LJ thought the wrongdoer was entitled to say that 'no breach would then have taken place' because 'there is a term of the contract which provides that, in the events which necessarily have happened, he would have been excused further performance'.[12]

The significance of these passages for exception clauses is obvious. On discharge, damages are to be assessed by asking what would have been the position of the parties had there been no repudiation, and by looking at the contract as a whole to see what the innocent party had lost. On that test, on what conceivable ground could it be possible to disregard a clause which in the events which had occurred limited damages (say) to £2,330? Similarly, if the contract contains a term which, in the events which have happened, excuses him (or limits his liability) or has the effect that no breach has taken place, why should the 'wrongdoer' not be able to rely on it?

The second case was *LEP Air Services v Rolloswin Investments Ltd*[13] which concerned a contract of guarantee. It had been argued for the guarantor that, since the principal contract had been discharged for breach, his own liability had ceased

[10] [1971] 1 QB 164. Noted (1971) 34 *MLR* 190; [1971] *CLJ* 11.
[11] [1971] 1 QB 164, 202.
[12] Ibid at 209.
[13] [1973] AC 331.

because the subject matter of the guarantee no longer existed. The Court of Appeal[14] which, perhaps significantly, included Edmund Davies and Megaw LJJ rejected this argument on the ground that, while discharge for breach affected future performances, the obligations of the parties remained unaffected by it. It was by reference to those obligations that damages fell to be assessed. This analysis was rejected on appeal by the House of Lords. They adopted the view that, on termination, all the obligations of the parties under the contract came to an end and were replaced by obligations to pay damages. These damages, however, were to be assessed by reference to the 'old' obligations.

At first sight, this analysis might appear to confirm the effects of the literal-termination theory of discharge for breach. The obligations to pay damages, it could be said, do not accrue until termination. By that time, the exception clauses have ceased to exist. But if this is so, the same must be true of contractual rights of termination which become exercisable only after the discharge. Yet it seems very unlikely that the House of Lords intended, by a side-wind, to overrule *The Mihalis Angelos*.[15] It all goes back to those original obligations by reference to which the substituted obligations to pay damages are required to be assessed. The House made no suggestion that those obligations were to be assessed by reference to anything other than the contract as a whole. The contract as a whole, then, it is submitted, could and should remain the measure of what the innocent party has lost. But, if that is accepted, it is impossible to maintain that the *mere* fact of termination deprives any part of the contract of all relevance thereafter.

The Function of Exception Clauses

The propositions that exception clauses operate only as mere defences, and that they are irrelevant to the definition of the obligations incurred under a contract, were both called into question in 1973 in *The Angelia*,[16] a decision of Kerr J.

A ship had been chartered to go to the port of Eilat and there load a cargo. The charterer was to have supplied the cargo from a given date but, because the required lorries were not available to bring the cargo to the port, there were substantial delays. Several issues arose but the relevant one here had to be decided on the assumption that the charterers were protected by an exception clause which covered loss or damage caused by delay from unavoidable hindrances. The argument for the shipowners was that, notwithstanding the exception clause, once the delay from unavoidable hindrances reached the proportions of a 'fundamental breach' the contract could be terminated. Thereupon, the exception clause would cease to apply. Understandably, Kerr J described this submission as 'far reaching if

14 [1971] 1 WLR 934.
15 [1971] 1 QB 164.
16 [1973] 2 All ER 144. Noted (1974) 37 *MLR* 209; (1973) 89 *LQR* 465.

not revolutionary'.[17] Even so, it falls well within the *Harbutt's 'Plasticine'* principle, and a similar approach has been the basis of at least one other decision at first instance since 1970,[18] and to some extent of the decision of Lord Denning MR in *Farnworth Finance Facilities v Attryde.*[19]

Kerr J thought the submission untenable. The presence of the exception clause meant that the charterers were not even in breach of warranty during the waiting period. Eventually, the contract would have been frustrated, but how could that be said to convert what had to that point not been a breach at all, into a fundamental breach? Moreover, how could it be argued that the supply of a cargo was an absolute and fundamental obligation when the exception clause provided that failure to supply a cargo should be no breach at all if due to unavoidable hindrances? The correct analysis was that the obligation was not absolute but qualified. Nor did it make any difference to this analysis that the obligation was expressed as 'I promise to supply a cargo but shall not be liable if I do not do so due to unavoidable hindrances' rather than 'I promise to supply a cargo unless prevented by unavoidable hindrances'.[20]

To reach this result, the learned judge had to treat the exception clause as relevant, not just as a mere defence at the point of adjudication, but as going to the definition of the obligations undertaken by the charterer.[21] The question whether a fundamental breach had occurred was decided not by looking at the contract apart from the exempting clauses, but by having regard to the contract as a whole. And, of course, the exception clause was not treated as having ceased to apply just because the contract had (notionally) been terminated.

Though it does not appear to have been mentioned to him in argument, Kerr J's approach to this aspect of the case can be supported by the not dissimilar (and very well-known) case of *Jackson v Union Marine Insurance Co.*[22] Historically, that case was a forerunner of the modern doctrine of frustration. But it was actually decided

17 [1973] 2 All ER 144, 160.

18 *Eastman Chemical International AG v NMT Trading Co* [1972] 2 Lloyd's Rep 25.

19 [1970] 2 All ER 774, though not of the judgment of Fenton Atkinson LJ in that case. Cf *Arrow Transfer v Royal Bank of Canada* (1971) 19 DLR (3d) 420, affd (1972) 27 DLR (3d) 81.

20 [1973] 2 All ER 144, 161–63.

21 Arguments for the view that exception clauses, whether expressed in terms of obligation or of liability for breach, qualify the rights and obligations of the parties and are more than mere defences to accrued rights of action, are set out in *Exception Clauses* Ch 1 and Appendix. Dicta since 1964 which support that analysis are listed in Coote [1970] *CLJ* 221, 229, fn 55 reprinted as Chapter 8 Part I in this volume. Other recent judicial support, partial or otherwise (in addition to that of Kerr J in *The Angelia* (above), includes Donaldson J in *Kenyon, Son & Craven Ltd v Baxter Hoare & Co Ltd* [1971] 1 WLR 519, 522; Barwick CJ in *State Government Insurance Office, Queensland v Brisbane Stevedoring* (1969) 43 ALJR 456, 461 and (rather ambiguously) *Arrow Transfer v Royal Bank of Canada* (1971) 19 DLR (3d) 420, 432. Exception clauses were treated as defining obligation in *George Wimpey v Territory Enterprises* (1970) 45 ALJR 38 and *Bata v City Parking Canada Ltd* (1974) 43 DLR (3d) 190. See also fn 35 below. For an illuminating discussion of the common law propensity for treating a qualified obligation as an absolute obligation with a defence, see Nicholas, 'Rules and Terms—Civil Law and Common Law' (1974) 48 *Tul L Rev* 946 and also Weir, above note 6 at 189.

22 (1874) LR 10 CP 125.

on more traditional common law principles. A ship had undertaken to proceed with all possible dispatch, dangers and accidents of navigation excepted, to a port of loading. En route, it ran aground and was delayed to an extent which frustrated the commercial adventure. It was held that the charterer had been released from his obligation to proceed with the adventure through the failure of a condition precedent as to the time of arrival. But reference was also made, incidentally, to the collateral question whether the shipowner could have been liable to the charterer for his failure to arrive. On a full *Harbutt's 'Plasticine'* approach, he would have been liable because he had failed to proceed with all possible dispatch and his exception of dangers and accidents of navigation would, because of the termination of the contract, have been rendered irrelevant. But this was not the attitude adopted either by Bramwell B, giving the judgment of the majority, or by Cleasby B, who dissented. For them, the exception of dangers and accidents of navigation had the effect that there was 'no breach' by the ship.[23] 'No cause of action' arose against it.[24]

While the obiter dicta of a High Court judge are no doubt a small thing to set against the ratio of a decision of the Court of Appeal, it is submitted that the fact situation assumed in *The Angelia* and Kerr J's approach to it at least give cause to question the reasoning behind *Harbutt's 'Plasticine'*.

Can *Harbutt's 'Plasticine'* be Distinguished?

Since a judge at first instance is bound to follow a Court of Appeal decision,[25] it is perhaps not surprising that ways have been advanced by which *Harbutt's 'Plasticine'* might be limited or confined. One, based on a dictum by Donaldson J in *Kenyon, Son & Craven Ltd v Baxter Hoare & Co Ltd*[26] was, at least by inference, used by Kerr J in *The Angelia*.[27] Another was employed by Donaldson J himself in the *Kenyon v Baxter Hoare* case.

The Type of Clause Used

The dictum of Donaldson J to which Kerr J adverted in *The Angelia* suggested that there were three types of 'protective' clause:

> [F]irst, those which limit or reduce what would otherwise be the defendant's duty; second, those which exclude the defendant's liability for breach of specified aspects of

[23] Ibid at 133 per Cleasby B.
[24] Ibid at 143 per Bramwell B.
[25] *Williams v Glasbrook Bros* [1947] 2 All ER 884.
[26] [1971] 1 WLR 519.
[27] [1973] 2 All ER 144.

> that duty and third, those which limit the extent to which the defendant is bound to indemnify the plaintiff in respect of the consequences of breaches of that duty.[28]

By his third category, the learned judge obviously referred to clauses like those which limit recovery to a given sum per package or unit, and those which place time limitations on claims. The second presumably includes exception clauses which are expressed to exclude 'liability' while the first covers those which explicitly qualify the proferens' duty. Donaldson J did not say whether he saw any significant difference in effect between the clauses comprehended under groups one and two. However, it was a clause in the second group which was at issue in *The Angelia*. Kerr J accepted Donaldson J's categories and then categorised the exception clause before him as one which qualified obligation. Its effect, he said, could not be made to depend on 'the semantic question' whether the contract used the expression 'but shall not be liable' rather than 'unless prevented'.[29]

The question then arises whether Donaldson J's third category represents clauses of a quite different order. If so, *Harbutt's 'Plasticine'* might be confined or distinguished on the basis that the exception clause in that case was a mere limitation of the amount recoverable for breach. Naturally, the limitation clause used in that case could have had no effect on the initial question whether a discharging breach had occurred. But for that to be a sufficient distinction it would still be necessary to show that limitation clauses within this third category operate as mere defences and, as such, cease to have any application once termination has occurred.[30] Here again, it is submitted, the decision of the House of Lords in *LEP Air Services Ltd v Rolloswin*[31] is relevant.

In his judgment in that case, Lord Diplock expressed the same view of the effect of discharge for breach as did the other noble Lords, but in the language of jurisprudence, when he said that upon such a discharge

> for his [the wrongdoer's] primary obligations there is substituted by operation of law a secondary obligation to pay to the other party a sum of money to compensate him for the loss he has sustained as a result of the failure to perform the primary obligations.

He then added the sentence:

> This secondary obligation is just as much an obligation arising from the contract as are the primary obligations that it replaces.[32]

[28] [1971] 1 WLR 519, 522; Legh-Jones and Pickering (1970), above note 9 at 520, 523.

[29] [1973] 2 All ER 144, 163.

[30] Legh-Jones and Pickering (1971), above note 9 at 520, favour the view that clauses limiting the quantum of damages are not definitive of obligation but agree that, if the contrary view is finally adopted, the effect of *Harbutt's 'Plasticine'* would be 'altogether short-circuited'. Cf also, Treitel, above note 8 at 548–49.

[31] [1973] AC 331.

[32] Ibid at 350.

Lord Diplock was here echoing judgments he had given in two earlier cases as a member of the Court of Appeal. In one of them, *C Czarnikow Ltd v Koufos*,[33] he said:

> The obligation to pay damages for breach of contract is a consensual obligation. When a party enters into a contract with another party the obligations towards the other party which he thereby undertakes to fulfil and the rights against the other party to which he is entitled are those and only those which by his words and conduct at the time of the contract he has reasonably induced the other party to believe that he is accepting a legal obligation to fulfil or asserting a legal right to claim. This is so not only in respect of ... primary obligations and rights ... but also in respect of the secondary rights and obligations'.[34]

In the paragraph immediately following, Diplock LJ (as he then was) expressly referred to the effect of liquidated damages and exemption clauses upon the acceptance of secondary obligations. The reader is left in no doubt that, in the learned Lord Justice's view, the limiting effect of such provisions occurred at the time the contract was entered into.

The consequence of Lord Diplock's analysis is that if, as I enter into a contract, I limit my potential liability to, say, £2,330, there is no question of the other party's acquiring unlimited secondary rights to which the limitation is a mere procedural answer. On the contrary, the presence of the clause ensures that, upon discharge (and always assuming that upon its proper construction it applies to the events which have occurred), no secondary rights beyond those to £2,330 come into existence. To put the matter in another way, what limits the damages recoverable in contract is the contemplation of the parties. Beyond that contemplation, no rights to damages can ever accrue. What a clause limiting the quantum of damages does is to give expression to the contemplation of the parties and, in so doing, to prevent the accrual of any rights to damages beyond the expressed limit. To allow a plaintiff to recover sums beyond that limit would be to allow him a bonus for which he had never bargained.

It is submitted, then, that *Harbutt's 'Plasticine'* is not to be distinguished or explained on the basis that the exception clause merely limited the quantum of damages. Though the presence of that clause could not affect the question whether a discharging breach had occurred, the mere fact of termination could not have affected the quantum of damages which became payable on discharge.[35]

[33] [1966] 1 Lloyd's Rep 595.

[34] Ibid at 607.

[35] Mr FMB Reynolds tells me that its application to Donaldson J's third category is the part of the 'exception clauses-as-qualifications' theory which causes most difficulty (at least in Oxford). This aspect of the question does not appear to have prompted very much judicial analysis. Perhaps the strongest statement is that of Barwick CJ in *State Government Insurance Office, Queensland v Brisbane Stevedoring* (1969) 43 ALJR 456, who said (461): 'A passenger purchasing an air or rail ticket with exclusion of liability or with limitations or liability never has the "excluded" rights'. (I am indebted to Mr MP Furmston for this reference.) Apart from the views of Lord Diplock reproduced in the text, there is the decision of the House of Lords in *Atlantic Shipping Co v Dreyfus* [1922] 2 AC 250 which very clearly

'Deviatory' Breach

The ground put forward by Donaldson J in the *Kenyon v Baxter Hoare* case[36] for distinguishing *Harbutt's 'Plasticine'* was that the principle in the latter case applied only to breaches of a 'deviatory' kind. He said:

> As I understand *Suisse Atlantique*, it is only in cases in which the performance is non-contractual in the sense that it is totally different from that which the contract contemplated, that one can ignore the construction of the exception clause or treat it as inapplicable notwithstanding that, as a matter of construction, it covers the loss which has occurred.[37]

The learned judge relied on the judgment of Lord Wilberforce in the *Suisse Atlantique* case.

Whatever its attractions, it is submitted that this suggested distinction cannot be justified.[38] The first objection is that, as formulated, it is a straightforward reinstatement of the substantive fundamental breach principle which was discarded by the House of Lords in the *Suisse Atlantique* case. The second objection is that the *Harbutt's 'Plasticine'* result depends not on the character of the breach itself, but on the fact of termination. It is because the contract has come to an end that the exception clause is supposed no longer to have any effect. Clearly, breaches do not have to make the performance non-contractual before they can justify discharge for breach. A simple breach of condition can have that effect.

characterises limitation clauses, both as to time and as to amount, as indistinguishable in principle from other forms of exception clause. A similar position has since been taken by Devlin J in *Smeaton Hanscomb v Sassoon I Setty* [1953] 1 WLR 1468, 1470; by Lord Wilberforce in the *Suisse Atlantique* case [1967] 1 AC 361, 431; and by the High Court of Australia in *H & E Van Der Sterren v Cibernetics (Holdings) Ltd* (1970) 44 ALJR 157.

In the *Atlantic Shipping Co* case, Lord Sumner (259) rejected the suggestion that a time limitation on claims was a mere procedural provision. Limitation clauses, whether as to time or as to amount, limited or excluded liability (260, 261). In particular, a time limitation excepted out of the shipowners' general liability losses the assertion of which was belated (261). There was no difference in principle between words which saved the proferens from having to pay at all, and those which saved him from paying as much as he would otherwise have had to pay (260). On this basis, therefore, such clauses, while not going to the question whether a breach has occurred, should otherwise be regarded as having an effect similar to those in Donaldson J's second category. In other words, the argument is not whether third category exception clauses are alone mere defences to accrued rights of action. Categories two and three in this respect fall to be considered together (as to which see note 21, above).

Two other relevant cases are *The Auditor* (1924) 18 Ll L Rep 464 and *Grein v Imperial Airways Ltd* [1937] 1 KB 50. In the first, Duke P held that a clause limiting the amount recoverable was in effect at the time the casualty occurred and left the goods owner without any claims or right. In the other case, Greene LJ said of a contract which contained a limitation as to amount that the liability *ex contractu* came into existence with the limitation annexed to it. Both statements are, of course, inconsistent with the 'exceptions-as-mere-defences' position.

36 [1971] 1 WLR 519.

37 Ibid at 531. Cf Treitel, above note 8 at 548–49.

38 See also the criticism by FMB Reynolds in *Benjamin's Sale of Goods*, above note 9 at 441 and Legh-Jones and Pickering (1971), above note 9 at 522–23.

The third objection, it is submitted, is that Lord Wilberforce did not make the distinction ascribed to him. Like the others of their Lordships in the *Suisse Atlantique* case,[39] Lord Wilberforce saw the effect of an exception clause as depending on its construction. The one case he allowed of unexcludable obligation was where a clause had been used which was so widely expressed that to interpret it literally would deprive one party's stipulations of all contractual effect. If the agreement were indeed a contract and not a mere declaration of intent, a limited interpretation would have to be applied if the contract were to be saved.[40] But short of this, he said, it must be a question of contractual intention whether a particular breach were covered. The courts were entitled to insist, as they did, that the more radical the breach, the clearer must be the language if it were to be covered. Lord Wilberforce then went on to give examples of cases in which 'through ascertainment of the parties' contractual intention' radical breaches had been held to fall outside the exception clauses used.[41] In none of them would a contrary interpretation have prevented the formation of a contract.

Two factors have tended to give the impression that Lord Wilberforce, in giving his examples of unexcluded radical breaches, was describing an unexcludable category. One was that he used the expression 'the clause cannot be taken to refer to such a breach'.[42] In its total context, it is submitted, the word 'cannot' referred to a strong prima facie inference, not a legal imperative. If he had meant to convey that the radical breaches of which he gave examples were unexcludable as a matter of law, he would hardly have referred to the more extreme case of clauses which would deprive the contract of legal effect as the one case where, 'to this extent', a rule of law might be said to apply.

The other factor was a distinction which Lord Wilberforce drew between two uses of the expression 'fundamental breach'.[43] The first denoted a performance totally different from that contemplated by the contract. This, clearly, was the type of breach more fundamental than a breach of condition which, since 1953, it had been said, as a matter of substantive law, no exception clause could exclude. It could still be seen to be relevant to the question of construction, whether an exception clause in the particular contract applied to a particular breach. And, generally, a breach sufficiently serious to fall outside the exception clause would also be sufficiently serious to give a right to discharge for breach. Under the other meaning, 'fundamental breach' denoted a breach which did give a right to discharge.[44] It did not follow that a breach which, apart from the exempting clause, would be a discharging one would on that account not be covered by the clause. It might be reduced in effect or made not a breach at all by the terms of the clause.[45]

39 [1967] 1 AC 361.
40 Ibid at 432.
41 Ibid at 432–34.
42 Ibid at 432.
43 Ibid at 431.
44 Ibid.
45 Ibid.

The distinction Lord Wilberforce was drawing, then, was between the process of construction on the one hand, and the consequences of the construction on the other. As to the process, the more radical the difference between the actual performance and that contemplated by the contract the clearer the words must be if the exception clause were to apply.[46] But if the words used were sufficiently clear, the mere fact that, apart from them, the contract could be discharged would not prevent their taking effect.[47] Thus understood, Lord Wilberforce's judgment, far from supporting the *Harbutt's 'Plasticine'* approach to the extent that it involves radical breaches, is fundamentally inconsistent with it.

Exception Clauses as Dependent Promises

An attempt to justify *Harbutt's 'Plasticine'* has recently been made by Mr Francis Dawson in an article in the *Law Quarterly Review*.[48] His argument proceeds from two premises. The first is that discharge for breach is best understood in terms of dependent and independent promises. The second is that limitations of contractual liability within Donaldson J's third category and, in some (unspecified) cases, exceptions of contractual liability within his second category,[49] are promises of immunity made to the proferens. It is argued that in cases like *Harbutt's 'Plasticine'*, the other party's promise of immunity is dependent on substantial performance by the proferens. On the facts of that case, it would mean that the defendant company was unable to rely on the plaintiff's 'promise' to limit liability to £2,330 because the defendant had not himself fulfilled his own promises.

The present writer has considerable sympathy with the premise that discharge for breach is best understood in terms of dependent and independent promises. The law today would be a great deal more certain than it is had that analysis not been displaced by misleading analogies with conditions subsequent, 'rescission', and the like. But the other premise, that some exceptions, and all limitations, of contractual liability are promises of immunity, it is submitted, quite misconceives their function. Exception clauses are not promises made *to* the proferens, but exceptions *from* (ie, qualifications of) what the proferens himself promises to undertake. And, as has already been argued earlier in this article, this is as true of limitations of liability as it is of exclusions.[50]

The only authority adduced by Mr Dawson for his proposition that exception clauses are promises is the decision of the Privy Council in *New Zealand Shipping*

[46] Ibid at 432.
[47] This follows from the dicta cited by Lord Wilberforce at 432.
[48] 'Fundamental Breach of Contract' (1975) 91 *LQR* 380.
[49] Above at note 22.
[50] Above at note 35, and in the text.

Co Ltd v AM Satterthwaite & Co Ltd.[51] But that case involved a limitation of liability in tort, not in contract. In *Midland Silicones Ltd v Scruttons Ltd*[52] the House of Lords had proceeded on the by no means universally accepted assumption that a contract was necessary for the exclusion or limitation of liability in tort. On this assumption, the Privy Council in the *Satterthwaite* case constructed a unilateral contract under which, in return for the act of unloading goods, the damages recoverable by the goods owner against stevedores were limited to the amounts specified in the head contract of carriage. A first point, therefore, is that statements in *Satterthwaite* about 'promises' and 'offers' to exempt were dictated by the (many would say false) premise that a contract was a precondition of any limitation of liability at all. More important, though, is a second point, that the sources of liability in contract and in tort are different, liability under the one being assumed consensually and under the other being imposed *ab extra*. Even assuming that a limitation of liability in tort is constituted by the act of the party who stands to suffer the loss or injury, the same is by no means necessarily true of contractual liability. There is just no call for a 'promise' of immunity in a situation where the liability itself can never accrue, whether because it goes beyond the contemplation of the parties or because it is never assumed in the first place.

Moreover, even if both premises were correct, it would not follow that *Harbutt's 'Plasticine'* was correctly decided. A dependent–independent promise analysis explains that case only if the plaintiff's 'promise' of immunity was in fact dependent on substantial performance by the defendant. If the 'promise' of immunity were interpreted as applying, notwithstanding destruction of the premises by fire as the result of the defendant's breach of contract, the promises would not be dependent but independent. And, of course, all the judgments in the Court of Appeal in the *Harbutt's 'Plasticine'* case do in fact proceed on the basis that the limitation clause covered what had occurred.[53] It follows that if the 'promise' of immunity in that case were indeed a dependent promise, the learned Lord Justices must, in interpreting it, have meant something less than they appear to have said. And if they did mean that the exception clause was not, after all, intended to apply to what actually happened, that, by itself, would have been sufficient, on any view, to dispose of the case. There would have been no point in going on to hold, as their Lordships did, that a discharge for breach had deprived the limitation clause of effect if, on its proper interpretation, it could have had no effect anyway.

It is submitted that on a dependent–independent covenant or promise analysis, to say that the exception clauses are dependent on the proferens' substantial performance of his promises is to beg the all-important question of what he promised in the first place. It is not until the extent of the parties' promises has been determined in the light of any exception or limitation clauses that questions of dependency or independency can arise.

[51] [1975] AC 154; [1974] 1 NZLR 505.
[52] [1962] AC 446.
[53] [1970] 1 QB 447, 464E per Lord Denning MR, 470G per Widgery LJ, 474E per Cross LJ.

Two Recent Cases

At least until recently there would have been general agreement that the effect of the terms of a contract should depend on their proper interpretation and construction. Even in the case of a discharge for breach, it would have been conceded that a provision intended to operate upon such an event could do so.[54] In the case of an exception clause, it is submitted the real issue ought always to be whether or not the clause was intended to apply in the events which have occurred. To hold that a purported discharge for breach of itself robs an exception clause of its effect is to beg the prime question of whether the clause was intended to apply in just such an event. Indeed, if the parties so intend by their clause, the supposed discharging breach may not constitute a breach at all.

The simplicity of this construction approach with its single question for decision stands in marked contrast to the difficulties raised by the *Harbutt's 'Plasticine'* rationale, as is illustrated by two cases decided by the Court of Appeal in 1975.

The first of these two cases was *Wathes (Western) Ltd v Austins (Menswear) Ltd*[55] which arose out of a contract to supply and install an air conditioning plant to and in the defendants' premises. While the plant itself worked well, its machinery made a noise which caused a nuisance to an adjoining occupier. This nuisance led to a claim which the defendants settled. The plaintiffs claimed the price of the plant and the defendants counterclaimed for damages for breach of contract. As a defence to this counterclaim, the plaintiffs relied on a clause which stated that 'The Company shall be under no liability for any consequential loss damage claims or liabilities of any kind arising from any cause whatever'. The appeal proceeded on the basis that this clause would protect the plaintiff in respect of everything short of a fundamental breach.

On a traditional construction approach, the issue raised by this clause would have been the quite simple one of whether it covered the events which had occurred. In the absence of any subsequent novation, variation, or waiver, the answer, whichever way it went, would have concluded the matter without more. Adopting the *Harbutt's 'Plasticine'* approach, however, the Court of Appeal had first to consider the difference between a fundamental breach and the breach of a fundamental term (and, en route, to consider the defendant's right to alter his pleadings so as to raise the one as well as the other). It then decided that there had been a fundamental breach but (since the contract had been affirmed) had to consider at what point the defendants had had that right to rescind which they had not in fact exercised. It was held that the defendants had had a right to rescind. Counsel for the plaintiffs had conceded (no doubt on the basis of *Harbutt's 'Plasticine'*) that, had the defendants in fact terminated the contract, the exception

[54] *Heyman v Darwins Ltd* [1942] AC 356.
[55] [1976] 1 Lloyd's Rep 14. Noted (1976) 92 *LQR* 172.

clause would not protect his clients. The Court next had to consider whether the defendants' acceptance of the plant was a waiver of their right to treat the breach as fundamental for the purpose of defeating the exception clause. It being held on the authorities that there had been no such waiver, the Court at last reached the stage of considering the meaning of the clause, but even here, it did so only obliquely. Instead of asking whether the exception clause was intended to cover consequential loss from a nuisance caused by the plant, the Court looked instead at *Charterhouse Credit Co Ltd v Tolly*[56] where it was held that an exception clause could never avail the party in breach against a fundamental breach of contract. Their Lordships recognised that the *Suisse Atlantique* case[57] had substituted a construction test for the substantive rule of law applied in *Charterhouse Credit Co Ltd v Tolly*, but it was thought that the new test would give no different results in the absence of any very clearly expressed intention that the clause was to cover fundamental breaches as such.

That the Court had to follow a line of reasoning as lengthy as this and could reach a result without at any stage having had to construe the actual contract, of itself, it is submitted, suggests that there is something artificial (to say the least) about the *Harbutt's 'Plasticine'* approach. But that approach also creates hurdles out of what should not be issues at all. On a true construction approach, the relative seriousness of the events which have occurred is, of course, relevant to the question whether the exception clause covers them. If, apart from the exception clause, they would have constituted a fundamental breach (or the breach of a fundamental term), that is no doubt one indication of their seriousness. But to require that they actually constitute a fundamental breach and be pleaded as such is to treat an aid to construction as the substantive determinant of what the construction should be. It is to discount completely the possibility that something less than a fundamental breach may fall outside the exception clause.

Again, it seems the height of artificiality, in a case where there could be no suggestion of a discharge for breach having occurred, that close consideration should have had to be given to the purely hypothetical question whether the defendant would have had such a right if he had chosen to use it. That in turn raised the equally hypothetical question of the time at which the right to discharge would have accrued. All this was seen as relevant only because the characterisation of what had occurred as a 'fundamental breach' was seen as the sole determinant of whether the exception clause applied or not, as a matter of 'construction'. At least it can be said for *Harbutt's 'Plasticine'* that it did not involve this error. In that case, it was the actual happening of a discharge for breach which was said to deprive the exception clause of its effect, not the characterisation of the breach as being 'fundamental' or not.

[56] [1963] 2 QB 683 (CA).
[57] [1967] 1 AC 361.

The artificialities induced by the *Harbutt's 'Plasticine'* type of approach were subsequently further illustrated by the unreported case of *Prince v Brown Brothers and Merseyside & North Wales Electricity Board.*[58] There, the plaintiff, a painter, successfully claimed damages for injuries sustained when, as an employee of the first defendant, he was painting a power transformer belonging to the second defendant. By the neglect of the second defendant, the transformer was still 'live' when painting work on it commenced. The employers claimed contribution from the Electricity Board, which in turn relied on an exclusion and indemnity clause in its contract with the employers. This in terms extended to liability for any injury whatsoever arising under any statute or at common law out of or in the course of or caused by the execution of the work specified in the contract. The employers conceded, on the authority of *Gillespie Brothers Ltd v Roy Bowles Ltd*[59] that this clause covered the negligence of the Electricity Board but they argued that it did not cover fundamental breach or the breach of a fundamental term. The Court decided that there was no breach of a fundamental term because a term which would require the Board to see that the transformers were not live was far too narrow and detailed to be the subject of implication. Neither was there a fundamental breach, because once the transformer ceased to be live, work could and did proceed satisfactorily. The second defendants were therefore protected by their indemnity clause.

Once again, because of the approach which was taken, the Court failed to face the real issue, whether the exception and indemnity clause was intended to cover the events which had occurred. If this latter approach had been followed by counsel and the Court, two things would have been obvious. One would have been that *Gillespie v Bowles* was distinguishable. The negligence which was held to be covered in that case was the carelessness of a driver which had resulted in the theft of goods from his van, an act far removed from that of the Board in failing to neutralise the extremely dangerous electrical equipment which was to be painted. That went beyond mere negligence. It was a breach of a statutory duty which involved extreme risk to life and limb and was in all probability a breach of the duty of common humanity as well.[60] The second thing that would have been obvious was that whether the Board's failure was the breach of a particular implied fundamental term was in no way conclusive. There was no doubt that, apart from the indemnity clause, the Board was under a duty. The question to be decided was whether the words used in the indemnity clause, on their true construction, covered what the Board had done. For that purpose it was the character of the Board's acts, rather than their characterisation, which was important. Equally, the fact that the employers were able, once the risk had been removed, to complete their contract, was not a sufficient reason for concluding that the Board's creation of that risk fell within the terms of the indemnity.

[58] Judgment dated 25 July 1975.

[59] [1973] 1 QB 400.

[60] Coote, 'Exception Clauses and Common Humanity' (1975) 125 *NLJ* 752.

To the extent that the *Prince* case concerned the allocation of an insurance risk between two commercial parties, it could hardly be suggested that the actual result was unjust, provided always that a party in the position of the employers ought to have realised that under the contract he would have to take the legal risk, inter alia, that the transformer would be live because of the Board's neglect.[61] But there was in fact more than the allocation of an insurance risk at stake. A finding that the Board's acts fell within the exception and indemnity clause meant that, in a contract to paint a potentially lethal piece of electrical plant, the employers had bargained away the obligation to take precautions for the physical safety of their workmen of the only party in a position to ensure that the transformer was not live. Whether that really was what the parties intended was something which, on the approach adopted, was not and could not even be considered.

Conclusion

Developments since *Harbutt's 'Plasticine'* have gone some way towards confirming the criticisms made at the time. There have been understandable attempts to limit and confine the effects of the decision but it is submitted that neither of the methods described above can be sustained. And, as was to be expected, the initial distortion of the law by *Harbutt's 'Plasticine'* had led to further distortions, and there may be more to come.

Thus, by way of postscript, it is worth noting that a finding, under the amended section 55 of the Sale of Goods Act 1893, that an exception clause was 'reasonable' could not save it from the effect of *Harbutt's 'Plasticine'*. It would have to be held inapplicable on a discharge for breach, unless the contract were affirmed. Nor, so long as the contract-apart-from-the-exempting clauses approach to interpretation is followed, could the presence of a 'reasonable' clause, so held, prevent a finding that an event excused by the clause was nevertheless a discharging breach.[62]

[61] Cf *Hollier v Rambler Motors (AMC) Ltd* [1972] 2 QB 71.

[62] Cf *Benjamin's Sale of Goods*, above note 9 at 454–55. The difficulty is recognised by the English and Scottish Law Commissions in their Second Report on Exemption Clauses, 1975, Law Com No 69, Scot Law Com No 39, 77.

9

Another Look at *Bowmakers v Barnet Instruments*

On the evidence of current textbooks,[1] *Bowmakers v Barnet Instruments*[2] seems no nearer to universal acceptance now than when it was first decided. Many lawyers, one suspects, see it as an anomaly which, someday, the House of Lords will overrule as being both inconsistent with principle and long the subject of general criticism. Yet it would surely be unfortunate if it were ever to suffer that fate. The common law on illegal contracts is Draconian enough, in all conscience, and the rule in *Bowmakers v Barnet Instruments* does offer a measure of relief, even if only in a rather limited sphere. Accordingly, if, as is believed, there is a way in which the decision can be supported both in logic and in law, it is the more desirable that it should be put forward, even at this late stage.

In the *Bowmakers* case, it will be recalled, the plantiffs as owners claimed damages for the conversion of some machine tools held by the defendants under a series of three hire-purchase agreements. These agreements were identified in the statement of claim, as they have been ever since, as agreements 1, 2, and 3. The plaintiffs had originally purchased the tools the subject of agreements 1 and 2 from one Smith under an illegal contract of sale. All three hire-purchase agreements were also illegal. The defendants had, to their own advantage, sold off the tools under the second agreement, but had failed to yield them up on demand. The remaining facts are stated only sketchily in the report, but it is a reasonable inference that the defendants had defaulted in payment of hire. Again, though the report does not say whether the agreements contained any clause allowing termination for non-payment of hire, it is reasonable to suppose that there was such a clause, since the agreements were stated to be 'in familiar form'.[3]

At the hearing, the defendants conceded that, notwithstanding the illegality, property in the tools the subject of agreements 1 and 2 had passed from Smith to the plaintiffs.[4] For their part, the plaintiffs conceded that, because all three

[1] Cheshire and Fifoot, *The Law of Contract* (7th edn, 1969) 305–06; *Anson's Law of Contract* (23rd edn, 1969) 362–63; *Sutton and Shannon on Contracts* (7th edn, 1970) 283n; Treitel, *Law of Contract* (3rd edn, 1970) 422–24; Guest, *The Law of Hire Purchase* (1966) 438; *Chitty on Contracts*, vol 1 (23rd edn, 1968) 440–41; Paton, *Bailment in the Common Law* (1952) 34–36.

[2] [1945] KB 65.

[3] Ibid at 66.

[4] Ibid at 70.

hire-purchase agreements were illegal, they were unable to rely on them. Their claim was based simply on the proposition that the machines belonged to them.[5] The Court of Appeal gave judgment for the plaintiffs in respect of all three groups of machine tools. The principle they purported to apply in doing so was stated by du Parcq LJ (delivering the judgment of the Court) to be as follows:

> [A] man's right to possess his own chattels will as a general rule be enforced against one who, without any claim of right, is detaining them, or has converted them to his own use, even though it may appear either from the pleadings, or in the course of the trial, that the chattels in question came into the defendant's possession by reason of an illegal contract between himself and the plaintiff, provided that the plaintiff does not seek, and is not forced, either to found his claim on the illegal contract or to plead its illegality in order to support his claim.[6]

The Lord Justice allowed that there might be limited exceptions to this rule,[7] and it will be necessary to return to this point later.

Three main criticisms have been levelled against the *Bowmakers* decision. The first, which involves all three hire-purchase agreements, is that it offends against the *in pari delicto* rule. The second, which in general accepts the correctness of the principle stated by the Court of Appeal, claims that it was incorrectly applied to the tools the subject of the second hire-purchase agreement. The third criticism is that, whether or not the decision can be justified in law, its effects in practice are likely to be undesirable or even grotesque. It is proposed to consider these objections in turn.

The First Line of Criticism

The first-stated criticism[8] derives from three main premises. The first is that an illegal contract is void and therefore a nullity. The second is that the courts will not assist a party to an illegal contract (*ex turpi causa non oritur actio*). The third is that, apart from certain exceptions concerned primarily with the relative degrees of fault of the parties, the advantage in an illegal contract lies with the defendant or the party in possession (*in pari delicto potior est condition defendentis* (*possidentis*)). The argument based on these premises is that since illegal contracts are void, they cannot pass property anyway.[9] Hence, the most that a transferee can

[5] Ibid at 69–70.

[6] Ibid at 71. See also *Scott v Brown, Doering, McNab & Co* [1892] 2 QB 724, 729; *Farmers' Mart v Milne* [1915] AC 106 (HL) 113.

[7] [1945] KB 65, 72.

[8] A sustained statement of this line of criticism is contained in an unpublished PhD dissertation by MJ Higgins, 'Enforcement and Restitution under Illegal Contracts' (1961) esp 259 *et seq*, 354 *et seq*, deposited in the Cambridge University Library. A parallel argument on the South African cases appears in De Wet and Yeats, *Die Suid-Afrikannse Kontraktereg en Handelsreg* (3rd edn, 1964) 79.

[9] The case for this view is argued by MJ Higgins, 'The Transfer of Property under Illegal Transactions' (1962) 25 *MLR* 149. Cf Treitel, above note 1 at 337; Grodecki, '*In Pari Delicto*' (1955) 71 *LQR* 254, 266. Cheshire and Fifoot, above note 1 at 303, describe the illegal contract as 'totally void'.

get under any illegal contract is possession.[10] Accordingly, to say that a party can recover by relying on his ownership is meaningless, since, if that were so, every transferor could recover. Whether the court allows recovery should depend solely on public policy and, by and large, the only parties who can hope for assistance under this head are those whose guilt is the less in certain technical ways,[11] or who have repented timeously,[12] or whom it was the policy of a statute to protect.[13] Otherwise, the loss lies where it falls. The party in possession of the subject matter retains it.[14]

To someone holding these views, the *Bowmakers* decision must appear somewhat cynical. A party to an illegal contract, he could be expected to say, is no more or less guilty because he has taken the precaution of entering into a bailment rather than a sale. Likewise, to allow recovery on the ground that ownership remains in the plaintiff not only misconceives the *in pari delicto* rule and gives an effect of sorts to a contract which is *ex hypothesi* a nullity;[15] it may also allow questions of public policy to depend on the accidents of pleading.[16]

Given the premise that illegal contracts are nullities, this argument against *Bowmakers* appears both attractive and coherent. On the modern authorities, however, it is not at all clear that that premise is a valid one. Of course, there are innumerable statements in the books to the effect that illegal contracts are 'void'. The same is true of infants' contracts, yet, as every student knows, infants themselves are able to enforce them. In the same way, there are any number of dicta to the effect that contracts are rescinded on discharge by breach, yet, as common lawyers[17] know, such 'rescission' does nothing to prevent the injured party recovering damages thereafter. The word 'void', when used in connection with illegal contracts, no doubt serves a useful purpose as a label but, like so many common law labels, it may be misleading if taken too literally.

No one could doubt that, in ordinary circumstances, no court will enforce a claim founded on an illegal contract.[18] There is, however, ground for saying nowadays that illegality does no more than make contracts or agreements founded on them unenforceable and that, once executed, they are effective to transfer property or other rights.[19] The leading case is probably *Singh v Ali*,[20] a decision of the Privy

[10] Cf Higgins, above note 9 at 151, 153.

[11] See, eg, Cheshire and Fifoot, above note 1 at 327–28.

[12] *Kearley v Thomson* (1890) 24 QBD 742; *Bigos v Bousted* [1951] 1 All ER 92; *Petherpermal Chetty v Servai* (1908) 24 TLR 462 (PC).

[13] *Kiriri Cotton Co v Dewani* [1960] AC 192 (PC).

[14] *Holman v Johnson* (1775) 1 Cowp 341, 343.

[15] Cf *Miles v Watson* [1953] NZLR 154, 158.

[16] Gooderson, 'Turpitude and Title in England and India' [1958] CLJ 199, 210; Grodecki, above note 9 at 269–70.

[17] Mr MJ Pritchard reminds me that not all equity lawyers make the distinction: see, eg, Farrand, *Contract and Conveyance* (1968) 247–48.

[18] *Holman v Johnson* (1775) 1 Cowp 341, 343.

[19] See CJ Hamson, 'Illegal Contracts and Limited Interests' (1949) 10 *CLJ* 249, 258; [1964] *CLJ* 20, 22–23; Chitty, above note 1 at 439; Anson, above note 1 at 362; *Benjamin on Sale* (8th edn, 1950) 494.

[20] [1960] AC 167. And see now *Belvoir Finance Co v Stapleton* [1971] 1 QB 210; [1970] 3 All ER 664 (CA) the report of which became available after this article had been written.

Council, in which it was held that the buyer of motor vehicles under an illegal sale had obtained a property in them which he could maintain against the seller when the latter attempted to repossess the vehicles from him. There is a long line of cases and dicta to support such a conclusion.[21] An objection which might be raised immediately is that the idea that ownership can pass under an illegal contract is inconsistent with the *in pari delicto* rule in at least two ways. One would be that, by resting the rights of the transferee on the ownership passed to him under the contract, it makes the *in pari delicto* rule largely superfluous.[22] The other would be that if ownership does indeed pass, it would be difficult to justify the established right of transferors not *in pari delicto* to recover property the subject of illegal contract. The answer to these objections is that there are enough rights other than those of ownership to give the maxim adequate content, and that its chief significance may lie in the power it confers on the court to come to the rescue of the more innocent party. The exceptions to the *in pari delicto* rule fall within a rather narrow compass. Most of them are concerned with the effect of such things as fraud, duress, and undue influence upon one of the parties. When the law allows recovery in such cases, despite an effective transfer of property, it is doing no more than it would in the case of a legal contract. The other two main cases, the *locus poenitentiae* rule and the granting of recovery where the policy of a statute is to protect one party against the other, are both explicable on grounds of public policy or on the application of statutes. Again, there have been the rather different cases where property has been held not to pass under an illegal contract because the statute made the contract not only illegal but also ineffective.[23] That this has been so tends, if anything, to confirm that an executed contract does have effect when it is made merely illegal by statute and no more.

It may not be possible yet to be certain that executed illegal contracts are effective to transfer rights. What can be claimed is that the trend is strongly towards that view.[24] Much more important for present purposes, however, is the effect which acceptance of that view has upon the first line of criticism of the *Bowmakers* decision. If executed illegal contracts do effectively transfer rights, a transferee is enabled to retain whatever has passed to him, not merely because he can take fortuitous advantage of a rule of public policy, but because he has effectively become the owner. The *ex turpi causa* rule applies as before and neither party can expect the courts to enforce any right created by the illegal contract. What they

[21] *Scarfe v Morgan* (1838) 4 M & W 270, 281; *Gas, Light & Coke v Turner* (1839) 5 Bing NC 666, 677; *Feret v Hill* (1854) 15 CB 207; *Taylor v Chester* (1869) LR 4 QB 309; *Elder v Kelly* [1919] 2 KB 179; *Kingsley v Sterling Industries Securities* [1967] 2 QB 747; *Singh v Ali* [1960] AC 167 (PC); *Chettiar v Chettiar* [1962] AC 294 (PC); *Roberts v Roberts* [1957] Tas SR 84 (FCt); *Joe v Young* [1964] NZLR 24 (CA); *Belvoir Finance Co v Stapleton* [1971] 1 QB 210; [1970] 3 All ER 664 (CA). This last decision directly contradicts the view expressed in Treitel, above note 1 at 421 that in such cases property passes, not by contract, but by delivery.

[22] Cf Higgins, above note 9 at 151.

[23] *Joe v Young* [1964] NZLR 24 (CA); *Amar Singh v Kulubya* [1964] AC 142 (PC); *Gopal v Cohen* 1946 TPD 283.

[24] *Hamson* [1964] *CLJ* 20; Chitty, above note 1 at 439–40.

can expect, however, is that the court will recognise the effectiveness of any transfer that has taken place. Moreover, since the effect of illegality is no more than a refusal by the courts to enforce illegal contracts, the idea that the courts might enforce rights not created by the illegal contract can be seen as not only consistent but almost inevitable. There would have to be some additional element present, it could be said, before the courts should extend disqualification from suit to rights which the wrongdoer held independently of the illegal contract.

On this basis, there is no longer anything particularly cynical about the rule stated in the *Bowmakers* case. On the contrary, it makes good sense. Nor is recovery by the owner merely the unmeritorious result of an accident of pleading. What the *Bowmakers* rule means is that he will obtain restitution if his claim is based on rights which belong to him independently of the illegal contract. He will not recover if he has, before suit, effectively transferred his rights away under an executed illegal contract. This, it may be added, is substantially the effect of a dictum by Watermeyer JA of the South African Appellate Division in *Jajbhay v Cassim*,[25] which for many years has appeared in successive editions of Cheshire and Fifoot on *The Law of Contract*.[26] According to that learned judge:

> [T]he Court will not assist a party to recover what he has paid or transferred to defendant in terms of the illegal contract, save in exceptional circumstances, but there is no need to go further and to deprive him of rights which he has not transferred to defendant.[27]

On this line of reasoning, or something like it, the *Bowmakers* decision has been accepted by many commentators to be correct, so far as agreements 1 and 3 are concerned.[28] The plaintiffs were able to plead their ownership and there was no reason for them to rely in any way on the illegal hire-purchase agreements in order to establish their immediate right to restitution. The explanation offered by the commentators for this latter point was that the defendants' act of selling the tools had automatically revested in the plaintiffs a right to immediate possession.[29] Because of a similarly automatic revesting, the argument runs, the plaintiffs could equally have recovered possession once the term of the bailment contract had expired by effluxion of time.[30] They might even have done so upon default in payment of hire, if the contract had contained a clause which terminated the bailment automatically for non-payment.[31] By the same token, a lessor would be able to recover his land on the expiry of the term of an illegal lease.[32]

[25] 1939 AD 537.

[26] In the seventh edition, it appears at 327. See also Chitty, above note 1 at 440; Anson, above note 1 at 362.

[27] 1939 AD 537, 557.

[28] This is true of those listed in note 1 above.

[29] Cheshire and Fifoot, above note 1 at 305–06; 422. The case cited by them is *North Central Wagon and Finance Co v Graham* [1950] 2 KB 7 (CA).

[30] Eg, Lloyd, *Public Policy* (1958) 103; Treitel, above note 1 at 422; Cheshire and Fifoot, above note 1 at 327.

[31] Treitel, above note 1 at 423.

[32] Cheshire and Fifoot, above note 1 at 327; Treitel, above note 1 at 423–24, where he confines the analogy to termination by expiry of the term; Anson, above note 1 at 362, Chitty, above note 1 at 440; Lloyd, above note 30 at 103; and cf Hamson (1949) 10 *CLJ* 249, 258.

The Second Line of Criticism

But these arguments (and this is of course the second of the three main criticisms of the *Bowmakers* decision referred to earlier) do not, the critics say, cover the circumstances of the second hire-purchase agreement, for in that case there had been no conversion of the tools, and therefore no automatic termination of the bailment. The defendants had failed to comply with a demand for the return of the tools, but the plaintiffs, to show that they were entitled to make the demand, would have been driven back onto the cesser provisions of the contract. To enable them to recover in those circumstances would be to recognise and enforce a right of termination given them by the illegal contract.[33] Such enforcement would be contrary to the *ex turpi causa* rule.

The fact that this line of reasoning leaves unexplained the Court of Appeal's decision on the second agreement is not its only disadvantage. It rests the Court's decision in respect of agreements 1 and 3 on the quite fortuitous circumstance that a conversion of bailed goods, while it apparently does not automatically terminate the bailment contract,[34] does revest an immediate right to possession in the bailor. Not only was this a factor not adverted to by du Parcq LJ when he delivered the judgment of the Court; it also has the effect of confining the decision substantially to bailment contracts, since there seems to be no equivalent automatic revesting under the law governing leases. It also seems to exclude the possibility of recovery on repudiatory breach generally,[35] since termination in such cases is ordinarily not automatic but depends on an election by the injured party.[36]

Despite the weight of opinion to the contrary, it is submitted that there do exist at least two ways in which both aspects of the *Bowmakers* decision can be justified. The first finds its basis in the dictum of Watermeyer JA in *Jajbhay v Cassim*[37] which has already been referred to, and in the line of South African cases which derive from it. The other involves a direct application of the principle which the Court of Appeal itself purported to apply in the *Bowmakers* case.

The First Justification: The South African Cases

From the number of times it has been cited in later cases, *Jajbhay v Cassim* appears to occupy in the South African law of illegal contracts an even more important

[33] Lloyd, above note 30 at 103; Treitel, above note 1 at 424; *Watson v Miles* [1953] NZLR 958 (CA), 968, 969.

[34] *Reliance Car Facilities Ltd v Roding Motors* [1952] 2 QB 844 (CA).

[35] Quaere, Treitel, above note 1 at 422 contra? In *Roberts v Roberts* [1957] Tas SR 84, 106, it is suggested that termination on repudiatory breach is not the exercise of a right under the contract, but only acquiescence in a state of affairs brought about by the other side. Hence, it is said, no reliance on a term of the contract is involved.

[36] *Reliance Car Facilities Ltd v Roding Motors* [1952] 2 QB 844 (CA).

[37] 1939 AD 537, 557.

position than does, say, *St John Shipping Corp v Rank*[38] in English and Commonwealth jurisdictions. It is one of those germinal cases, like *Donoghue v Stevenson*,[39] where an appellate court has seized an opportunity to enunciate a general principle where previously there had been only particular instances. The facts were that the registered holder of a licence to occupy a stand in the Johannesburg Malay Location had sub-let it illegally. The sub-tenant entered into possession and thereafter observed all the conditions of his sub-tenancy. The licensee now claimed to eject the sub-tenant. He had taken no steps to terminate the sub-tenancy and his claim was based solely on grounds of illegality. The South African Appellate Division found for the sub-tenant, as indeed an English court would almost certainly have done, if *Feret v Hill*[40] is an accurate indicator. What has made the decision important in South Africa and also the subject of criticism from local commentators, is that the Court took the opportunity to look afresh at the *in pari delicto* rule. They saw the rule as a valuable discouragement to illegal transactions, but they emphasised that its application should always be subject to wider considerations of justice and public policy. The well-known exceptions arising from fraud, duress and *locus poenitentiae* were seen as mere examples of the application of these wider considerations. On the facts of the case before them, they said, they could find no considerations of justice or public policy which would compel them to deprive the sub-tenant of possession of the stand. The dictum already referred to of Watermeyer JA came at the end of his judgment, when he sought to meet an objection by counsel based on the hardship to an owner which such a result would cause. He said:

> It was suggested in argument that unless the Court came to the appellant's assistance, the respondent could remain in possession of the property in perpetuity. But this is not so. The appellant has not lost his dominium in the property, or rather what could be more correctly described in this case as his right of occupation. Delivery in pursuance of contracts of lease or loan does not transfer ownership in what is delivered and in this respect differs from delivery in pursuance of a contract of sale and from payment of money. Under the general principle which has been discussed in this judgment the Court will not assist a party to recover what he has paid or transferred to defendant in terms of the illegal contract save in exceptional cases, but there is no need to go further and to deprive him of rights which he has not transferred to defendant … So far as the rights of occupation which he has transferred to the defendant affect or modify his rights of occupation he cannot get relief but so far as they do not there is no reason why relief should be refused. It follows that the respondent cannot retain possession of the property against the appellant when the right of occupation given to him by the appellant terminates.[41]

A few months after *Jajbhay v Cassim* another action, *Petersen v Jajbhay*,[42] to eject a sub-tenant from a stand in the Johannesburg Malay Location, came before the

[38] [1957] 1 QB 267.
[39] [1932] AC 562 (HL).
[40] (1854) 15 CB 207.
[41] 1939 AD 537, 557.
[42] 1940 TPD 182.

Transvaal Provincial Division. This time, however, the sub-tenant had failed to pay his rent, and the illegal agreement contained a condition that failure to pay rent would render the sub-tenant liable to ejectment without notice. In these circumstances an order for ejectment was made. The Court declined to base its decision on the dictum of Watermeyer JA, taking the view that it was *obiter*. It preferred to apply what it took to be the *ratio* of *Jajbhay v Cassim*, that the application of the *in pari delicto* rule is subject to considerations of justice and public policy. It concluded that, on those grounds, the stand ought to be restored to the licensee-owner, since any right of occupation the sub-tenant might have had, had come to an end when the agreement terminated for non-payment of rent.[43] The *ratio* of *Jajbhay v Cassim* as stated by the Transvaal Provincial Division was subsequently confirmed by the Appellate Division itself in the 1948 case of *Kelly v Koke*.[44] In consequence, the *Jajbhay v Cassim* principle is seen in South Africa as an aspect of the *in pari delicto* rule, rather than as turning, as the *Bowmakers* case does, on whether the plaintiff need or need not ground his case upon an illegal contract.

The South African criticism of *Jajbhay v Cassim*,[45] and of its application to facts like those of *Petersen v Jajbhay*,[46] has been based on two main grounds. The first is the doctrinal point that there is no warrant in Roman-Dutch law for a discretion as wide as that enunciated by the Appellate Division.[47] The other criticism is based on the premise that, in Roman-Dutch law, illegal contracts are absolutely void.[48] As might be expected, those who argue from this premise can see little justification for determining questions of justice and public policy by reference to whether a tenant has or has not performed the non-existent obligations of an ineffective lease.[49]

For common law jurisdictions, however, the interest in the South African cases lies, not in their restatement of the *in pari delicto* principle, but in the obiter dictum of Watermeyer JA and the subsequent developments from it. For, if the common law does allow the effectiveness of an executed illegal contract to transfer rights, and permits the court to assist a party to an illegal contract, provided the rights he seeks to enforce arise independently of the illegal contract, the principle contained in the dictum is correct at common law, however suspect it may be in the Roman-Dutch context.

Until now, the Watermeyer principle, that while the courts will not assist a party to recover what he has transferred away, they will not deprive him of what he has retained, has been cited in England as support merely for the proposition that a bailor or lessor can recover possession on termination of the bailment or lease

[43] Cf *Mancherjee v Bala* 1946 WLD 182; *Jajbhay v Cassim* 1939 AD 537, 545 per Stratford CJ.

[44] 1948 (3) SALR 522.

[45] 1939 AD 537.

[46] 1940 TPD 182.

[47] 'Aquilus' (van den Heever J), 'Immorality and Illegality in Contract' (1941) 58 *SALJ* 337; (1942) 59 *SALJ* 16; LB Behrmann, '*Jajbhay v Cassim*' (1946) 63 *SALJ* 40; De Wet and Yeats, above note 8 at 79.

[48] Gibson, *South African Mercantile and Company Law* (2nd edn, 1963) 8, 56–58; Wille, *Principles of South African Law* (5th edn, 1961) 317.

[49] De Wet and Yeats, above note 8 at 79. Cf Kerr, *The Principles of the Law of Contract* (1967) 46–49.

by effluxion of time. If this were indeed the only significance of the principle, it would amount to no more than peripheral support for a conclusion already implicit in the English authorities. The real significance of the principle, it is submitted, is that it goes beyond that. What the South African cases show is that it justifies recovery by a lessor or bailor on earlier termination for failure to comply with the conditions of the agreement.

The question of earlier termination for breach of covenant was raised in *Petersen v Jajbhay*,[50] the next case to be heard after the decision of the Appellate Division. In the *Petersen* case, it will be remembered, the sub-tenant had failed to pay his rent and, under the terms of the illegal agreement, that made him liable to be ejected without notice. Not unnaturally, counsel for the sub-tenant sought to rely on the Watermeyer dictum. Counsel for the plaintiff, however, objected that, assuming the dictum justified recovery on termination by effluxion of time, it did nothing to justify earlier ejectment for non-payment of rent. Greenburg JP, delivering the judgment of the Provincial Division, answered counsel's objection in this way:

> According to the reasons given by Watermeyer JA, one must decide what the owner has transferred in terms of the illegal agreement. When such agreement gives the occupier the right of occupation for a fixed period, then the transfer is for a fixed period. Where it is for a monthly tenancy, the transfer is for a period terminable by a month's notice. In both cases, the terms of the agreement define the extent of the transfer. Where, as in the present case, the agreement is for an indefinite period, with rent payable monthly, but with a right to the owner to terminate on failure by the occupier to pay the rent by a certain date, this provision amounts to a limitation of the right to occupation in the same way as the definition of the term in the first of the two instances given, and the right to terminate by a month's notice in other.[51]

The Judge President's point, then, is that a condition in a lease providing for termination by the lessor is as much a definition of the term of the lease as is a condition stating a fixed period. Though he does not actually say so, it follows equally that a provision for earlier termination contained in a lease for a fixed term is also part of the definition of the term. What the lessee gets in such a case is something less than an absolute term. To allow him to remain in occupation notwithstanding an earlier termination in pursuance of the conditions of the lease is to grant him a larger right of possession than was transferred to him under the agreement. By the same token, to deny the lessor possession in such a case is to deprive him of a right which he did not transfer away.

An Explanation

At this stage, no doubt, the objection will be made that, whatever the theoretical justification for this point of view, it necessarily must fail because it involves the

[50] 1940 TPD 182.
[51] Ibid at 190.

enforcement by the court of a right of termination created by the illegal agreement and hence would be a breach of the *ex turpi causa rule*.[52] Two points need to be made in answer to this objection and the first of them, at least, also appears from the South African cases. A distinction has to be made between the enforcement of rights given by an illegal agreement, which would offend against the *ex turpi causa* rule, and reference to an illegal contract as a matter of evidence, which does not.[53] The leading case on this point, also, is probably *Singh v Ali*,[54] where the Privy Council had to know that the illegal contracts were sales before they could recognise that ownership had passed under them to the plaintiff. Similarly in *Taylor v Chester*[55] the illegal pledge confirmed the defendant's right to retain the half banknote, just as in *Feret v Hill*[56] the illegal lease evidenced the lessee's right to possession of the premises. The *ex turpi causa* rule, therefore, does not prevent a court's looking at an illegal agreement in order to discover what was retained and what was transferred away. In fact, its right to do so is implicit in the notion that recovery can be had after the expiry of a fixed term. The evidence for such expiry must be the illegal agreement.

The other, and more serious, point concerns the objection that to allow a termination for breach of the conditions of a lease or bailment is to enforce a right created by the illegal agreement. If this were indeed so, there would be a breach of the *ex turpi causa* rule and that would end the matter. The answer to this objection is, quite simply, that the owner's rights of termination for breach are not the creation of the illegal agreement. When an owner enters into a bailment or lease, he starts with the totality of ownership. Under his contract, he transfers away his rights of possession, to the extent which the contract defines. But the remaining incidents of his ownership, including his rights of reversion, are things he retains.[57] The contract does not create his reversionary rights; it merely evidences them. One can contrast this with an owner's claim for rent which, because it is founded on rights created by the illegal agreement, must fail.[58]

If this argument is accepted, we now have one principle by which the decision on all three agreements in the *Bowmakers* case can be justified. Whether the first and third agreements were terminated automatically, or by the act of the plaintiffs in bringing their action, is seen to be immaterial. Either way, the plaintiffs were relying on reversionary rights of ownership which they had never transferred away. The same, of course, was also true in the case of the second agreement,

[52] Cf Treitel, above note 1 at 424; Behrmann, above note 47 at 42; *Watson v Miles* [1953] NZLR 958 (CA) 968–69 per Gresson J.

[53] Chitty, above note 1 at 435; *Petersen v Jajbhay* 1940 TPD 182, 191; *Bowes v Foster* (1858) 27 LJ Ex 262; *Belvoir Finance Co v Stapleton* [1971] 1 QB 210; [1970] 3 All ER 664 (CA).

[54] [1960] AC 167.

[55] (1869) LR 4 QB 309.

[56] (1854) 15 CB 207.

[57] Cf *Roberts v Roberts* [1957] Tas SR 84, 105; also *Vandervell v IRC* [1967] 2 AC 291 (HL) 329.

[58] *Edler v Auerbach* [1950] 1 KB 359. Similarly, moneys paid by way of loan are irrevocable, since property passes to the borrower, the lender having only a chose in action.

always assuming it contained a provision allowing termination for non-payment of hire. As has already been mentioned, it is a fair inference from the report that this was the case.

The Second Explanation

The second possible explanation for both aspects of the *Bowmakers* decision involves a direct application of the principle which the Court purported to apply in that case. It will be recalled that du Parcq LJ stated the principle to be that the owner might recover possession provided he was not forced, either to found his claim on the illegal contract, or to plead its illegality in order to support his claim.[59]

To fall within the second leg of this principle, the plaintiffs, having effectively transferred possession of the tools to the defendants under the illegal contracts, would have had to have been claiming to vacate that transfer of possession for the very reason that it was illegal.[60] Had they done so, they would have been met with the answer that the courts will not nullify an executed illegal contract and restore the parties to their original position, except under the well-known but limited exceptions to the *in pari delicto* rule. None of these exceptions was applicable to the facts of the *Bowmakers* case.

In actual fact, of course, the plaintiffs were not asking the Court to vacate the agreements on account of their illegality. They pleaded and relied upon their ownership of the tools. In these circumstances, it fell to the defendants to rely on the illegal agreements in order to establish their rights to retain possession and resist the plaintiffs' demand for their return. So far as the tools the subject of agreements 1 and 3 were concerned, their act of selling them off had, fortuitously, revested an immediate right of possession in the plaintiffs, and that was an end to the matter so far as these agreements were concerned. As to the second agreement, however, the only right to possession they could show was one which, on a not unreasonable assumption of fact, had already come to an end, because terminated by the plaintiffs for non-payment of hire.[61] And since the termination had been by act of the *plaintiffs*, there was no question of the *Court's* being asked to enforce the cesser clause in the agreement. All they were asked to do was to notice what had already taken place.[62]

On this explanation, therefore, the correctness or otherwise of the *Bowmakers* decision turns upon whether a party can be said to be 'founding his claim' on an illegal contract when he asks the court, not to enforce it for him, but to recognise that he has already exercised a power reserved to him under it. In these

[59] [1945] KB 65, 71.

[60] Behrmann, above note 47 at 42, 43; Salmond and Winfield, *Law of Contracts* (1927) 150 *et seq.* Cf *Kalian v Moodley* 1948 (3) SALR 986, esp 990; *Belvoir Finance Co v Stapleton* [1971] 1 QB 210, 221; [1970] 3 All ER 664 (CA) 671.

[61] *Roberts v Roberts* [1957] Tas SR 84, 104. Cf Cornish (1964) 27 *MLR* 225, 228.

[62] Behrmann, above note 47 at 44. Cf *Kalian v Moodley* 1948 (3) SALR 986, esp 990; *Belvoir Finance Co v Stapleton* [1971] 1 QB 210, 221; [1970] 3 All ER 664 (CA) 671.

circumstances, for the court to refuse his claim would involve a reversal of its usual stance, which, while refusing to enforce the contract, is to recognise the effectiveness of what has been done under it.

The Third Line of Criticism

The third major objection to the *Bowmakers* decision arises from the potentially bizarre results its application might have in practice.[63] An extreme example would be an action by a gangster to recover a machinegun loaned to a confederate for the purposes of a murder. Actions of this kind could be regarded as an affront to the dignity of the court and it may well appear inconceivable that they should be allowed to succeed by an application of the *Bowmakers* principle. Yet the logic of the principle is that the owner should recover since he relies on his prior title and, *ex hypothesi*, there is no question of the enforcement of an illegal dealing. In other words, to justify refusal of relief there would have to be some factor present additional to the *Bowmakers* principle itself.

The problem was in fact adverted to by the Court of Appeal in the *Bowmakers* case.[64] It should not be thought, they said, that the rule they had enunciated was subject to no exceptions. They instanced the class of case where the goods claimed are of such a kind that it would be unlawful to deal in them at all. They gave the example of obscene books. Illicit drugs would not doubt fall within the same category, as conceivably would an unlicensed machinegun.

Beyond this kind of case, however, it is difficult to see upon what ground relief could be refused or, if it were, where the line should be drawn. Either of these things would involve the withholding of assistance on grounds external to the real issue. It would amount to denying the plaintiff his rights because the court disapproved of his behaviour, and this the courts seem disinclined to do. On the decided cases, they will not refuse recovery of money or goods just because the plaintiff has come by them illegally.[65] Indeed, there may be good sense in this for to adopt any other attitude would be to encourage the possibly greater evil of self-help.

One distinguished commentator has suggested, as a further exception, the type of case where a bailment agreement requires the bailee to commit an illegal act and where possession is sought for a breach of that requirement.[66] But on the view of the *Bowmakers* principle advanced in this present article, this kind of objection would not apply. Repossession would be sought, not on the grounds that the bailee had failed to comply with the illegal terms of the agreement, but because his right

[63] Hamson (1949) 10 *CLJ* 249, 254; Paton, above note 1 at 35. Professor Hamson at 255 suggests limits which might be placed upon the rule.

[64] [1945] KB 65, 72.

[65] Eg, *Gordon v Chief Commissioner of Metropolitan Police* [1910] 2 KB 1080 (CA); *Singh v Ali* [1960] AC 167 (PC).

[66] Hamson (1949) 10 *CLJ* 249, 254.

to possession would have come to an end. The plaintiff would not be relying on any right accruing to him from the breach as such, but on his pre-existing title.

Of course, this result is open to the objection that, whatever the position in theory, the consequence de facto is the enforcement of an illegal agreement. A bailee or lessee will be encouraged to perform his side of the illegal bargain because he will know that if he does not the courts will deprive him of possession. Unfortunate though this consequence may be, it cannot in itself be fatal to the *Bowmakers* principle and, indeed, has not proved to be so in South Africa. Even if the law were to be reversed, the results could be said to be just as unfortunate. A rule which made a de facto gift of title to an unscrupulous bailee or lessee would be just as deficient in moral appeal. The real difficulty lies in the arbitrary, all-or-nothing character of the common law governing illegal contracts. The same sort of criticism can be made of the law as to mistake[67] and used to apply to the law of frustration before the legislature intervened with the Law Reform (Frustrated Contracts) Act 1943, to enable the courts to strike a fairer balance between the parties.[68] It is perhaps relevant that when New Zealand sought recently to solve the problem of illegal contracts, it did so by according wide discretionary powers to the courts.[69]

Perhaps all that can be said at this stage is that the Court of Appeal has recognised the possible existence of additional exceptions to its rule and has left the matter open for later courts to deal with. In the meantime, at a rather more empirical level, there remains at least one further factor which should tend to militate against any undue rush of applications. That is, of course, the risk of exposure. No doubt any criminal, minded to seek the assistance of the court to recover his ill-gotten gains, would be told by his legal advisers of the awful example of the two highwaymen.[70] One of them asked the court for an account of their spoils. Thus exposed, both of them ended up on the gallows.

Conclusion

In a sense, both *Bowmakers v Barnet Instruments* and *Jajbhay v Cassim* may have been decided too far in advance of their time. Twenty-five years ago, the proliferation of regulatory offences had already robbed illegality of much of its moral stigma. That trend has continued during the intervening period. But today society is, in addition, generally less censorious than it used to be. If, as is believed, the *Bowmakers* decision can be supported in logic and in law, there may be grounds for hope that it will be allowed to continue to stand, despite the criticism to which it has been subjected.

67 Cf *Ingram v Little* [1961] 1 QB 31 (CA) 74 per Devlin LJ.

68 See also the Law Reform (Married Women and Tortfeasors) Act 1935 and the Law Reform (Contributory Negligence) Act 1945.

69 Illegal Contracts Act 1970 (NZ) s 7.

70 *Everet v Williams* (1725) 9 LQR 197; Megarry, *Miscellany-at-Law* (1955) 76 *et seq.*

10

Chance and the Burden of Proof in Contract and Tort[1]

Introduction

The extent to which successful claims in contract and tort can be based on the chance that something is, will be, or might have been, is a question about which it seems very easy to disagree. Every law student knows that *Chaplin v Hicks*[2] established that damages can be recovered for the loss of a chance. In that case, the chance was of gaining a prize in a beauty competition. More recently, in *Hotson v East Berkshire Area Health Authority*[3] the English High Court and Court of Appeal decided that a patient who had received negligent treatment in a hospital should, by analogy with *Chaplin v Hicks*, be entitled to damages for loss of the chance of a better outcome for his affliction. But that decision has since been reversed by the House of Lords. In *Fink v Fink*[4] the High Court of Australia denied recovery to a woman separated from her husband because she could not show on the balance of probabilities that a reconciliation would have occurred. Yet in *Davies v Taylor*[5] the House of Lords held that a less-than-even chance of reconciliation could found a wife's action for damages under the *Fatal Accidents Acts* 1846–59 (England). In the *Davies* case Lord Reid said he could see no ground at all for saying that someone with a 40 per cent case should fail altogether while another with a 60 per cent case should recover 100 per cent. Yet in *Hotson* the possibility of a result of that sort seems to have been accepted with equanimity by the House of Lords. In the New Zealand case of *Takaro Properties v Rowling*[6] where a Minister of the Crown

[1] The writer is grateful for comments by Ms JM Manning and Mr TS Pitt-Payne on the penultimate draft.

[2] [1911] 2 KB 786.

[3] [1985] 1 WLR 1036 (Simon Brown J); [1987] 1 AC 750 (CA and HL).

[4] (1946) 74 CLR 127.

[5] [1974] AC 207, 213.

[6] [1986] 1 NZLR 22 (HC and CA); reversed [1988] AC 473; [1988] 2 WLR 418 (PC). Noted by Y Cripps [1987] *CLJ* 389. See also G Cooper, 'Damages for the Loss of a Chance in Contract and Tort' (1988) 6 *AULR* 39; J Stapleton, 'The Gist of Negligence' (1988) 104 *LQR* 213, 389, 390 *et seq.*

had been found negligently to have withheld an approval which might have enabled an unprofitable company to remain in business, the judge at first instance declined to award the company damages since it could not show on the balance of probabilities that it would ever have made a profit. The Court of Appeal disagreed on the ground that, while the company's prospects might not have been good, it had lost at least a chance of remaining in existence long enough to become profitable. When the matter subsequently came before the Privy Council their Lordships held that no negligence had been established which meant that they were spared having to decide between the competing views on damages expressed in the courts below. Their advice to the Sovereign nevertheless contains a hint that they would have preferred the view of the trial judge.[7]

As Lord Mackay of Clashfern put it in the *Hotson* case,[8] this is a 'difficult area of the law'. It would be unwise, therefore, for anyone at this stage to claim to have all the answers. Nevertheless, it is possible by reference to basic principles of contract and tort, and to some of the reported cases, substantially to reduce the areas of uncertainty.

The Need to Establish a Cause of Action

To succeed in a claim in tort or contract, a plaintiff must establish a cause of action. This means he or she must prove to the standard required in civil cases (that is, on the balance of probabilities) the facts necessary to show:

a. That a duty was owed to the plaintiff.
b. That an act or omission not conforming to that duty was committed which both
   i. was committed by the defendant and
   ii. caused or contributed to an injury suffered by the plaintiff.
c. If recovery is to be had for substantial damages, that the injury so suffered either was or caused the plaintiff loss of a legally compensable kind.
d. So far as possible, the measure of such loss.

In practice, no one seems seriously to have disputed that the plaintiff must establish on the balance of probabilities both that facts existed which gave rise to a duty and that the acts or omissions allegedly in breach of that duty occurred. It is in respect of the remaining elements in the plaintiff's case that questions of chance have arisen in the reported cases. Each will be considered in turn.

[7] *Takaro Properties v Rowling* [1988] AC 473; [1988] 2 WLR 418 (PC) 427.
[8] [1987] 1 AC 750 (CA and HL) 789.

That the Act or Omission which Caused or Contributed to the Injury was Committed by the Defendant

In the Canadian case of *Cook v Lewis*[9] the plaintiff had been shot in the face. Two persons had fired their rifles at the relevant time and the Supreme Court of Canada assumed for the purposes of judgment that it was not possible to decide which of them had caused the injury. The Court took the view that the two who fired shots had both been careless and that, in those circumstances, the onus fell on them to exonerate themselves if they could. Three members of the Court went further and concluded that if neither could discharge that onus, both should be held liable.

That conclusion had some support at the time from Dr Glanville Williams who made the point that to deny the plaintiff any remedy would mean that justice was certainly not done, whereas to give a remedy against both would mean a 50 per cent possibility that justice was done.[10] But, as Professor Hogan stated in a subsequent article, a careless act is not wrongful unless it causes an injury.[11] To hold both defendants liable would be to commit a 100 per cent injustice against one or other of them. An analogy here can be drawn with paternity suits. The fact that two or more persons could have fathered a child is no ground for making all of them liable to maintain it, in the absence of any statutory provision to the contrary.[12] Professor Hogan's conclusion was that in a case like *Cook v Lewis* the onus should properly remain with the plaintiff to prove, on the balance of probabilities, which of the defendants had committed the act which caused the injury. It is submitted that he must be right.

In this, as in other contexts, it is worth recalling that statistical probability by itself is never enough to establish the identity of a guilty party. In the *Hotson* case, Lord Mackay of Clashfern cited the hypothetical illustration, given in an American case, of a town in which there were only two taxi companies, one having three blue cabs and the other one yellow cab.[13] If a person were knocked down by a cab the colour of which had not been observed, it would be wrong to suggest that the first company would be liable solely because there was a 75 per cent chance that its cab had been the one involved. Additional information would be necessary. To resort

[9] [1951] SCR 830; [1952] 1 DLR 1.

[10] Case note in (1953) 31 *Can Bar Rev* 315, 317. There was also obiter support for the same principle from Denning LJ in *Roe v Minister of Health* [1954] 2 QB 66, 82.

[11] 'Cook v Lewis Re-examined' (1961) 24 *MLR* 331, 339–41.

[12] Eg, *Wilson: Children and the Law* (2nd edn, by J Wilson and M Tomlinson, 1986) 214.

[13] [1987] 1 AC 750, 789, citing *Herskovits v Group Health Cooperative of Puget Sound* (1983) 664 P 2d 474, 491 per Brachtenbach J. Cf *Taylor v O'Connor* [1971] AC 115, 140; *Mitchell v Mulholland (No 2)* [1972] 1 QB 65, 76–77.

again to the analogy of a paternity suit, it has recently been observed in the New Zealand High Court in relation to blood tests that

> even a high mathematical probability [in that case 99 per cent] does not [without more] translate into a forensic certainty.[14]

That the Act or Omission Committed by the Defendant Caused or Contributed to the Plaintiff's Injury

For the most part, the relevance of this step is to claims in tort rather than contract. In the latter, the act or omission complained of, the alleged breach of contract, is itself the injury. If a breach has been established on the balance of probabilities, so too has an injury. But in torts not actionable per se, and particularly in negligence, the plaintiff must usually show that physical injury, damage, or deprivation has occurred. In general, the onus of proof in such cases is very clear. The plaintiff must show on the balance of probabilities that the acts or omissions complained of caused or contributed to the physical injury, damage, or deprivation that he or she has suffered.[15] This means, of course, that an equal chance, and a fortiori a less than equal one, would not be enough. For example, in the Canadian case of *Levesque v Comeau*,[16] the plaintiff had suffered a severe blow to the head in a motor accident. Two months later she developed deafness, of which there had been no sign before the accident. The trial judge held that while the accident could have caused the plaintiff's condition, it was equally probable that it had resulted from some other cause. The Supreme Court of Canada held that on that finding, which a majority of the Court decided must stand, the plaintiff's claim must fail.

Despite the fact that this rule has been long established at the highest level, the English Court of Appeal has on three recent occasions departed from it. In each case, the plaintiff was held entitled to recover damages on the basis of a chance which (if quantifiable at all) was less than 51 per cent, that the injury complained of had been caused or contributed to by the defendant.

The first of the three cases was *Wilsher v Essex Area Health Authority*.[17] A prematurely born infant had been placed in a special unit at the hospital where he was born. He survived, but with an incurable condition of the retina which resulted in near-blindness. It was the case for the child that, through negligence for which the Board was vicariously responsible, he had been given too much oxygen and that this had been the cause of his affliction. On the evidence, excess oxygen was merely

[14] *Byers v Nichols* (unreported, NZ HC, judgment 13 August 1987), noted (1988) NZ *Recent Law* 92.

[15] Eg, *Bonnington Castings Ltd v Wardlaw* [1956] AC 613. It is, of course, no defence that other causes may also have contributed to the injury.

[16] (1970) 16 DLR (3d) 425.

[17] [1987] QB 730 (CA); [1988] AC 1074; [1988] 2 WLR 557 (HL).

one of several different factors, any of which could have caused or contributed to that condition. The plaintiff could therefore show no more than a chance that the negligence complained of had caused his blindness. Nevertheless, the trial judge found for him and awarded him the sum of £116,199 in damages. That judgment was affirmed by the Court of Appeal (Mustill and Glidewell LJJ, Sir Nicholas Browne-Wilkinson V-C dissenting).

The second case was *Hotson v East Berkshire Health Authority*.[18] The plaintiff, then aged 13 years, had injured his hip in a fall. Through negligence within the hospital to which he was taken, his condition was wrongly diagnosed and it was not until five days later that he received appropriate emergency treatment. The trial judge held that had his condition been diagnosed correctly on admission the plaintiff would have had a 25 per cent chance of a good recovery. That chance having, in his view, been lost through negligence for which the Board was vicariously responsible, he awarded the plaintiff 25 per cent of what would have been the full damages, which were assessed at £46,000. That judgment was subsequently affirmed by the Court of Appeal.

The third case was *Fitzgerald v Lane*.[19] The plaintiff had walked briskly onto a pedestrian crossing controlled by lights at a time when the lights were showing against him. At about the centre of the road he was struck by the car of the first defendant and was thrown to the other side of the road, into the path of a car driven in the opposite direction by the second defendant. The plaintiff suffered multiple injuries and in particular an injury to the neck which resulted in partial tetraplegia. It was not possible for the plaintiff to establish at what point the latter injury occurred. The trial judge held that the plaintiff and the drivers of both cars were all equally to blame. On appeal, the driver of the second car argued, inter alia, that it had not been shown on the balance of probabilities that the impact with his car had caused or materially contributed to the plaintiff's tetraplegia. That part of the appeal was dismissed on the ground that, though there were two separate possible causes of the plaintiff's injuries, and the existence and extent of the second defendant's contribution to causing those injuries could not be ascertained, his careless driving had created or increased the risk that such injuries would occur.

The willingness of the Court of Appeal in all three cases to allow departure from the ordinary requirement of proof on the balance of probabilities obviously needs to be explained. There were in fact two explanations.

The decisions in *Wilsher* and *Fitzgerald v Lane* were both based on an interpretation of the opinions delivered in the House of Lords in *McGhee v National Coal Board*.[20] There, the defendant employers had failed to provide washing facilities for the plaintiff and others of their employees who worked in a hot dusty atmosphere. As a result, the plaintiff had had to cycle home while still covered in dust.

[18] [1985] 1 WLR 1036 (Simon Brown J); [1987] 1 AC 750 (CA and HL).

[19] [1987] QB 781.

[20] [1973] 1 WLR 1. Applied also in *Bryce v Swan Hunter Group plc* [1988] 1 All ER 659 (Phillips J), though the decision could be justified as a direct application of *McGhee* and *Bonnington Castings* (above).

Before long, he contracted dermatitis. It was agreed that the employers were under no duty in respect of the actual working conditions, but they had been negligent in not providing facilities for their workmen to wash themselves. While it was established that the dust had caused the dermatitis, it was not possible in the then state of medical knowledge to tell whether that condition would have been prevented had the plaintiff been able to wash before he cycled home. What was clear, though, was that the plaintiff's having to cycle home unwashed had materially increased the risk of his contracting the disease. In the view of all of their Lordships, that was sufficient to make the employers liable. According to Lord Reid, there was no substantial difference between saying that what the employers did materially increased the risk of injury to the plaintiff and saying that what the employers did materially contributed to his injury.[21] This appears to have been the conclusion of them all.

From that decision and from various dicta of their Lordships in the *McGhee* case, Mustill LJ in the *Wilsher* case extracted the following principle:[22]

> If it is an established fact that conduct of a particular kind creates a risk that injury will be caused to another or increases an existing risk that injury will ensue, and if the two parties stand in such a relationship that the one party owes a duty not to conduct himself in that way, and if the party does conduct himself in that way, and if the other party does suffer injury of the kind to which the risk related, then the first party is taken to have caused the injury by his breach of duty even though the existence and extent of the contribution made by the breach cannot be ascertained.

That principle, which was in due course applied by the Court of Appeal in *Fitzgerald v Lane*, has since been rejected by the House of Lords in the *Wilsher* case on the ground that it was inconsistent with the ordinary requirement that the plaintiff establish, on the balance of probabilities, that the defendant's breach of duty caused or materially contributed to the injury suffered by the plaintiff.[23] *McGhee* was explained as being a case where the ordinary onus had been discharged. It would seem, therefore, that the coincidence identified by Lord Reid, between increasing the risk of an injury and materially contributing to the injury itself, can occur where the acts complained of affect the intensity of risk from a single cause (as in *McGhee*) but not where their consequence is to increase the number of potential causes (as in *Wilsher*).

In *Hotson v East Berkshire Health Authority* the judgments of the English High Court and the Court of Appeal proceeded on the basis that, on the analogy of *Chaplin v Hicks*, the plaintiff, in being denied the possibility of a more favourable outcome, had suffered the loss of a valuable chance. The decision of the Court of

[21] [1973] 1 WLR 1, 5.

[22] [1987] QB 730, 771–72. In *Vymer v Waldenberg Bros* [1946] KB 50, the English Court of Appeal held that in the case of the breach of a statutory safety provision, the onus was on an employer to show that the breach did not cause the injury. That decision was overruled by the House of Lords in *Bonnington Castings Ltd v Wardlaw* [1956] AC 613.

[23] See, also, *Kay v Ayrshire Area Health Board* [1987] 2 All ER 417 (HL); *Torrison v Colwill* (1987) 42 CCLT 51 (BCSC).

Appeal has since been reversed by the House of Lords, but on the narrow ground that, on the balance of probabilities, the plaintiff never did have any chance of a better outcome. It was specifically stated that this finding left open what the legal position would have been had such a chance existed, though Lord Bridge of Harwich and Lord Mackay of Clashfern, with whom Lord Brandon of Oakbrook and Lord Goff of Chieveley agreed, foresaw difficulties which they did not specify, but which Lord Bridge characterised as 'formidable'.[24] It is proposed to return to that question later in this article.

The *Hotson* case dealt with a chance of limiting the effects of physical injury which, if it had once existed, had been lost before the case came before the Court. If the difficulties in basing a cause of action on such a chance would be 'formidable', they would, of course, be no less so for a plaintiff who had not yet suffered any physical injury at all, and as to whom there was merely a chance that such an injury might some day occur.[25]

So far, under this heading, consideration has been confined to cases where physical loss, damage, or deprivation has had to be established before questions of economic loss could arise. However, in the last quarter of a century, cases like *Hedley Byrne & Co Ltd v Hiller & Partners Ltd*[26] and *Anns v Merton London Borough Council*[27] have led to the possibility of claims in negligence where the injury complained of has itself been economic loss. These cases are dealt with under the next heading.

That the Injury or Breach of Duty Caused or Occasioned Economic Loss of a Legally Compensable Kind

Under this heading fall cases where the plaintiff claims that

a. physical injury, damage and deprivation; or
b. a breach of contract; or
c. (in the case of a tort not dependent on physical loss, damage, or deprivation) a breach of duty

has caused or occasioned economic loss. Here again, the burden remains prima facie on the plaintiff to prove his or her case on the balance of probabilities. Indeed, *McGregor on Damages* suggests that the standard to be met is one of 'reasonable

[24] [1987] 1 AC 750, 782, 786, 789.

[25] In such cases much will turn on what constitutes the injury. If the plaintiff has been poisoned, was he injured when he ingested the toxic material or only when the physical symptoms appeared?

[26] [1964] AC 465.

[27] [1978] AC 728. More recently, the House of Lords, the Privy Council, and the High Court of Australia have all moved to limit the effect of Lord Wilberforce's famous two-stage test of liability; see the article by Stephen Quinlan and David Gardiner, 'New Developments with Respect to the Duty of Care in Tort' (1988) 62 *ALJ* 347.

certainty'.[28] Nevertheless, and notwithstanding the ordinary rule, this is one area where chance clearly can form an ingredient of a successful claim.

An example of this arises in relation to events which may occur in the future. Provided a plaintiff can show a present injury sufficient to establish a cause of action, he or she can recover damages in respect of loss or further injury which may in the future result from, or be occasioned by, the original injury. And this is so even though the chances of such injury are only even or less than even, provided they are not too insubstantial. The position was stated by Lord Diplock in *Mallett v McMonagle*[29] in this way:

> The role of the court in making an assessment of damages which depends on a view as to what will be and what would have been is to be contrasted with its ordinary function in civil actions of determining what was. In determining what did happen in the past a court decides on the balance of probabilities. Anything that is more probable than not it treats as certain. But in assessing damages which depend on its view as to what will happen in the future or would have happened in the future if something had not happened in the past, the court must make an estimate as to what are the chances that a particular thing will or would have happened and reflect those changes, whether they are more or less than even, in the amount of damages which it awards.

An obvious justification for thus departing from the ordinary burden of proof in the case of possible future events is the once-for-all nature of claims at common law. In respect of any one cause of action only one claim may be brought. If there is a real and not merely a speculative chance that an actionable injury will have consequences in the future which are not too remote, that chance must be taken into account at the time of the action if it is to be relevant at all. As Lord Diplock's dictum implies, the same approach is called for whether the original injury has the potential in the future either, on the one hand, to cause additional loss or damage or, on the other, to prevent the accrual or occurrence of a benefit. Thus, for example, in *Davies v Taylor*,[30] which was a claim under the Fatal Accidents Acts 1846–59 (England), the death of the plaintiff's husband had removed any chance there might have been that the separation between them would have ended and a reconciliation been effected. On the facts, the plaintiff was unable to show that a significant chance had existed and she was unable therefore to establish any dependency. But the House of Lords made it clear that while the chance of a reconciliation had to be significant, it did not have to be as high as 51 per cent and that any damages recoverable would be proportional to the strength of the chance. That case turned on the application of a statute which required the dependants to establish an 'injury', but the House seems to have treated the death of her husband as the injury to the plaintiff, and the potential loss of support as the economic consequences of that injury. That was the analysis adopted (it is submitted, correctly) by Croom-Johnson LJ in the Court of Appeal in the *Hotson* case.[31]

[28] (15th edn, 1988) 214–15.
[29] [1970] AC 166, 176.
[30] [1974] AC 207.
[31] [1987] 1 AC 750, 768.

Because of its reference to what will happen, or would have happened in the future, Lord Diplock's dictum in *Mallett v McMonagle* might be thought to exclude events which might have happened in the past had it not been for the injury suffered. And to have regard to events which might have happened in the past would lack the justification of the once-for-all nature of common law claims. On the other hand, it would be an odd result if, in a case like *Davies v Taylor*, success or failure for the plaintiff's case should have to turn on whether the chance of a reconciliation with her husband related to the period after, rather than before, the hearing of the action. Moreover, as it happens, while the second part of Lord Diplock's dictum refers to what would have happened in the future, his initial statement, about the distinction between what was on the one hand and what will be or what would have been on the other, is not so confined. Rather, the contrast drawn is between the actual and the necessarily hypothetical. That being so, it seems reasonable to conclude that when his Lordship spoke of what would have happened in the future if something had not happened in the past, the future to which he referred was intended to date from the occurrence of that 'something' rather than from the hearing of the action.

The other main instance under this heading of a chance forming an ingredient of a successful claim occurs where what has been lost is the opportunity to make an economically valuable gain. *Chaplin v Hicks* is, of course, the classic example. There, the plaintiff belonged to a limited class of 50 persons from amongst whom the twelve 'winners' of the beauty contest would be chosen. Statistically, therefore, her chance of gaining a prize was about one in four, though the jury, who had seen her in the witness box, may have estimated her own chance as higher than that. The Court of Appeal was satisfied that her chance of winning had itself an economic value, the quantum of which it was for the jury to assess.

Since that decision, a number of successful claims for the loss of an economically valuable chance have been reported. Some have concerned sporting competitions involving, for example, professional golf,[32] professional cycling,[33] ten-pin bowling,[34] and ballroom dancing.[35] Other examples include the loss of a chance of success in a ballot for land,[36] in obtaining an approval,[37] in a court action,[38] or with a planning objection,[39] of gains from the lease of a racehorse including

[32] *Mulvanie v Joseph* (1968) 112 Sol J 927.

[33] *Leis v Gardner* [1965] Qd R 181 (FC).

[34] *Hawrish v St John's Sportsmen's Club* (1964) 46 DLR (2d) 45.

[35] *Hall v Wheeler* [1962] QWN 40.

[36] *Markholm Construction Co Ltd v Wellington City Council* (unreported, NZ HC, judgment 6 August 1984) noted (1985) 3 BCB 61.

[37] *Aquaculture v NZ Green Mussel Co Ltd* (unreported, HC, judgment 4 November 1986) noted (1988) 14 *NZ Recent Law* 159. (FDA of the United States.)

[38] *Richards v Cox* [1943] KB 139; *Kitchen v Royal Air Force Association* [1958] 1 WLR 563 (CA); *Cook v Swinfen* [1967] 1 WLR 457 (CA).

[39] *Craig v East Coast Bays City Council* [1986] 1 NZLR 99 (CA).

the potential proceeds from bets,[40] of contracting a marriage,[41] of striking oil,[42] of remaining in the police force,[43] of retaining a valuable franchise,[44] and of a debt being paid through the debtor's remaining in custody.[45] These were all chances on which an economic value could be placed.

There are, however, certain established limits to claims of this kind. In the first place, while the chance need not be better than even, and may be relatively poor, it must at least be more than merely speculative. That was the problem the respective wives faced in *Davies v Taylor*[46] and *Fink v Fink*.[47] In the one case a reconciliation was on the evidence very unlikely, and in the other it was held that there were too many contingences.[48] Second, though a plaintiff may statistically appear to have a significant chance, there may be circumstances peculiar to him or her which mean that in fact the chance never existed. An analogous example of that was *Hotson v East Berkshire Area Health Authority*.[49] Third, if the reality of the chance depends on some action that the plaintiff would need to have taken, he or she must establish on the balance of probabilities that that action would in fact have been taken. Thus, plaintiffs have failed in claims in respect of negligent advice on the ground that they could not show that they would have followed the correct advice anyway.[50] Fourth, if the existence of the chance depends on the exercise of a choice by the defendant, it is assumed that he or she would exercise that choice in his or her own favour[51] provided and to the extent that that could be done legally and bona fide. As to this last proviso, it was held to be no defence in *Chaplin v Hicks* that the defendant could have chosen arbitrarily not to give the plaintiff a prize.[52] In *The Mihalis Angelos*[53] by contrast, it was held that since the defendant company had an express right to terminate the contract which it would certainly have exercised had the contract not already been discharged for the defendant's breach, no damages could be recovered by the plaintiff. Fifth, the chance must have some assessable economic value.[54]

40 *Howe v Teefy* (1927) 27 SR (NSW) 301 (FC).

41 *Graham v Fogarty* (1970) 92 WN (NSW) 452 (CA); *Jackson v Jackson* [1970] 2 NSWR 454 (CA) 458; *Taylor v Addems* [1932] 1 WWR 505.

42 *Carson v Willitts* [1930] 4 DLR 977.

43 *Moores v CWS Ltd* (London *Times*, 9 May 1955) cited in J Munkman, *Damages for Personal Injuries and Death* (5th edn, 1973) 84.

44 *Schilling v Kidd Garrett* [1972] 1 NZLR 243 (CA); cf *Hampton & Sons Ltd v George* [1939] 3 All ER 627; *Sanders v Parry* [1967] 1 WLR 753.

45 *Macrae v Clarke* (1866) LR 1 CP 403.

46 [1974] AC 207.

47 (1946) 74 CLR 127.

48 Cf *Murray v Bannerman* [1972] NZLR 411 (CA). Presumably a negligently destroyed ticket in a lottery yet to be drawn would at least be worth its cost price.

49 [1987] 1 AC 750; cf *Adams Express Co v Egbert* (1860) 36 Pa 360 cited in *Chaplin v Hicks* by Farwell LJ at 798; *Barnett v Chelsea Hospital* [1968] 1 All ER 1068.

50 *Sykes v Midland Bank Executors and Trustee Co* [1971] 1 QB 113 (CA).

51 *McGregor on Damages*, above note 28 at 228–30 and cases there cited.

52 See also *Abrahams v Reiach* [1922] 1 KB 477.

53 [1971] 1 QB 164 (CA).

54 *Howe v Teefy* (1927) 27 SR (NSW) 301 (FC) 306–07. Cf *Hardie v Fothergill* (1888) 13 App Cas 351 (HL) where a contingent liability to indemnify for breach of contract was held to have presently assessable value.

Thus, in the notable Australian case of *McRae v Commonwealth Disposals Commission*,[55] the plaintiff was held entitled to be reimbursed for expenses incurred in setting up a salvage expedition, but could recover nothing for the value of the non-existent vessel and cargo. There was no contract that the vessel and cargo would have any value. It was not a case like *Chaplin v Hicks* where the plaintiff had lost the chance of an ascertainable benefit. Rather, the chance lay in the nature of the thing contracted for.[56] Sixth, it is perhaps hardly necessary to add that the existence of the chance must itself be established on the balance of probabilities.[57]

It has sometimes been suggested that claims of the *Chaplin v Hicks* type are peculiar to contract, and certainly the point was made in that case that the chance to compete was something for which the plaintiff had specifically contracted.[58] Moreover, there is an argument in favour of such claims in contract which does not apply in tort. If someone is prepared to contract for a chance and a fortiori to give consideration for it, it would be inconsistent for the law to treat it as being of no value, particularly since 'value' in this context does not depend exclusively on profitability.[59] Nor can it be argued in such a contract case as it can be in tort that the loss of the chance may be too remote. Nevertheless, if the hurdles of value and remoteness can be surmounted it would seem that, in principle, claims for loss of the chance of an economic benefit can succeed in tort.

While in tort claims for loss of a chance the latter may frequently be too remote, that need not always be the case. The classic hypothetical case is of a running-down victim prevented from attending a meeting at which a lucrative deal was to have been concluded. One such case has occurred in Canada.[60] The plaintiff succeeded but the issues received little consideration in the reported judgment. However, in *Mulvaine v Joseph*,[61] a professional golfer, who had been injured through the negligence of a taxi driver, recovered damages, inter alia, for loss of a chance of winning prize money in golf tournaments.

In both the above cases, the plaintiff had suffered physical injury, the loss of the chance being a consequence of that injury. That still leaves for consideration claims in those torts where the injury can be economic loss per se rather than loss resulting from physical injury, damage, or deprivation. Assuming that such claims arise from torts which are not actionable per se, establishment that on the balance of probabilities loss had been occasioned by the defendant's breach of duty would be an essential element in the plaintiff's cause of action. It was doubtless for this reason that at first instance in *Takaro Properties v Rowling*,[62] Quilliam J considered it necessary that the plaintiff company establish on the balance of

[55] (1951) 84 CLR 377.

[56] Ibid at 412.

[57] Eg, *Hornach v Paterson* (1967) 62 DLR (2d) 289, 298.

[58] [1911] 2 KB 786, 795.

[59] *The Greta Holme* [1897] AC 596; *The Mediana* [1900] AC 113; *Howe v Teefy* (1927) 27 SR (NSW) 301 (FC) 304.

[60] *Phillips v McKay* [1931] 2 WWR 98.

[61] (1968) 112 *Sol J* 927.

[62] [1986] 1 NZLR 22 (HC and CA); [1988] AC 473; [1988] 2 WLR 418 (PC).

probabilities that the alleged negligence of Mr Rowling in denying approval had been the cause of loss to it. Because he considered the company had a much less than even chance of ever becoming profitable, he held that the burden of proof had not been discharged. On that point his judgment was reversed in the Court of Appeal. Woodhouse P commented:[63]

> In the present case Quilliam J did not attempt to assess the chance of success because of an assumed onus upon the plaintiffs to demonstrate that success for their project was more profitable than not. It is an approach which fails to distinguish between the difficulty of assessing the level of an admitted chance with evidence which shows the chance was actually present. Thus an additional onus was set up against the plaintiffs—an onus not merely to show on reasonable grounds that the project would have had the chance to trade its way out of trouble once the added share capital had been injected but to show that the chance was a better one than 50 per cent.

For his part, Cooke J took the view that if there were some real possibility of success the project must have had some commercial value, however hard to assess, and damages should be awarded accordingly.[64]

What the New Zealand Court of Appeal seems to have been affirming is that in torts based on economic loss, as in contract, provided the plaintiff can show on the balance of probabilities that he or she has lost a chance which itself has or had economic value, it does not have to be a chance which is more likely than not to occur. That view is also consistent with the slightly earlier decision of the same Court in *Craig v East Coast Bays City Council*[65] where, through negligence of the Council, a property owner lost his chance of objecting to a certain planning application. It was held that he was entitled to damages for loss of that chance. The *Takaro Properties* case went to the Privy Council[66] which allowed the appeal on the ground that, assuming the Minister had been under a duty of care, it had not been shown that he was negligent. On the question of damages their Lordships commented that this finding meant they did not have to

> deal with the issue of causation (as to which there was an acute division of opinion between Quilliam J and the Court of Appeal) or with the issue of damages.[67]

However, there was an earlier reference to the point in these terms:[68]

> Despite Quilliam J's express finding of fact that he could see nothing but disaster for the scheme, damages were calculated [by the Court of Appeal] by reference to the loss of the chance that the plaintiff, which was probably insolvent on 21 March 1974, might have become prosperous if the Minister had on that date legalised the issue of shares to Mitsubishi.

63 Ibid at 64.
64 Ibid at 69.
65 [1986] 1 NZLR 99 (CA).
66 [1988] AC 473; [1988] 2 WLR 418.
67 Ibid at 512; 440.
68 Ibid at 499; 427.

So far as that passage may be taken to imply a negative reaction to the award of damages, the further implication could be drawn that the reaction was due not to the fact that damages had been given for loss of a chance as such but rather to an inference that, on the findings in the High Court, there had been no chance in the first place. It is submitted that where economic loss has to be established it should in principle be sufficient that a chance of economic gain has been lost, provided always that the chance itself has or had present value.

The Measure of the Loss Suffered

In the *Hotson* case[69] at first instance, Simon Brown J drew a distinction between causation of loss on the one hand and quantification on the other. The former he thought had to be established on the balance of probabilities but in respect of the latter regard could be had to chances of less than 51 per cent. Applying that distinction to the case before him, he classified the plaintiff's chance of a better recovery as a matter of quantification. That classification was rejected on appeal. But Sir John Donaldson MR in the Court of Appeal also rejected any suggestion that the assessment of damages and the establishment of loss involved different burdens of proof. In his view:[70]

> Having identified and proved [a] loss, the loss then has to be valued. Identification and valuation are distinct and separate processes but … it is for the plaintiff to prove both the identified loss and its value and to do so in each case on the balance of probabilities.

This dictum appears in general to be correct, though some qualifications have to be made. So far as quantification or valuation of loss is susceptible of proof, the onus should in principle be on the plaintiff to adduce that evidence and establish his or her case on the balance of probabilities. As was said by Bowen LJ in *Ratcliffe v Evans*,[71] 'as much certainty and particularity must be insisted on, both in pleading and proof of damage, as is reasonable'. A corollary to this is that if proof is not reasonably practicable but it is nevertheless clear that loss of damage has been suffered, the burden is relaxed and the court will do the best it can with what is available. In the words of Vaughan Williams LJ in *Chaplin v Hicks*,[72]

> the fact that damages cannot be assessed with certainty does not relieve the wrongdoer of the necessity of paying damages.

Accordingly, in relation to future or contingent events which could affect or might have affected the quantum of loss (and whether by increasing or diminishing it),

[69] [1985] 1 WLR 1036, 1044.

[70] [1987] 1 AC 750, 760.

[71] [1892] QB 524, 532–33.

[72] [1911] 2 KB 786, 792. See also *Biggin & Co Ltd v Permanite Ltd* [1951] 1 KB 422; *Callaghan v William C Lynch Pty Ltd* [1962] NSWR 871 (FC) 877; *Enzed Holdings Ltd v Wynthen Pty Ltd* (1984) 57 ALR 167.

the court may well have to pay regard to chances and possibilities which, though 'significant', cannot be shown to be more likely than not to occur. So, for example, in jurisdictions which permit claims for personal injury, courts may well take into account in quantifying damages such chances as those of obtaining a higher paid position, length of working life, physical recovery or deterioration, remarriage, and the like.[73]

Areas of Uncertainty Remaining

If the foregoing analysis has been correct, there are really only two areas where the law relating to the loss of a chance is still uncertain. One concerns claims in tort where the injury relied on is the loss of the chance of an economic benefit. It has already been submitted that in principle, and despite any doubts which might be inferred from comments of the Privy Council in the *Takaro Properties* case, all that need be established in such cases on the balance of probabilities is that the chance existed and that it had economic value.

The other area of uncertainty concerns recovery for the loss of the chance of avoiding physical harm, or at least of achieving a result which would have been less physically damaging. This was the question deliberately left open by the House of Lords in *Hotson v East Berkshire Area Health Authority*. Here, the eventual answer may turn on whether the claim is brought in contract or in tort, even though that could have unfortunate effects in practice. It could mean, for example, in jurisdictions where claims can still be brought for personal injury, that a patient's rights or recovery might depend, for example, on whether the hospital responsible for negligent treatment was a public or a private one.

The situation in contract is relatively straightforward, there being no good reason at common law why a party should not contract for the benefit of a chance of avoiding physical harm or damage. For example, persons with suicidal tendencies can contract with others for protection from the chance that they might destroy themselves.[74] If a medical practitioner can offer a 30 per cent chance of success for a particular procedure, there is again no reason in principle why it should not be possible to contract for the benefit of that chance however unlikely it might be in practice that a practitioner would enter into such a contract. Since breach of contract is actionable per se, a plaintiff should be able to recover substantial damages if he or she is wrongfully denied the benefit of the chance contracted for, provided always that the chance can be valued in economic terms.

[73] Cf *Mallett v McMonagle* [1970] AC 166, 176–77 per Lord Diplock.

[74] Cf *Pallister v Waikato Hospital Bd* [1975] 2 NZLR 725 esp 736, 741 *et seq* discussed in Coote, 'Suicide and the Claims of Dependants' [1976] *NZLJ* 54.

But in the case of a tort of the kind where the very existence of the cause of action depends on establishing that the plaintiff has been caused physical loss, damage, or deprivation, the existence of such physical loss, damage, or deprivation and its cause have to be established before any question of its economic consequences can arise. The ordinary requirement is that the plaintiffs establish on the balance of probabilities that the defendant caused or contributed to the physical condition complained of. Argument that a chance of less than 51 per cent should be accepted as sufficient could presumably take one of three forms. One would be that a chance of that kind should be accepted as the *equivalent* of a present injury, rather as the loss of a chance of financial gain can represent a present economic loss. The second would be that a lesser standard of probability would be appropriate in a case where the defendant's breach of duty had made it impossible to be sure what the outcome would otherwise have been. A third argument, and one which appealed to the lower courts in the *Hotson* case, would be that the defendant's breach of duty had deprived the plaintiff of the benefit of a chance of recovery and that the loss of that benefit was *itself* the injury needed to establish the cause of the action. It is submitted that none of these arguments should succeed.

As to the first argument, the loss of a chance of financial gain goes to establishing the existence of the actionable tort only where the nature of the tort or, as regards negligence, the category of the case, is such that economic loss is sufficient for the purpose. Loss of the chance complies with the requirement because the chance itself has an economic value. No artificiality is involved. There would be such artificiality, though, if the chance of physical injury or the loss of a chance of physical recovery were to be treated by the courts as amounting to a form of injury in itself. The second possible argument has the merit of seeking to avoid the injustice of allowing a wrongdoer to shelter behind an uncertainty brought about by his or her own breach of duty. But that could be said to have been the situation in *Hotson*, *Wilsher*, and *Fitzgerald v Lane* and, though the last has still to be reviewed by the House of Lords, the evidence of the other two decisions is that there is no disposition in that tribunal to modify the ordinary burden of proof to take account of hard cases. The third argument would seek to substitute the loss of a valuable benefit for the requirement of physical injury or damage. So long as the existence of a tort depends on the presence of such injury or damage, the loss of a mere valuable benefit could not be a sufficient compliance with that requirement.[75] The tort itself would first have to be changed.

[75] Cf HLA Hart and AM Honore, *Causation in the Law*, 2nd edn (Clarendon Press, Oxford, 1985) where (at 418) it is suggested that to allow such claims would be to treat the plaintiff's chance of recovery as something like a lottery ticket of which the defendant had deprived him.

Conclusion

On the basis of the foregoing analysis the position can be summarised at least tentatively in the following way:

1. If a claim in contract or tort is to succeed, the plaintiff's cause of action must be established on the balance of probabilities.
2. So far as the cause of action depends on establishing economic loss, the loss of a chance of economic gain will be sufficient for the purpose if the chance itself has or had economic value.
3. Where a cause of action depends on establishing physical loss, damage, or deprivation, a chance that such loss, damage, or deprivation will occur or could have been avoided will be insufficient if it is less than 51 per cent.
4. Once a cause of action has been established on the balance of probabilities, the courts, in part because of the once-for-all nature of common law actions, will have regard, in assessing damages, to chances of less than 51 per cent that events or developments both physical and economic which may diminish or increase the economic consequences of the defendant's wrongful acts or omissions will occur in the future as the result of those wrongful acts or omissions (or alternatively, where appropriate, would have occurred, whether in the past or in the future, had it not been for them).

11

Damages, *The Liesbosch*, and Impecuniosity

'The damages for which the defendant is liable cannot be increased by reason of the want of funds of the plaintiff'. So said the edition of *Salmond on Torts*[1] used by my generation of undergraduates. The authority cited was *Owners of Dredger Liesbosch v Owners of Steamship Edison*[2] (hereinafter *The Liesbosch*), a decision of the House of Lords in 1933.

In fact, though, even in 1933 there were circumstances in which a plaintiff's impecuniosity could have the effect of increasing the amount recoverable in damages. And in the years since then, some important developments have changed relevant aspects of the law of damages. So it is hardly surprising that since that passage appeared in *Salmond*, *The Liesbosch* has been doubted,[3] distinguished,[4] even confined to its own facts,[5] not to say misunderstood.[6] Nevertheless, it still appears in Torts textbooks in England, Canada, Australia, and New Zealand.

Recently, the Privy Council in *Alcoa Minerals of Jamaica Inc v Herbert Broderick*,[7] on appeal from the Court of Appeal of Jamaica, was invited by counsel to hold that *The Liesbosch* was no longer part of the law of that country. Their Lordships chose not to consider that question, it being unnecessary to their decision to do so. In the result, how far, if at all, impecuniosity is or ought to be relevant to damages is still in issue and that is the question to which the present paper is directed.

The Liesbosch: The Facts

The plaintiff owners of the Liesbosch, a dredger, were a syndicate of civil engineers who had contracted with the Harbour Board at Patras for the construction there of piers and quay walls under heavy penalties for default. The works included

[1] *Salmond's Law of Torts*, 10th edn by WTS Stallybrass (Sweet & Maxwell Ltd, London, 1945) 125.
[2] [1933] AC 449.
[3] *Dodd Properties Kent Ltd v Canterbury City Council* [1980] 1 WLR 433, 458.
[4] Ibid at 452.
[5] Eg, *Perry v Sydney Phillips & Son* [1982] 1 WLR 1297, 1302; *Attorney-General v Geothermal Produce NZ Ltd* [1987] 2 NZLR 348, 355.
[6] Eg, *Martindale v Duncan* [1973] 1 WLR 574, 577.
[7] [2002] 1 AC 371; [2000] 3 WLR 23.

a considerable amount of dredging, for the purpose of which the plaintiffs had bought the Liesbosch at a cost of £4,000 plus an additional £2,000 for fitting it out and transporting it to Patras. On 26 November 1928, the defendants' ship, Edison, fouled the moorings of the Liesbosch, dragging it out into the open sea where it sank and became a total loss.

Because its funds had all been committed to the construction contract, and to the payment of a deposit which it had been required to make thereunder, the syndicate had no moneys available to purchase a replacement dredger. What it did, therefore, was at high rates to hire the Adria (a rather larger dredger) plus a tug and two hopper barges. It was not until 17 June 1929 that these had arrived at Patras and could be put to use. Until then, work on the contract had to be suspended. In the event, the high cost of hire proved such a burden that the Harbour Board, in order to assist the plaintiffs, bought the Adria for £9,177 and resold it to them on relatively easy terms. In May 1930, almost a year after the arrival of the substitute vessels, the owners of the Edison finally admitted liability.

Before the Admiralty Registrar and Merchants, the syndicate claimed £23,514 made up as follows:

(i) The actual value of the lost Liesbosch, together with certain expenses attendant upon the purchase of the Adria.
(ii) Expenses incurred during the time when the plaintiffs were unable to carry on any of the work of dredging but were obliged to maintain certain members of their staff and minor items of plant.
(iii) The hiring expenses of the Adria from May 1929 to June 1930.
(iv) The extra cost of operating the Adria as compared with the Liesbosch.
(v) Loss of profit owing to cessation of all work under the contract for the period November 1928 to June 1929.

Under (i) the Registrar allowed, as the actual value of the Liesbosch, the sum of £9,177,[8] being the amount for which the Harbour Commissioners had bought the Adria in June 1930. With certain reductions, he also allowed the greater part of (ii), (iii), and (iv) and about one-third of the amount claimed under (v), totalling in all the sum of £19,820. He also held that 'having regard to all existing circumstances, such as the severe terms of their contract in regard to penalties and their want of liquid resources', the plaintiffs had acted reasonably and that the hiring of the Adria was a 'direct and natural' result of the collision. They were entitled to take all reasonable steps to carry out their contract with as little delay as possible. They were equally bound to minimise the damages flowing from the sinking, which they had done.

The owners of the Edison next moved in the Probate Division to vary the Registrar's report, substantially on the ground that they were being called upon to pay much more than twice the value of the sunken dredger, merely because the plaintiffs had been too poor to buy a substitute. The proceedings before the Probate

[8] [1933] AC 449, 450–51.

Division and the appeals which followed are illustrations of the truth that the answers a court will, or should, give depend crucially on how it classifies the problem before it. The Probate Division seems to have seen the main issue as being one of mitigation. In the Court of Appeal, the emphasis was on the measure of damages and in the House of Lords it was to an important degree on causation and remoteness. Accordingly, at one point or another as the case proceeded through its various stages, four basic components of the law of damages were canvassed, each of them having discernibly different incidents. It is important to an understanding of *The Liesbosch* and of its continuing significance that these four aspects of damages be treated separately, at least for the purpose of analysis.

The Probate Division: Mitigation

Argument and Judgment

Before Langton J in the Probate Division,[9] the defendants argued that it was not a normal consequence of a tort that a plaintiff should be too poor to carry on his business. Any loss, therefore, beyond the value of the sunken dredger, would be too remote. In response, the syndicate submitted that the question at issue was not of remoteness but of mitigation.[10] An innocent party ought not to be under an obligation to keep or reserve funds on hand just for the benefit of potential wrongdoers, or to mitigate damages at his own expense.

In his judgment, Langton J accepted the Registrar's finding that the hiring of the Adria was a direct and natural result of the collision.[11] That being so, he seems to have accepted the submission that the problem became in large measure one of mitigation. The correct approach, he considered, was to test each item claimed by the plain criterion whether it was properly and reasonably incurred. He referred with approval to the passage, already mentioned, of the Registrar's report in which it was stated that the plaintiffs were not only entitled to take all reasonable steps to carry out their contract with as little delay as possible, but were equally bound to minimise the damages flowing from the sinking of the Liesbosch. The defendants' motion to vary the Registrar's report was therefore dismissed.

The Mitigation Point

Although it was apparently not cited until *The Liesbosch* reached the House of Lords, part of the speech of Lord Collins in *Clippins Oil Co v Edinburgh and*

[9] *Sub nom The Edison* [1930] P 230, 231–32.
[10] Ibid at 232.
[11] Ibid at 238.

District Water Trustees[12] would have been very much in point if the question at issue had correctly been one of mitigation. There his Lordship had referred to a point taken by the appellants which they contended showed that a wrong measure of damages had been applied and that, in consequence, the amount awarded had been improperly reduced. For this point they relied mainly on a passage from the judgment of Lord Dunedin, below, in which it was stated: 'The defenders are not to be prejudiced by the fact that the times were bad and that the company was not rich. Accordingly a claim upon total loss is, I think, inadmissible'. Lord Collins continued:

> It was contended that this implied that the defenders were entitled to measure the damages on the footing that it was the duty of the company to do all that was reasonably possible to mitigate the loss, and that if, through lack of funds, they were unable to incur the necessary expense of such remedial measures the defenders ought not to suffer from it. If this were the true construction to put upon the passage cited, I think there would be force in the observation, for in my opinion the wrongdoer must take his victim *talem qualem*, and if the position of the latter is aggravated because he is without the means of mitigating it, so much the worse for the wrongdoer, who has got to be answerable for the consequences flowing from his tortious act.[13]

In his speech in *The Liesbosch*, Lord Wright, who delivered the leading judgment in the House of Lords, did not question the correctness of this passage. He simply distinguished it on the ground that it was concerned only with a victim's duty to minimise damage[14] and was therefore irrelevant to the case before him. Much more recently, Megaw LJ has stated that 'a plaintiff who is under a duty to mitigate is not obliged, in order to reduce the damages, to do what he cannot afford to do'.[15] There is no reason to doubt the correctness of what Lord Collins and Megaw LJ were saying. Certainly, *The Liesbosch* is no authority to the contrary. However, in a couple of more recent cases before the Court of Appeal, where mitigation had been postponed by the plaintiffs at least in part because of impecuniosity, there had been judicial reluctance to distinguish *The Liesbosch* on the mitigation point. The Court has chosen, instead, to accept other reasons to justify the delay.

The first of these cases was *Martindale v Duncan*[16] where the plaintiff, who was impecunious and whose motor car had been damaged in a collision with another belonging to the defendant, waited until liability had been admitted and the insurers of both parties had approved the repairer's estimate before authorising the repairs to go ahead. At issue in the appeal was an award of £220 for 10 weeks' loss of use of his car, at the rate of £22 a week, that being the cost of hiring a substitute vehicle. The appeal was dismissed on the ground that, until both insurers were

[12] [1907] AC 291, 303.

[13] His Lordship went on to add 'On the other hand, the victim being in fact a poor man is not entitled to claim damages in respect of lost opportunities which he could not have utilised unless he had been rich', words as true now as they were then.

[14] [1933] AC 449, 461.

[15] *Dodd Properties Kent Ltd v Canterbury City Council* [1980] 1 WLR 433, 453.

[16] [1973] 1 WLR 574.

satisfied, the plaintiff could not be certain of retaining his no claims bonus or his good standing with his own insurance company. It was this, rather than his inability to pay, which was taken to justify his delaying the repairs and prolonging the period of hire.

The second case was *Perry v Sydney Phillips & Son*.[17] In reliance on a surveyor's report, the plaintiff had bought a house property which turned out to have serious defects. The surveyor denied liability and the plaintiff, who could not himself afford any major expense, executed only minor repairs. On a claim for distress and discomfort, the defendant contended that whatever the plaintiff had suffered was due to his own failure to carry out sufficient repairs. That defence was rejected at first instance and by the Court of Appeal. Lord Denning MR took the view that, so far as *The Liesbosch* had laid down that loss due to impecuniosity was not recoverable, it should be restricted to its own facts.[18] On the other hand, Oliver LJ identified the real question as being:[19]

> Was it reasonable in all the circumstances for the plaintiff not to mitigate his damage by carrying out the repairs which were required? One reason, no doubt, was the plaintiff's poverty. As I said, if that were the only reason, *The Liesbosch* might well provide an answer for the defendants. But in fact the plaintiff's conduct in not carrying out the repairs was quite reasonable for a number of other reasons; and one of the reasons why he did not do them was because the defendants were strenuously resisting any liability at all for the repairs and denying that they were responsible.

Kerr LJ agreed that these reasons were sufficient and thought that if it were reasonably foreseeable that the plaintiff might be unable to mitigate as soon as he would have done had he been provided with the necessary funds to do so from the other party, *The Liesbosch* would no longer apply in its full rigour.[20]

To the extent that the problem before them was correctly one of the duty to mitigate, the reluctance to accept that impecuniosity went to the reasonableness of a plaintiff's behaviour seems much too cautious. The explanation may be that, in *Martindale v Duncan*,[21] Davies LJ, with whom the other members of the Court agreed, asserted that *The Liesbosch* was 'authority for the proposition that impecuniosity is no excuse for not mitigating damage'. While that was clearly not correct, it doubtless reflected the sort of view of *The Liesbosch* evidenced by the passage from *Salmond on Torts* cited at the beginning of this article.[22]

A more important reason for caution may have been the fact that while the matters actually at issue before the Court of Appeal in the two cases were loss of use, and vexation and inconvenience, respectively, and therefore involved questions of mitigation, in both, the loss had arisen from delays in the execution of repairs with a consequent increase in their costs. That increase in the cost of repairs, as such,

17 [1982] 1 WLR 1297.
18 Ibid at 1302.
19 Ibid at 1305.
20 Ibid at 1307. Foreseeability has not commonly been seen as an element of the 'duty' to mitigate.
21 [1973] 1 WLR 574, 577.
22 See text above, at note 1.

raised questions, not of mitigation but of the measure of damages for a primary loss. It is a distinction which, as we shall see, was to prove fatal to the syndicate's case when *The Liesbosch* reached the Court of Appeal.

The Court of Appeal: Measure of Damages

The Conventional Measure

The irony of the position in which the syndicate found itself in *The Liesbosch* was that, had the Edison merely damaged the dredger, there was ample authority for allowing it the cost of hiring another vessel while its own was being repaired. Thus, in an earlier case concerning a damaged dredger, *The Greta Holme*, Lord Herschell stated that:

> If the appellants had hired a dredger instead of purchasing one, and had they during the months they were deprived of its use been bound to pay for its hire, it cannot be doubted that the sum so paid could have been recovered.[23]

Lord Herschell added that out of pocket expenses would also have been recoverable, together with interest, and general damages for delay.

In *The Liesbosch*, the root cause of the plaintiffs' troubles in the Court of Appeal and, subsequently, in the House of Lords, was that instead of merely damaging the dredger, the defendants had destroyed it. As Scrutton LJ said, that made the situation quite different.[24] Behind that difference lay a universal rule, obtaining then and until the 1970s, that damages were to be fixed as at the time of loss. In the case, say, of a motor car or vessel which had merely been *damaged*, the cost of the repairs themselves, whenever done, was measured by reference to the charges which would reasonably have been incurred as at the time of the accident (or immediately thereafter). To that calculation, mitigation was necessarily irrelevant. On claims for loss of use, on the other hand, losses continued to accrue until the repairs had in fact been done and claims could be subject to the defendant's duty to mitigate. When chattels were *destroyed*, damages were also to be measured by value as at the date of loss. But it seems that the plaintiff was for other purposes treated as though he had actually gone into the market and obtained a substitute, however unreal that possibility might be in practice given his lack of funds.[25] That it did not turn on the realities of the situation is evidenced by the analogous case of the non-delivery of goods where, again, the measure was value as at the date of loss. It was established quite early that it would make no difference to the result if

[23] *Steam Sand Pump Dredger No 7 (Owners of) v Owners of SS Greta Holme* [1897] AC 596, 605.
[24] *The Edison* [1932] P 52, 64.
[25] Cf Goode, *Commercial Law*, 2nd edn (Penguin Books, London, 1995) 415–16.

the plaintiff buyer had prepaid the purchase price and was, therefore, so much the less likely to have funds for a substitute purchase readily available.[26]

This conventional assumption, independent of the realities, that the plaintiff could and would obtain a substitute if one were available, had the unfortunate result for the owner of a sunken vessel that, being notionally in the early possession of the substitute, he could have no claim for the subsequent loss of use or loss of profits unless he could show good reason to the contrary. In the Court of Appeal, it was held that the owners of the Liesbosch were entitled to be paid only its 'value' as at the time of the loss, plus interest from then until the date of judgment. On the other hand 'value' for these purposes was not necessarily limited to the market price at that time. In the case of a vessel which was under a charter (a common occurrence) its value could reflect its worth to the plaintiff 'as a going concern',[27] based on the usual rates of hire, provided always, as Greer LJ stated,[28] the plaintiff had not been entitled under the charter to employ a substitute vessel to perform it. Scrutton LJ added that the valuation as a going concern should be 'at that place' since, if the vessel had to be replaced at the point where it had been lost, expense and time might have to be added to the cost of the substitute.[29] From this it follows that in appropriate cases the Court of Appeal would have allowed the possibility of recompense for a notional short-term loss of use and loss of profits, but this would have been only as an element in the valuation of the lost vessel. That being so, the plaintiffs' actual inability, from lack of funds, to replace the sunken dredger would have been wholly irrelevant. And, as Scrutton LJ said, to allow expenditure incurred because of the owners' poverty, in addition to the value of the vessel so assessed, would be to give them its value twice over.[30] In the result, the Court of Appeal reversed the judgment of Langton J in part. The figure of £9,177, which the Registrar had based on the cost of the replacement dredger, was treated instead by the Court as if it were the value of the Liesbosch as a going concern. Interest on that sum was allowed as from the date of the sinking.

The Assessment Date

As is well known, there has since the 1970s been a significant weakening of the rule that damages are to be assessed as at the date of loss. An important illustration of that for present purposes was afforded by the decision of the Court of Appeal in *Dodd Properties Kent Ltd v Canterbury City Council*.[31] There, work on the foundations of a new car park had damaged adjoining business premises known as Marlowe Garage. At the time of the trial, the relevant repairs had not

26 *Startup v Coriazzi* (1935) 2 CM & R 165; 150 ER 71.
27 [1932] P 52, 65.
28 At 73.
29 At 65.
30 At 67.
31 [1980] 1 WLR 433 (HC and CA).

yet been done and the question at issue was whether the date as at which damages should be assessed should be 1968, when the damage was discovered, 1970, which the experts on both sides agreed was the earliest it would have been reasonable to begin repairs, or 1978, being the time of the judgment. Because of inflation, the 1970 figure of £15,483 had risen to £42,278 by 1978.

In his judgment at first instance, Cantley J drew attention to the distinction between the measure of damage and the duty to mitigate.[32] The normal measure in the case of chattels damaged and destroyed was, he said, respectively the cost of repair, or the market value, at the time of the loss. He also saw the irrelevance to these enquiries of the plaintiff's inability to purchase a substitute. It would have made no difference to the amount recovered in *The Liesbosch*, he said, had the owners spent 10 years saving to buy a similar dredger to the one they had lost. These comments by Cantley J were premised on the continued application of the principle that damages were to be assessed as at the date when the damage occurred and he cited Denning LJ in *Phillips v Ward*[33] to that effect. However, he recognised that even under this rule, there could be circumstances under which it would be necessary or prudent to delay commencement of repairs while necessary inspections were done, a contractor found, and the damage itself had stabilised. He generalised from this to the proposition that 'the appropriate damages are the cost of repairs at the time when it was reasonable to begin repairs' and he thought that what was reasonable for this purpose should be judged 'objectively', without taking account of the impecuniosity or financial stringency of the plaintiff.[34] On that basis, he chose the cost as at 1970, rather than at 1968 when the damage occurred.

In the Court of Appeal, the valuation date chosen was the date of judgment in 1978. The Court did this in reliance on such cases as *Miliangos v George Frank (Textiles) Ltd*,[35] *Radford v De Froberville*,[36] and *Johnson v Agnew*,[37] all then very recent, which had established that while the date of loss was still generally the appropriate date, it was no longer universally so. Rather, it could be said the appropriate date had become that which best did justice between the parties. Like Cantley J, their Lordships accepted that the relevant date should be that at which it would have been 'reasonable' to begin repairs. But they considered that, questions of impecuniosity apart, there were sufficient other grounds, *including* the plaintiff's financial stringency,[38] to make it reasonable for the commencement of repairs to be delayed until the date of judgment and they allowed the appeal accordingly.

[32] Ibid at 443.
[33] [1956] 1 WLR 471, 474.
[34] [1980] 1 WLR 433, 444–45.
[35] [1976] AC 443.
[36] [1977] 1 WLR 1262.
[37] [1980] AC 367. A more recent example is *Smith New Court Securities Ltd v Citibank NA* [1997] AC 254.
[38] [1980] 1 WLR 433, 453 per Megaw LJ; 459 per Donaldson LJ.

In reaching this conclusion, they relied on the following passage from Cantley J's judgment:

> I find that the first plaintiffs could probably have raised the money for the repairs but this would have increased their annual losses and their financial stringency. As a commercial decision, judged exclusively from the point of view of the immediate and short-term welfare of the companies, it was reasonable to postpone incurring the very considerable expense of these repairs while no harm was being done to the building by the delay in repairing it and while these three rich defendants with apparent if not genuine belief in the validity of their defences were firmly denying liability to make even a contribution.[39]

Reasonableness

At this point, two tests of reasonableness would seem to be operating, the first concerning the measure of damages for a primary loss and the second, the date as at which those damages nowadays fall to be assessed. If Cantley J is right and the former is properly objective in the sense of having no regard to factors personal to the plaintiff,[40] it has to be contrasted with the latter which does seem to allow for the inclusion of such personal factors as financial stringency.

Additional authority for the application of a reasonableness test to the fixing of the assessment date can be found, for example, in the speech of Lord Wilberforce in *Johnson v Agnew*[41] and in the judgment of Oliver J in *Radford v De Froberville.*[42] But that test has also been seen as analogous to a third reasonableness requirement: the one which qualifies the duty to mitigate. That appears from what was said by Oliver J in the *Radford* case[43] and it is also reflected in the judgments of Megaw LJ and Donaldson LJ in *Dodd Properties*[44] itself. Thus, according to Megaw LJ:[45]

> Once it is accepted that the plaintiff was not in breach of any duty owed by him to the defendant in failing to carry out repairs earlier than the time when it was reasonable for all the repairs to be put in hand, this becomes, for all practical purposes, if not in theory, equated with a plaintiff's ordinary duty to mitigate his damages. Lord Wright in his speech in *The Liesbosch*, accepted Lord Collins' dictum in *Clippins Oil Co Ltd v Edinburgh and District Water Trustees*: 'in my opinion the wrongdoer must take his victim *talem qualem*, and if the position of the latter is aggravated because he is without the means of mitigating it, so much the worse for the wrong-doer'.

[39] [1980] 1 WLR 433, 442.
[40] Brown LJ, 456, queried the use of the word 'objective'.
[41] [1980] AC 367, 401.
[42] [1977] 1 WLR 1262, 1287.
[43] Ibid at 1285, 1286.
[44] [1980] 1 WLR 433.
[45] At 453.

Donaldson LJ took a not dissimilar view, stating that whether the fixing of a reasonable date was

> regarded as arising out of the primary measure of damage, ie, that the relevant time is when the property should have been reinstated, or whether it is regarded as being a reflection of a plaintiff's duty to mitigate his loss, may not matter.[46]

If this analogy is correctly drawn, it would follow that the standard of reasonableness required for fixing an assessment date ought to be no higher than the relatively relaxed standard required of mitigation.[47] It ought also to follow, given what was said by Lord Collins in *Clippins Oil*[48] about taking a victim *talem qualem*, that there should be no barrier to having regard to a plaintiff's impecuniosity when settling an assessment date. And if that is so where a chattel has been damaged and requires repairs, it is not immediately obvious why, on the same reasoning, it should not nowadays also be the case where the chattel has been destroyed and has to be replaced. Nevertheless, it has to be recorded that in *Ramwade Ltd v WJ Emson & Co Ltd*,[49] decided six years after *Dodd Properties*, where there had been the total loss of a motor lorry, the hire of a substitute vehicle while the plaintiff waited for damages to be paid was held by the Court of Appeal to flow from the plaintiff's impecuniosity and, therefore, to be irrecoverable under the principles stated in *The Liesbosch*. On the other hand, it does not appear from the judgments that the possible significance of cases like *Johnson v Agnew* was actually drawn to the attention of the Court or considered by it.

The House of Lords: Causation and Remoteness

The Judgment

When *The Liesbosch* reached the House of Lords, the conclusions arrived at in the leading judgment, given by Lord Wright, were not too dissimilar from those reached by the Court of Appeal. He, too, saw the question at issue as being, basically, the measure of damages for a primary loss to be assessed as at the date of the loss.[50] He also agreed that the value of the dredger as at that date must include elements additional to the mere market price of a comparable substitute. But he supposed that in awarding what was in substance the purchase price of the replacement dredger, the Court of Appeal intended to give simply the replacement cost of the Liesbosch without including, in its value, allowance for any other factor.[51]

[46] At 458.

[47] See, eg, vol 12(1) *Halsbury's Laws of England*, 4th edn reissue (Butterworths, London, 1998) para 859.

[48] [1907] AC 291, 303.

[49] [1987] RTR 72.

[50] [1933] AC 449, eg at 468.

[51] At 467–68.

With respect, that conclusion is not always easy to accept. It was clear from the judgment of Scrutton LJ that the Liesbosch had to be valued as 'a profit-earning dredger' and, as we have seen, that had to include allowance for the expense of, and the time taken in, getting the replacement to Patras.[52] What the learned Lord Justice did say was that the Registrar had given, as the value of the Liesbosch, the sum of £9,000-odd, that being half as much again as the original cost to its owner of buying her and getting her to Patras. It was also more than half as much again as her insurance value. That therefore seemed to him to be 'an ample measure' of the dredger's value as a going concern.[53]

What Lord Wright and the House of Lords chose to do was to refer back to the Registrar ascertainment of the true value on the following basis:

> The value of the Liesbosch to the appellants, capitalized as at the date of the loss, must be assessed by taking into account: (1) the market price of a comparable dredger in substitution; (2) costs of adaptation, transport, insurance, etc, to Patras; (3) compensation for disturbance and loss in carrying out their contract over the period of delay between the loss of the Liesbosch and the time at which the substituted dredger could reasonably been available for use in Patras, including in that loss such items as overhead charges, expenses of staff and equipment, and so forth thrown away, but neglecting any special loss due to the appellants' financial position.[54]

On the capitalised sum so assessed interest was to run from the date of the loss.

Pace Lord Wright, the Court of Appeal's global figure of about £9,000 was certainly intended to cover much the same ground. However, taken on his own terms, what Lord Wright wanted (while purporting to remain within the principle that damages be assessed as at the date of loss and that the lost dredger be valued as at that date) was in effect to allow the plaintiff damages based not on the assumption that the Liesbosch had been replaced instantly, but on the basis of its having been replaced and made available within a reasonable time. But that reasonable time was to be fixed without reference to the plaintiffs' financial difficulties.[55] In consequence, the plaintiffs, in addition to getting the value of the lost dredger, were to be recompensed for the costs incurred and losses suffered between its sinking and its notional replacement at the 'reasonable' later date. In that respect, he was doing rather as did Cantley J, later, in the *Dodd Properties* case, when that learned judge fixed 1970 as the date at which repairs were to be costed, rather than 1968, the date the damage occurred, or 1978, the date of judgment.

Given the non-existent purchase taken to have occurred at an artificially determined time leading in turn to an inflated valuation, it might have been assumed that the House of Lords would have treated the plaintiffs' impecuniosity as totally

[52] See text at notes 27–30.

[53] [1932] P 52, 58, 59, 67.

[54] [1933] AC 449, 468.

[55] This, presumably, was what Cantley J had in mind (above, note 33) when in the *Dodd* case he spoke of an objectively reasonable time. The Court of Appeal in that case appear to have concluded that, in relation to the newly emerging test of reasonableness in fixing the date at which damages should be assessed, different criteria should apply.

irrelevant. But that is not how Lord Wright saw it. Having remarked that the impecuniosity was not traceable to the respondents' acts and was in his opinion outside the legal purview of the consequences of those acts,[56] he went on to state in the most often cited sentence from his speech:

> In the present case if the appellants' financial embarrassment is to be regarded as a consequence of the respondents' tort, I think it is too remote, but I prefer to regard it as an independent cause, though its operative effect was conditioned by the loss of the dredger.[57]

It would appear to follow from this dictum that if a causal link could have been shown between the sinking of the Liesbosch, the plaintiffs' impecuniosity and their eventual losses, and if the remoteness hurdle could have been overcome, those extra losses could have been added to the three groups of losses listed above by Lord Wright. They would then presumably, on the same reasoning, have all formed part of the 'valuation' of the lost vessel. The third group would seem to include some degree of loss of use and it has only recently been said in the House of Lords that loss of use is a capital account loss.[58] The same third group would also, potentially, include loss of profits. However, in those cases, it would doubtless have been incumbent on the plaintiffs to mitigate the additional loss by hiring a substitute dredger, as in fact had been done in *The Liesbosch*. On the capitalised sum finally arrived at, the defendants would have to pay interest as from the date of the sinking.

But if contortions of these kinds are really required by Lord Wright's reasoning, it could only be because of his desire to give the plaintiffs something more than the replacement cost of their lost dredger, within the confines of the rule that damages be quantified as at the date of the loss. And that is a requirement which, as we have seen, no longer necessarily exists.

Causation

Lord Wright obviously saw causation and remoteness as separate concepts. In practice, they can easily be confused, especially when, as we shall see was for a time established in *In re Polemis and Furness Withy & Co Ltd*,[59] the notion of a direct cause is treated also as the test for remoteness.

On the question of causation, Lord Wright's first point was that the plaintiffs' impecuniosity was a separate and concurrent cause, extraneous to and distinct in character from the tort.[60] Second, the impecuniosity was not traceable to acts of the defendants. Third, even if the plaintiffs' financial embarrassment were

[56] [1933] AC 449, 461.

[57] Ibid at 461.

[58] *Dimond v Lovell* [2002] 1 AC 384, 406; [2000] 2 WLR 1121, 1139 per Lord Hobhouse of Woodborough.

[59] [1921] 3 KB 560. See text below at note 82 *et seq*.

[60] [1933] AC 449, 460–61.

regarded as a consequence of the defendants' tort, it was too remote. Fourth, he preferred to regard it as an independent cause, though its operative effect was conditioned by the loss of the dredger. Fifth, he distinguished *In re Polemis* on the ground that it dealt with the immediate physical consequences of the negligent act and not with the cooperation of an extraneous matter such as the plaintiffs' want of means. Finally, he stated that the plaintiffs' financial disability was not to be compared with 'that physical delicacy or weakness which may aggravate the damage in the case of personal injuries'.

That list is not without its problems, the first of which is in what circumstances the plaintiffs' impecuniosity can be said to have been the result of the plaintiffs' acts. On one approach, the financial problems of the owners of the Liesbosch were entirely the result of the defendants' wrongful act in the sense that, but for the loss of the dredger, they would have had no shortage of funds. In *Dodd Properties*,[61] where a similar situation arose, Megaw LJ made the point that the 'financial stringency' of the plaintiffs in that case 'arose, as a matter of common sense, if not a matter of law, solely as a consequence of the defendants' wrongdoing'. Clearly, Lord Wright must have had in mind something other than a cause in that sense.

In the cases decided since *The Liesbosch*, at least two types of situation have been identified where a causal connection can exist. In one, the wrongful act has so injured the plaintiff that he has been unable to earn the funds to enable him to replace what he has lost. Thus, in the New Zealand case, *Attorney-General v Geothermal Produce NZ Ltd*[62] the plaintiff, his initial plantings having been destroyed by the wrongful act, was deprived of earnings from them which would have made further plantings possible. And in a recent West Australian case, *Watts v Turpin*,[63] the plaintiff, through injuries suffered in a motor accident, was unable to earn the income which could have enabled him to replant lost trees.

The second type of situation arises where a party who has undertaken to supply funds has failed to do so. An early example was *Muhammad Issa el Sheikh Ahwad v Ali*[64] on appeal to the Privy Council from the Supreme Court of Palestine. The owner of land which he had already contracted to sell, resold it to a third person, receiving in return an indemnity from that person against any claims the original purchaser might have against the vendor. The original purchaser, having sued, received judgment but the final purchaser defaulted on his indemnity. The vendor, despite having previously received the purchase price from the first purchaser, lacked the funds to himself satisfy the judgment. Other property of his was taken into execution and sold at a heavy loss. It was held that that loss was not too remote and was recoverable. Another early example was *General Securities Ltd v Don Ingram Ltd*,[65] before the Supreme Court of Canada. There, a finance company

[61] [1980] 1 WLR 433, 453.
[62] [1987] 2 NZLR 348.
[63] (1999) 21 WAR 402.
[64] [1947] AC 414.
[65] [1940] 3 DLR 641.

had repudiated its contract to finance a car sales company's purchase of cars from a manufacturer under an exclusive franchise. The sales company was unable to obtain funds elsewhere in the time available and, amongst other things, lost its franchise. An analogous New Zealand case was *Dods v Coopers Creek Ltd*[66] where the defendant's failure to pay a debt owed to the plaintiffs meant that they had to borrow money at some cost.

An additional point emerging from *Attorney-General v Geothermal Produce NZ Ltd*[67] is that the causal link between wrongful act, impecuniosity, and eventual loss would not be broken just because the majority shareholders in the plaintiff company could have raised funds by selling other property. That would seem to be consistent with a statement by Scrutton LJ in *The Liesbosch* appeal[68] that ships themselves were treated in the authorities as the claimants and 'an isolated account taken as if the injured ship were the whole business of the shipowner'.

A second problem with Lord Wright's references to causation stems from his distinguishing financial from physical 'delicacy'. Ordinarily, supervening events will not be treated as causes if they are unforeseeable. But in the case of existing circumstances, a causal connection will not ordinarily be negatived however abnormal those circumstances might be, the most commonly cited example being the plaintiff with an eggshell skull.[69] In *The Liesbosch*, the plaintiff's lack of liquid resources was an already existing state at the time of the sinking. In *Clippins Oil*[70] Lord Collins affirmed that a wrongdoer must take his victim *talem qualem* and he very clearly saw an impecunious plaintiff as such a victim. Lord Wright chose to confine what Lord Collins had said to mitigation but, with respect, that dismissal, at least on that ground, cannot be correct. What Lord Collins was addressing when he referred to taking the victim *talem qualem* included a question of causation. As Donaldson LJ was to observe years later in *Dodd Properties*: 'It is not at once apparent why a tortfeasor must take his victim as he finds him in terms of exceptionally high or low profit-earning capacity, but not in terms of pecuniosity or impecuniosity which may be their manifestation'.[71]

Lord Wright's statement that the syndicate's financial disability could not be compared with a physical delicacy or weakness has been taken by subsequent commentators to have been based on policy grounds alone.[72] Hart and Honore have suggested[73] that the law is often reluctant, as a matter of general policy, to take

[66] [1987] 1 NZLR 530, applying the ratio of *Wadsworth v Lydall* [1981] 1 WLR 598. It was pointed out by Holland J in *Krehic v Clark* [1991] 1 NZLR 703, 709, that this approach can have the effect of conferring an advantage on the impecunious which is denied to those who have funds available. See also *Jarvis v Richards & Co* (1980) 124 *Sol J* 793.

[67] [1987] 2 NZLR 348.

[68] [1932] P 52, 61.

[69] Eg, Hart and Honore, *Causation in the Law*, 2nd edn (Clarendon Press, Oxford, 1985) 172 *et seq*; *Halsbury's Laws of England*, above note 47 at para 858; *McGregor on Damages*, 16th edn (Sweet & Maxwell, London, 1997) paras 210 *et seq*.

[70] [1907] AC 291, 303.

[71] [1980] 1 WLR 433, 458.

[72] Eg, *McGregor on Damages*, above note 69 at para 210.

[73] At 175.

steps to extricate parties from predicaments into which they would not have fallen but for lack of means. (From him that hath, it would seem, shall be taken even that he hath!) But if such a policy does apply in the case of existing circumstances, it might be asked why it should not also apply in the case of mitigation. Fortunately, no policy is set in stone and it would always be open to a court of final resort to take a different view.

Remoteness

The modern law of remoteness, both in contract and in tort, is descended from the often quoted dictum of Alderson B in *Hadley v Baxendale* in which he said:

> Where two parties have made a contract which one of them has broken the damages which the other party ought to receive in respect of such breach of contract should be such as may fairly and reasonably be considered either arising naturally, ie, according to the usual course of things, from such breach of contracts itself, or such as may reasonably be supposed to have been in contemplation of both parties at the time they made the contract, as the probable result of the breach of it.[74]

But, as was pointed out, for example, by Bowen LJ a few years later in *The Argentino*,[75] there was at that time seen to be a crucial difference in the application of this dictum to contract as distinct from tort. In both, damages could be such as 'flow directly' and in 'the usual course of things' from the wrongful act. In the case of contract, though, the law uniquely super-added such damages 'as may reasonably be supposed to have been in the contemplation of the parties at the time they made the contract as the probable result of its breach'.

It became significant that while the passage from *Hadley v Baxendale* spoke of damages arising 'naturally, ie, according to the usual course of things', Bowen LJ substituted the word 'directly' in that phrase and Lord Esher MR in the same case[76] cited with approval the fourth edition of *Mayne on Damages*[77] which spoke of damage 'immediately and necessarily' flowing from the cause of action. When *The Argentino* went on appeal to the House of Lords,[78] Lord Herschell used the expression 'directly and naturally, or in the ordinary course of things'. In the period between *The Argentino* and *The Liesbosch*, two different approaches to remoteness developed from those varied but seemingly similar ways of stating the test. Under the one, 'natural' was taken to require that the damage be foreseeable. The second approach owed most to the speech of Lord Sumner in *Weld-Blundell v Stephens*,[79] a case in which accountants engaged by the plaintiff to report on a company

[74] (1854) 9 Ex 341, 354; 156 ER 145, 151.
[75] (1888) 13 PD 191, 201 (affirmed (1889) 14 App Cas 519).
[76] At 197.
[77] He referred to p 44 of that edition.
[78] (1889) 14 App Cas 519, 523.
[79] [1920] AC 956.

negligently left the plaintiff's letter of instructions in the company's office. It contained libellous statements which, when found, led to a successful claim against the plaintiffs by the persons defamed. The plaintiff sought to recover the damages and costs he had had to pay in the libel action. By a majority of three to two, the House of Lords held against the plaintiff on the ground that the damages for libel were not the result of the defendants' breach of duty.

In his speech, Lord Sumner dismissed each element of the test of 'natural probable and necessary' consequences and preferred instead the expression 'direct' cause.[80] He then added:

> What a defendant ought to have anticipated as a reasonable man is material when the question is whether or not he was guilty of negligence, that is, of want of due care according to the circumstances. This, however, goes to culpability, not to compensation.[81]

These words of Lord Sumner strongly influenced the decision of the Court of Appeal the following year in *In re Polemis and Furness Withy & Co Ltd.*[82] In that celebrated case, tins of petrol stowed in a ship had leaked with the result that when it reached Casablanca there was a considerable quantity of petrol vapour in the hold. Stevedores engaged by the charterers negligently caused a heavy plank to fall into the hold where four or five Arab labourers were working at the time. The plank must have struck two pieces of metal together, causing a spark. There was an instantaneous rush of flame resulting in the destruction of the vessel.[83] London arbitrators decided that while some damage to the ship might have been anticipated, it could not reasonably have been anticipated that a spark could have resulted from the descent of the plank. They nevertheless awarded the shipowners the full value of the lost ship.

In the Court of Appeal, Mr RA Wright KC (as Lord Wright then was) argued for the charterers that from the requirement that the damage be the 'natural and probable' consequence of the negligent act, it followed that the damages had to be those which could reasonably have been anticipated.[84] On the other hand, counsel for the owners argued that all damages which flowed 'directly' from the negligent act should be recoverable and they relied in particular on what had been said by Lord Sumner in *Weld-Blundell v Stephens.*[85] The Lords Justices recognised that two conflicting views existed but they preferred the one stated by Lord Sumner. It was, they held, sufficient to create liability that damage of some kind could have been anticipated from the act complained of. Once that was established, the wrongdoer was responsible in law for all damage directly resulting or, in other words, direct causation was to be the test for remoteness.

[80] At 983–84.
[81] At 984.
[82] [1921] 3 KB 560.
[83] We are not told what became of the four or five Arab workmen!
[84] At 564–66.
[85] At 567.

When *The Liesbosch* reached the House of Lords, Lord Wright distinguished *In re Polemis* on the ground that it was concerned with the immediate physical consequences of the negligent act and not with the cooperation of an extraneous matter such as the plaintiffs' want of means.[86] Since he did not suggest that the tests adopted by the Court of Appeal in that case had been wrong, it can be inferred he accepted that they were correct. If that is so, it would follow that when he earlier stated 'if the appellants' financial embarrassment is to be regarded as a consequence of the respondents' tort, I think it is too remote,'[87] he must have had in mind not that it was too remote because not reasonably foreseeable but, rather, too remote because it was not the 'immediate physical' (that is, 'direct') result of the tort. His going on to say that he preferred to regard it as an independent cause again hardly indicates a preference for a test of foreseeability.

That makes all the more puzzling Lord Wright's other often quoted dictum on impecuniosity when, in *Monarch Steamship Co Ltd v Karlshamns Oljefabriker (A|B)*, he said:

> In *Liesbosch (Owners) v Edison (Owners)* it was held that loss due to the party's impecuniosity was too remote and therefore to be neglected in the calculation of damages: it was special loss due to his financial position. A different conclusion was arrived at in *Muhammad Issa el Sheikh Ahwad v Ali*, where damages consequent on impecuniosity were held not too remote, because, as I understand, the loss was such as might reasonably be expected to be in the contemplation of the parties as likely to flow from breach of the obligation undertaken.[88]

If that were where the dictum had ended, it could easily enough be explained in terms of the *In re Polemis* approach, once regard is had to the use of the expression 'special loss'. Earlier in his speech, Lord Wright had defined 'special' by reference to the second category of loss identified in *Hadley v Baxendale*.[89] And that, as we have seen, was confined in *The Argentino* to loss resulting from breach of contract[90] (*Monarch* was a contract case). In the first part of his dictum he could be understood as saying that loss due to impecuniosity was 'special' in that sense and therefore not recoverable in tort. On the other hand, in a contract case like *Ali*, it could be recoverable if in contemplation, provided a causal link could be found, as it had been in that case.

The problem with this interpretation is that Lord Wright immediately went on to say, 'The difference in results did not depend on the differences (if any) between contract and tort in this connection'. That does rather suggest that his Lordship was again espousing the foreseeability test for remoteness in tort which he had argued as counsel in *In re Polemis*. If so, that could well explain the shift from his stated preference in *The Liesbosch* for a causation explanation to his choice of

86 [1933] AC 449, 461.
87 Ibid at 460.
88 [1949] AC 196, 224.
89 Ibid at 221.
90 See text above, at note 75.

remoteness in his *Monarch* dictum. More importantly, it would show that Lord Wright himself now took the view that the law had moved on since *In re Polemis* and *The Liesbosch*, with the result that the latter was now of doubtful authority on the relation of a plaintiff's impecuniosity to questions of remoteness.

The directness test of remoteness in tort was, of course, finally rejected by the Privy Council in *Overseas Tankships (UK) Ltd v Morts Dock & Engineering Co Ltd (The Wagon Mound)*[91] and the foreseeability test confirmed. That might, incidentally, have been expected to spell the effective end of the 'existing state' rule of causation since, *ex hypothesi*, a loss due to an improbable existing state would be unlikely to be reasonably foreseeable. In practice, though, that has not happened, as was confirmed in recent years by the House of Lords in *Page v Smith*.[92] In consequence the eggshell skull rule was unaffected and could potentially still apply to an existing state of impecuniosity.

This, then, is the background to the recent decision of the Privy Council.

The *Alcoa Minerals* Case

In *Alcoa Minerals of Jamaica Inc v Broderick*,[93] the defendant company, Alcoa, operated a smelting plant which for many years had discharged pollutants, noxious gases, and corrosive dust over the surrounding area. In what was, effectively, a test case, the plaintiff, Broderick, a local resident, claimed in nuisance for the resulting damage to the roof of his house. His claim initially was for some \$200,000 (Jamaican) being the then cost of repairing the roof. The defendant denied liability and the plaintiff was not, himself, able to afford to have the repairs done. Due mainly to inflation, the cost of repairs escalated and, four years after beginning his action, the plaintiff was permitted to increase the amount of his claim to \$938,000. An award of that amount was subsequently upheld by the Jamaican Court of Appeal.

As will by now be apparent, the facts in *Alcoa* were closely analogous to those in *Dodd Properties Kent Ltd v Canterbury City Council*[94] and the issue raised was, as in that case, the measure of damages for a primary loss, namely the cost of repairs. Again as in *Dodd*, the plaintiff had not himself had the repairs done, the cost of which had increased in the meantime. The task of the Privy Council, therefore, was to fix the date at which the cost of repairs should be assessed and that, in turn, depended on what justice required and on whether the plaintiffs' delay had been reasonable. On both counts, the Privy Council, in a judgment delivered by Lord Slynn of Hadley, held for the plaintiff. The Court of Appeal below had accepted that Broderick had been told that Alcoa would pay for the repairs and that this had justified his waiting. Alcoa denied this but the alternative was that they had

91 [1961] AC 388.
92 [1966] AC 155.
93 [2002] 1 AC 371; [2000] 3 WLR 23.
94 [1980] 1 WLR 433.

been refusing to accept liability. The facts had been complex and the outcome of the case had not been so obvious that Broderick ought to have borrowed at a high rate of interest in order to have the repairs done at his own expense. It was reasonable for him to wait until either Alcoa paid or liability had been established.[95] The Privy Council seems to have reached this conclusion independently of whether the plaintiff, from his shortage of funds, would in fact have had any realistic alternative. On the general question of whether impecuniosity could in principle be a reasonable ground for fixing a later assessment date, their Lordships were somewhat less than bold. After a review of the cases they summarised the present law thus:

> It seems generally to be accepted that there is no absolute rule that where the plaintiff at the date of breach did not have the funds to repair the damage that his impecuniosity is to be ignored in all cases when deciding the appropriate date for the assessment of damages.[96]

In an earlier passage they were equally tentative:

> In a case where repairs have to be done at what is a heavy cost in relation to the plaintiff's financial position there may be stronger grounds for delaying the date of assessment than in a case where the plaintiff has undertaken a contractual obligation to buy and pay for the goods, where he could go out into the market and buy the goods at or near the same price.[97]

On this view, it would seem that a plaintiff's impecuniosity is relevant to the fixing of the assessment date, if at all, only as one supporting factor amongst others. But in any event, in *Alcoa* itself, there was on previous authority, the *Dodd Properties* case in particular, no need to have any recourse to Broderick's financial position.

It should be noted that by the time the case reached the Privy Council no question of causation, remoteness, or mitigation was in issue, unless, in the latter case, by way of analogy to the requirement of reasonableness in relation to the assessment date. Accordingly, as Oliver LJ said of the *Dodd Properties* case in *Perry v Sidney Phillips & Son*,[98]

> it could not be suggested that there was any other measure of damages than the cost of repair, the only question being the date at which the repairs ought to have been carried out; and the debate there was as to the date at which it was reasonable for plaintiffs to have carried out the repairs … the question was what loss the plaintiff, acting reasonably, had actually suffered.

Nevertheless, their Lordships seemed to have felt constrained also to say that 'the real question [here] is whether Mr Broderick was in breach of his duty to mitigate his damage'. They added that it seemed to them to have been obviously foreseeable that the plaintiff would not, or might not, have had the wherewithal to do the repairs.[99]

95 [2002] 1 AC 371, 383; [2000] 3 WLR 23, 32.
96 Ibid at 382; 30.
97 Ibid at 378; 26–27.
98 [1982] 1 WLR 1297, 1304.
99 [2002] 1 AC 371, 383; [2000] 3 WLR 23, 31.

With respect, those observations may be no more than a reflection of the confused state of some earlier authority. Certainly, they were addressed only to questions of mitigation and remoteness. But if an inference to be drawn is that before a factor can be taken into account in fixing an assessment date it must have been reasonably foreseeable by the tortfeasor, or in contemplation, it is submitted a significant departure from previous understandings would have occurred. In such cases as *Johnson v Agnew,*[100] *Radford v De Froberville,*[101] and *Dodd Properties Kent Ltd v Canterbury City Council,*[102] the requirement laid down was, as we have seen, not foreseeability but remoteness. That, after all, is why it was thought an analogy could be drawn with mitigation, which has nothing at all to do with foreseeability.

Contract

So far as it relates to impecuniosity, *The Liesbosch* is not usually to be found cited in the Contract textbooks of Commonwealth countries, Canada being an exception. It seems not unlikely that the reason for this dismissal of the case stems from a perception that, in *Muhammad Issa v Ali,*[103] the Privy Council showed that, at least in that respect, it had no application to contract cases. If this is indeed the case, it is (in the phrase used by Donaldson LJ)[104] 'not at once apparent' why it should have been so. *The Liesbosch* is not mentioned in the Privy Council judgment and, in any event, the plaintiff's impecuniosity and the ultimate loss were held to be the 'direct result' of the breach of contract. That apart, it is not easy to find any features distinguishing contract from tort when the four aspects of damages are considered separately. The rules relating to mitigation are the same in both cases and in relation to remoteness the difference is merely between foreseeability and contemplation and so hardly relevant for present purposes. Likewise, the rules relating to causation are also the same. That leaves only the measure of primary loss. The modern rules relating to the date of loss owe at least as much to contract cases as they do to tort cases. The only obvious difference concerns sale of goods cases where the assessment date is required by statute to be the date of loss. That particular exception can be regarded as an important protection of certainty in commercial cases or, alternatively, as an illustration of the potential disadvantages of statutory codification.

[100] [1980] AC 367.
[101] [1977] 1 WLR 1262.
[102] [1980] 1 WLR 433.
[103] [1947] AC 414.
[104] Cited above, at note 71.

Summary

It is submitted that the relevance of impecuniosity to the four aspects of damages can be summarised in the following way.

Torts

Mitigation[105]

As Megaw LJ said in the *Dodd* case, a plaintiff who is under a duty to mitigate is not obliged, in order to reduce the damages, to do what he cannot afford to do. In other words, whether a plaintiff is impecunious is relevant to the question whether he has taken reasonable steps to mitigate his loss. Lord Collins said as much in *Clippins Oil* and when, in *The Liesbosch*, Lord Wright referred to that passage he did not question its correctness. The uncertainty apparent in subsequent cases seems largely to have been the result of a misunderstanding of the effect and extent of the *Liesbosch* decision.

The Measure of Damages for Primary Loss[106]

The crucial determinant of the result in *The Liesbosch*, at both Court of Appeal and House of Lords levels, was not the plaintiff's impecuniosity but the fact that the claim arose from the *destruction* of the dredger. For that, the primary measure of damages in 1933 was its value as a going concern as at the date of the loss. To the measure thus arrived at, the plaintiff's inability from his own resources to afford to replace the vessel was strictly irrelevant. In the 1970s the rule that damages be assessed as at the date of loss ceased to be invariable and it was established that some other date could be fixed should justice so require. The question then became one of fixing a date at which it would have been reasonable for the plaintiff to have acted. In cases where the primary loss has been the cost of repair, it seems now to have been accepted that, in determining what is reasonable, the plaintiff's impecuniosity can be taken into account at least as one factor amongst others. But if, in this context, an analogy between reasonableness in relation to the date of loss and reasonableness in relation to mitigation is accepted, as seems increasingly to be the case, any lingering reluctance to have regard to impecuniosity in the case of destruction ought to disappear. On the evidence of the decision of the Court of Appeal in *Ramswade Ltd v WJ Emson & Co Ltd*, the changes of the 1970s have yet

[105] See text at notes 9–22.
[106] See text at notes 23–58.

to be taken into account in cases calling for replacement rather than mere repair. On the other hand, those changes do not appear from the reports to have been argued, or considered, by the Court in that case.[107]

Causation[108]

Where a causal link exists between the wrongful act, the plaintiff's impecuniosity, and the eventual loss, there can be no doubt that recovery can be had. *The Liesbosch* allowed for it and it has been confirmed in subsequent decisions. Where *The Liesbosch* created a difficulty was deciding in effect that the plaintiff's impecuniosity could not be treated like other existing states (the 'eggshell skull' rule) despite the assertion by Lord Collins that a wrongdoer must take his (impecunious) victims *talem qualem*. As Donaldson LJ has said, it is not at once apparent why such an exception should exist. Commentators have attempted to justify it on grounds of policy but these are increasingly difficult to maintain in the face of the contrary position in mitigation and the developing position in relation to the date of loss. As Donaldson LJ hinted later in the passage just referred to, the only reason for the continuation of the exception is the rule stare decisis.

Remoteness[109]

The Liesbosch was decided not long after *In re Polemis* in a climate where directness of causation was the test for remoteness of damage in tort. By the time of his speech in *The Monarch SS Co* case, Lord Wright himself appears to have moved away from directness in favour of a test of foreseeability. Any doubt about the correct test for remoteness was finally removed in favour of foreseeability by *The Wagon Mound* and there can no longer be any reason, other than stare decisis, for denying that reasonably foreseeable impecuniosity is relevant to questions of remoteness.

Contract[110]

Statutory provision apart, there is no conceptual reason why the treatment of impecuniosity should differ as between contract and tort. Certainly, *Muhammad Issa v Ali* is no authority to the contrary.

[107] See, now, *Glenmont Investments Pty Ltd v O'Loughlin* (2001) 79 SASR 151, a case of destruction, where Millhouse J, in fixing the date at which damages for the primary loss were to be assessed, took account of the plaintiff's impecuniosity. He did, though, appear to see the question as one of mitigation.

[108] See text at notes 59–73.

[109] See text at notes 74–92.

[110] See text at notes 103–04.

Conclusion

Developments in the law since *The Liesbosch* was decided in 1933 have made it increasingly difficult in principle to justify special treatment of the plaintiff's impecuniosity in the context of any of the four aspects of damages considered in this article. Almost certainly, had *The Liesbosch* not been a decision of the House of Lords, it would before now have been overruled. To state the obvious, litigation by the impecunious is not frequently taken to the very highest level. Even when it is, the Court may still not feel prompted or required to undertake a fundamental reconsideration. *Alcoa* was such a case and an opportunity was missed.

Postscript: Impecuniosity Pays Off

Lagden v O'Connor [2003] UKHL 64; [2004] 1 AC 1067; [2003] 3 WLR 1571 (hereinafter *Lagden*) will be remembered for its treatment of impecuniosity, but it is interesting too for what it says or implies about the purpose of damages in tort.

Lagden was the third round of a contest between the motor insurance industry and credit (or accident) hire companies. The latter have evolved to meet the needs of owners whose motor cars have been damaged through no fault of their own and who want the use of a substitute vehicle while theirs are being repaired. In the past, many such owners would have chosen to go without, because the cost of hire was not covered by their own policies, or because they lacked the ready cash to pay upfront and had no wish to borrow or were unable to do so, or just because they did not wish to take the risk of finding themselves unable to recover the cost of hire from the other party. What the credit hire companies do is supply substitute cars for which the hirers need produce no money either at the time of hiring or at all. The hire company pursues the allegedly negligent drivers' insurers and brings and conducts court proceedings if need be.

Together, these services cost more than an ordinary hire at local spot rates. In *Lagden*, for example, the plaintiff had entered into four agreements with related companies. There was a hire agreement, a supplementary credit hire agreement, a credit repair agreement, and an insurance agreement in case recovery from the other party could not be had. The total cost of these services was £659.76 whereas, according to the judge at first instance, the ordinary spot hire rate would have been some 70 per cent of that amount. These developments were unwelcome to the motor insurance companies and not just because of the prospect of having to bear costs additional to the ordinary rate. Their emergence meant that accident victims could and would hire substitute vehicles which they, for the sorts of reason already mentioned, would not otherwise have done so. The point here is that if no substitute were in fact hired by the victim, the amount recoverable by him in general damages for loss of use could be considerably less even than the ordinary spot rate (*Steam Sand Pump Dredger No 7 (Owners of) v Owners of SS Greta Holme (The Greta Holme)* [1897] AC 596). Admittedly, there were suggestions in *Steamship Mediana (Owners of) v Owners, Master and Crew of the Lightship Comet (The Mediana)* [1900] AC 113 that a jury might, in practice, award the amount which would have been payable had a notional substitute been hired. But it appears that if no vehicle has been hired the county courts, by which most such claims are heard, routinely award general damages for loss of use at the rate of about £10 a day, a figure two or three times less than an actual hire could cost.

The insurance industry's first line of attack was to claim that credit hire agreements were champertous and therefore void. That argument was rejected by the House of Lords in *Giles v Thompson* [1994] AC 142.

In the second round the industry was much more successful. In *Dimond v Lovell* [2002] 1 AC 384 (hereinafter *Dimond*), the House of Lords held that the credit hire agreements before them failed to comply with the requirements of the Consumer Credit Act 1974 and were therefore unenforceable. However, that defect being a technical one curable by a change in drafting, three of their Lordships (Lord Browne-Wilkinson, Lord Hoffmann, and Lord Hobhouse of Woodborough) went on to say that, even had the agreements been enforceable, the plaintiff could have recovered no more than the reasonable cost of a simple hire at local spot rates. Their reasoning was that the credit hire system conferred benefits additional to the use of a car and that, under *British Westinghouse Electric and Manufacturing Co Ltd v Underground Electric Railways Co of London Ltd* [1912] AC 673, these needed to be brought into account when calculating damages (at 401, 402, 407). Alternatively, the additional benefits were not attributable to the cost of mitigating the plaintiff's loss of use (at 407). It was pointed out that awards of statutory interest and costs could enable recovery for some of the cost of the additional benefits, in another form (at 409).

By contrast, Lord Nicholls of Birkenhead thought credit car hire arrangements provided a reasonable basis by which no-fault victims could in fact obtain the benefit of what he called 'the right' which the common law and compulsory third-party insurance sought to give them against careless drivers (at 391). The right he had in mind appears to have been the provision of substitute hire vehicles. For his part, Lord Saville of Newdigate saw the question as one of great importance and difficulty which he preferred to consider in a case where it actually arose for decision (at 403).

Dimond was a considerable setback for the credit hire companies, but they were able to mount a partial counter attack in *Lagden* on the grounds that the plaintiff was impecunious, that the credit hire system provided his only practicable means of securing the use of a substitute vehicle, and that *Dimond* was distinguishable on that basis. The House of Lords by a majority (Lord Nicholls, Lord Slynn of Hadley, and Lord Hope of Craighead), Lord Scott of Foscote and Lord Walker of Gestingthorpe dissenting) accepted those arguments and held the plaintiff entitled to recover the whole of the cost of his credit hire arrangements. It was a premise of that decision that what Lord Wright had said about the irrelevance of impecuniosity in *Liesbosch Dredger (Owners of) v Owners of SS Edison* [1933] AC 449 (hereinafter *The Liesbosch*) should no longer be considered authoritative. Lord Scott and Lord Walker both accepted that premise but nevertheless considered themselves bound by *Dimond* to hold that the additional benefits accruing to the plaintiff were incapable of being the subject of damages at common law.

A potential problem was and is the application in practice of the concept of impecuniosity, with the attendant risk of increased litigation. For Lord Nicholls (at [9]) the test was whether the plaintiff could pay without making sacrifices he could not reasonably be expected to bear while Lord Hope (at [37]) thought it could turn on whether he had the benefit of a recognised credit or debit card. Both expected the insurance and credit hire companies to reach their own solutions. The question of what constitutes impecuniosity seems to have received little discussion in earlier reports, one exception being *Attorney-General v Geothermal Produce NZ Ltd* [1987] 2 NZLR 348 where it was held that the causal link between the wrongful act, impecuniosity, and eventual loss would not be broken just because the majority shareholders in the plaintiff company could have raised funds by selling other property (and see also Scrutton LJ in *The Liesbosch* [1932] P 52, 61). The scope for uncertainty might increase if, as Lord Hope suggested (at [16]), recovery could similarly be had if a plaintiff's lack of choice were to arise from other reasonably foreseeable causes.

How far *Lagden* has altered the general law on impecuniosity and damages depends mainly on whether the context being considered is one of mitigation, causation, remoteness, or measure. In the context of mitigation, impecuniosity has long been treated as relevant and Lord Wright did not suggest otherwise. For him the question at issue in *The Liesbosch* was not one of mitigation. Instead, he saw the plaintiffs' lack of funds as either an independent cause or too remote (at 461). As Megaw LJ said in *Dodd Properties Kent Ltd v Canterbury City Council* [1980] 1 WLR 433, 453, 'a plaintiff who is under a duty to mitigate is not obliged, in order to reduce the damages, to do what he cannot afford to do'. In *Dimond*, Lord Hoffmann and Lord Hobhouse (at 401, 407) saw the actions of the plaintiff as a reasonable attempt to mitigate her loss of use, but as going beyond mitigation to the extent that the credit hire agreements included additional benefits. Similarly, in *Lagden*, Lord Hope seems also to have seen the issue before the House as primarily one of mitigation but with the difference that he treated the additional costs as being themselves mitigatory (at [34], [61]). On that view, the novelty of *Lagden* would be, not that impecuniosity was treated as relevant to mitigation but, rather, that the plaintiff's impecuniosity widened the range of what could be classed as mitigation.

As to causation, it was similarly the case before *Lagden* that, where there were causal links between the wrongful act, the plaintiff's want of funds, and the eventual loss, recovery could be had. Again, Lord Wright did not suggest otherwise. On the other hand, for obvious reasons, supervening impecuniosity not the result of the wrongful act could not then and still cannot be treated as relevant. In *The Liesbosch* the impecuniosity was pre-existing. The problem here was

Lord Wright's insistence that that sort of impecuniosity was not to be treated like other existing conditions (the 'eggshell skull' principle) and that, in this respect, the plaintiff was therefore not to be taken *talem qualem*. It followed that, in the climate created by *In re Polemis and Furness Withy & Co Ltd* [1921] 3 KB 560, the want of funds, not being the direct result of the wrongful act, for that reason had to be too remote. Since *The Liesbosch*, the law as to remoteness has moved on, the test now being one of reasonable foreseeability (or in contract, contemplation) as Lord Hope recognised in *Lagden* (at [61]). But in any event, in *Lagden*, the plaintiff's impecuniosity was an existing state. Lord Nicholls and Lord Hope both stated expressly that the defendant must take his victim as he found him (at [6], [61]). Lord Slynn agreed with Lord Nicholls.

That leaves measure of damages and here the effect of *Lagden* is in one respect perhaps less clear. Historically, where property was damaged and could be repaired, the measure of damages was the market cost of those repairs as at the date the damage occurred or within a reasonable time thereafter. To the fixing of that date, impecuniosity would have been irrelevant. However, since the 1970s, and decisions such as *Johnson v Agnew* [1980] AC 367, the date at which loss is to be assessed has become more flexible. Thus, in *Dodd Properties Kent Ltd v Canterbury City Council* [1980] 1 WLR 433, the Court of Appeal accepted that where defendants were unreasonably denying liability and where raising money for repairs would have increased the plaintiff's annual losses and their financial stringency, it was reasonable for them to defer repairs until a judgment was obtained. Accordingly, it was as at the date of judgment that damages for the cost of repairs were assessed. Subsequently, in *Alcoa Minerals of Jamaica Inc v Broderick* [2002] 1 AC 371 where the facts were conceptually similar, the Privy Council reached a similar conclusion, impecuniosity being seen as one supporting factor among others. In *Lagden* the date as at which the cost of repairs should be fixed was not in issue. Nevertheless, it seems likely that impecuniosity could now by itself be a sufficient reason for fixing a date much later than that when the damage occurred. Lord Nicholls was of the view that Lord Wright's dictum about not taking into account a claimant's want of means when assessing the 'amount' of his loss would no longer be regarded as authoritative (at [8]). Lord Slynn said much the same (at [12]) while Lord Hope's characterisation (at [51]) of a distinction Lord Wright had made between measure and mitigation as 'a distinction without a difference' seems to imply that damages ought no longer be measured as if the injured party had done what he could not afford to do. Lord Walker, too, thought the differences between mitigation and measure were by no means obvious (at [97], [102]) and said that he understood the House to be unanimous that 'what is left of' *The Liesbosch* should now be laid to rest (at [90]).

Less certain is the position when the wrongful act destroys and not merely damages the plaintiff's property. *The Liesbosch* was just such a case, the dredger having been a total loss. The plaintiffs could not afford to buy a replacement until some time later and in the meantime were forced to hire another dredger at unfavourable terms. In both the Court of Appeal and the House of Lords, it was taken for granted that the proper measure of damages was the value of the *Liesbosch* as a going concern, as at the date of the accident. That value was to be assessed as including allowance for costs and expenses reasonably incurred and losses suffered during the period between the sinking and the time at which a substitute could reasonably have been brought on site and become available for use. The difference between the Court of Appeal and the House of Lords was that, in assessing the value of the *Liesbosch*, the former took as a sufficient estimate of that value the approximate cost of the substitute dredger which the plaintiffs hired and were eventually able to purchase. If it is unrealistic to assess a complainant's damages as if he had been able to afford immediate repairs despite his inability to do so, it could arguably be no more realistic to ignore his inability when his property has been destroyed. After all, impecunious victims are now to be taken *talem qualem*. Nevertheless, none of their Lordships in *Lagden* said in so many words that *The Liesbosch* was being overruled. On the one hand, the observations of Lord Nicholls and Lord Slynn about taking into account a claimant's want of means when assessing the 'amount' of his loss were not in terms restricted to damage as distinct from destruction. The other member of the majority, Lord Hope, also said the rule laid down in *The Liesbosch* 'should now be departed from'. On the other hand, he added that it was 'not necessary' to say that the case itself had been wrongly decided (at [61]). Lord Walker went further, declaring (at [102]) that the actual decision could readily be justified by the reasoning of Scrutton and Greer LJJ in the Court of Appeal. He may have had particularly in mind the fact that the sum awarded by that Court was in effect the actual cost of the substitute dredger, albeit expressed as an approximate valuation of the *Liesbosch* as a going concern as at the time of its loss. If, as seems at least possible, damages for destruction of property are still to be assessed as at the date of loss despite the victim's impecuniosity, it may well be the single remaining exception, though nonetheless welcome to the insurance industry.

A final point concerns the contrasting ways in which the majority and the minority of the House treated the provision of a substitute car. As Lord Hope said (at [30]), it is an elementary rule that the purpose of an award of damages is to place the injured party as nearly as possible in the same position as he was in before the accident. For Lord Scott and Lord Walker, this meant that, since the plaintiff had in fact secured a substitute car, his entitlement was to damages measured by the reasonable market rate of hire. It was, in other words, to a sum of money, the quantum of which was to be fixed objectively, without regard to what he might or might not have been able to afford and independently of what the actual cost to him of securing a substitute would have been. Accordingly, the extra costs he had incurred because of his impecuniosity were to be treated as being for additional benefits.

The approach of the majority was rather different. For them, it seems, placing the plaintiff in the position he was in before the accident meant in effect making possible the actual use of a substitute car. Lord Nicholls spoke (at [6]) of an innocent plaintiff's being enabled to 'obtain the use' of such a car, and it will be remembered that in *Dimond* he seemed to have spoken of the use of an alternative car as a 'right'. Lord Hope, when referring to the motorist's minimising his loss of use by hiring an alternative, spoke (at [43]) not of his 'duty' to mitigate but of his not being deprived of an 'opportunity' to do so. He talked, too, (at [34]) of the extra benefits under the credit hire agreement as being incidental to the step the plaintiff was 'entitled' to take in the mitigation of his loss. Moreover, he said (at [30]), if the plaintiff could not recover all he had had to spend he would be at risk of being worse off than he was before the accident. He also cited (at [24]) Lord Nicholls' comment on the need to 'yield money in time to be of use to' the victim. What seemingly is being described, therefore, is not just compensation for going without one's car but, rather, a right to obtain the actual use of a substitute. On this view, the so-called additional benefits would simply be part of the cost of credit. (Indeed, their intended function would almost certainly have been to provide security for the credit hire.) Accordingly, if an impecunious plaintiff has to borrow to secure his right, he can now recover his cost of credit as well as the sum borrowed. Lord Hope implied as much (at [61]).

If this analysis is correct, we appear to have in *Lagden* a perceived function of damages in tort not too unlike protection of the performance interest in contract and a division of approach in some ways reminiscent of that in *Alfred McAlpine Construction Co Ltd v Panatown Ltd* [2001] 1 AC 518 (discussed in Coote, 'The Performance Interest and the Problem of Loss' (2001) 117 *LQR* 81 reprinted as Chapter 9 of *Assumption*).

12

Contract as Assumption and Remoteness of Damage

The judgments of Lord Hoffmann in *Banque Bruxelles Lambert SA v Eagle Star Insurance Ltd*[1] (hereinafter *Eagle Star*) and of Lord Hoffmann and Lord Hope of Craighead, respectively, in *Transfield Shipping Inc v Mercator Shipping Inc*[2] (hereinafter *The Achilleas*) have already attracted so many published comments[3] that to add yet another may seem, at best, gratuitous. The focus of all this attention has been what their Lordships had to say about assumption of liability in contract and its relationship to remoteness of damage. Happily, for the purposes of this present note it will not be necessary to rehearse in detail the numerous points already covered by others. The objective here is merely the much more limited

[1] [1997] AC 191, sub nom *South Australia Asset Management Corp v York Montague Ltd* [1996] 3 All ER 365.

[2] [2009] 1 AC 61.

[3] An exhaustive list would be far too lengthy to set out here. But a sample would include:

(a) On *Eagle Star*: J Stapleton, 'Negligent Valuers and Falls in the Property Market' (1992) 113 *LQR* 1; J Wrightman, 'Negligent Valuations and a Drop in the Property Market: The Limits of the Expectation Loss Principle' (1998) 61 *MLR* 68; J O'Sullivan, 'Negligent Professional Advice and Market Movements' [1997] *CLJ* 19; SM Waddams, 'Liability of Values: *Kenny & Good Pty Ltd v MGICA (1992) Ltd* (1997) 5 *Torts LJ* 218; DW McLauchlan, 'Negligent Value Liability: The Paradox Remains?' (1997) 113 *LQR* 421; DW McLauchlan, 'A Damages Dilemma' (1997) 12 *JCL* 114; A Robertson, 'The Basis of the Remoteness Rule in Contract' (2008) 28 *Legal Studies* 192; A Kramer, 'An Agreement-Centred Approach to Remoteness and Damages' in Cohen and McKendrick (eds), *Comparative Remedies for Breach of Contract* (Hart Publishing, Oxford, 2005); Lord Hoffmann, 'Causation' (2005) 121 *LQR* 592; A Tettenborn, '*Hadley v Baxendale* Foreseeability: A Principle Beyond its Sell-by-Date' (2007) 23 *JCL* 120. See also AM Dugdale, 'Purposive Analysis of Professional Advice: Reflections on the BBL Decision' [1995] *JBL* 533; Francis Dawson, 'Reflections on Certain Aspects of the Law of Damages for Breach of Contract' (1995) 9 *JCL* 125; DW McLauchlan and CEF Rickett, '*SAAMCO* in the High Court of Australia' (2000) 116 *LQR* 1.

(b) On *The Achilleas*: J O'Sullivan, 'Damages for Lost Profits for Late Redelivery: How Remote is Too Remote' [2009] *CLJ* 34; G Gordon, '*Hadley v Baxendale* Revisited: *Transfield Shipping Inc v Mercator Shipping Inc* (2009) 13 *Edinburgh LR* 125; R Halson, 'Time Charters, Damages and Remoteness' (2008) *LMCLQ* 119; D Foxton, 'Damages for Late Or Early Redelivery Under Time Charter Parties' [2008] *LMCLQ* 461; DW McLauchlan, 'Remoteness Re-Invented?' (2009) 9 *OUCLJ* 109; E Peel, 'Remoteness Revisited' (2009) 125 *LQR* 6; J Halliday, 'Remoteness of Contractual Damages' (2009) 21 *Denning LJ* 173; Lord Hoffmann, '*The Achilleas*: Custom and Practice or Foreseeability?' (2010) 14 *Edinburgh LR* 47; PCK Wee, 'Contractual Interpretation and Remoteness' [2010] *LMCLQ* 150.

one of attempting to show how far, if at all, the views expressed by their Lordships are consistent with, or may even support, a thesis the writer has been exploring in print, on and off, since the 1960s.[4]

A Premise

It is a thesis with a number of aspects, but the one most relevant to the present enquiry starts with the premise that promises involve assumptions of obligation, usually of a moral, social, or religious kind. Promises are made in order to assure promisees that they can rely on what has been promised because the promisor has thereby accepted a corresponding level of responsibility. But there are situations where an assumption of merely moral, social, or religious responsibility will be insufficient to inspire the required degree of assurance and where only a legally enforceable responsibility will suffice. It is to enable the assumption of just such a responsibility that the institution of contract has been provided by society and the state. That contractual promises should be binding and enforceable at law is thus central to the very notion of a contract and is, in fact, their raison d'etre. Contractual duties and obligations, and their corresponding rights and liabilities (hereinafter referred to as primary and secondary obligations), are each essential to the purpose and existence of the other and are in effect like two sides of the one coin. That being so, an assumption of primary contractual obligations necessarily also requires and involves an assumption of the secondary obligations that go with them. In other words, both primary and secondary contractual obligations, even when implied by law, are incurred on the creation of a contract, not because they have been imposed by law *ab extra*, but because, in the act of entering into a contract, the parties have, by thus assuming them, taken them upon themselves. What at first sight might appear to be exceptions are the so-called contracts of imperfect obligation where a merely procedural inability to sue has been imposed *ab extra*. Contracts barred by statutes of limitations and contracts with foreign sovereigns are examples. In these cases the obligations which have been assumed become enforceable if the procedural inability to sue is removed as, for instance, by the foreign sovereign submitting to the jurisdiction.

However, the conclusion that the parties have in effect imposed contractual obligations on themselves does not, of itself, show whether and how far the actual content of the secondary obligations thus assumed is as determined by the parties themselves or, instead, is as prescribed and dictated by law. Whichever of these might be the case, the law does allow the parties by express agreement to modify much of the content of their secondary obligations. That content can, for example, be reduced directly by the use of exception clauses, or by clauses limiting the

[4] A dozen of these pieces were republished in *Assumption*. For practical reasons, treatment of *The Achilleas* was there restricted to a two-page addendum. Hence this current piece.

time within which claims can be brought, or the amount of damages which can be recovered. The amount recoverable on breach can also be reduced by the use of liquidated damages clauses. And because of the interdependence of primary and secondary obligations, a reduction of either type of obligation has an equivalent effect on the other. Thus, the exclusion of all secondary liability in respect of some particular aspect of what would otherwise be a contracted part of a promise has the result that no corresponding primary obligation in respect of that part can arise.

The law also allows the parties by express provision even to increase the content of their secondary obligations, again, for example, through the use of liquidated damages clauses, provided the increase falls short of being penal. Another example of an increase was referred to in argument by counsel for the defendants in *Hadley v Baxendale*[5] (one of whom, interestingly, was the future Willes J). The argument was that, since the defendants were, as common carriers, required to carry for all comers, it was only if they had made a 'special acceptance' that they could be made liable for the loss which had been caused through the mill being unable to operate for want of the shaft. In other words, before any question of remoteness could arise, it had to be determined whether any special measure of liability had been assumed. As Alderson B himself recognised[6] 'had the special circumstances been known, the parties might have specially provided for the breach of contract by special terms as to the damages in that case'. But in the absence of any such special provision the second limb of his famous formula would still apply. The plaintiff's claim for loss of profits failed because, as he said,[7]

> such loss would neither have flowed naturally from the breach of this contract in the great multitude of such cases occurring under ordinary circumstances, nor were the special circumstances, *which, perhaps, would have made it a reasonable and natural consequence of such breach* of contract, communicated to or known by the defendants (italics supplied).

Two Questions

But while it is clear enough that parties may at least by express provision limit, modify, or exclude their secondary obligations, there remain two questions, the answers to which do not follow automatically from the proposition that, like primary obligations, secondary obligations are assumed at the point of formation. It would not *necessarily* be inconsistent with that premise for those parts of the secondary obligations left after any express modifications have been made to be recognised as having been assumed, but with their residual content as imposed by

[5] (1854) 9 Exch 341, 352; 156 ER 145, 151.
[6] (1854) 9 Exch 341, 354–55; 156 ER 145, 151.
[7] (1854) 9 Exch 341, 356; 156 ER 145, 151.

law. Two questions then remain: first, whether the parties are permitted in law to modify their secondary obligations by implicit or implied, as well as by express, agreement; and second, whether it is correct that the content remaining after modification is dictated by force of law *ab extra* or is, instead, governed by the agreement of the parties. If the latter were the case, it would mean that the rules of remoteness of damage, as laid down in *Hadley v Baxendale* and its successors,[8] could function as no more than doubtless strong, but rebuttable, indications or presumptions of what the parties intended. While, in practice, the answer to the first of these two questions could potentially be of some importance, the answer to the second might in practice make less difference to the result in many, if not most, cases. But the answer would still not be unimportant since, if liability were to be treated as having been imposed by law *ab extra*, it could be expected there would be at least some bias towards applying the imposed rule or rules, in full force and with a minimum of exceptions. On the other hand, any bias could well be the other way if the rules as to remoteness gave rise to no more than indications, assumptions, or rebuttable presumptions. *The Achilleas* may provide examples of both approaches.[9] For present purposes, it is to these two questions, posed above, that the views expressed and applied by Lord Hoffmann and Lord Hope have particular relevance.

The Two Cases

Given all the attention *Eagle Star* and *The Achilleas* have received, their facts and results are likely to be already well known. In any event, they can (again, for present purposes) be summarised quite briefly. In *Eagle Star*, the central issue was the potential damages liability of valuers, on the security of whose negligently inflated valuations of properties moneys had been advanced. In particular, did the losses for which they were liable include those caused when a subsequent fall in market values reduced the extent of the lender's security? In the courts below, the case had been approached on the basis that, under the principle in *Robinson v Harman*,[10] damages should, as nearly as possible, place plaintiffs in the position they would have occupied had they not been injured. From the Appeal Cases report, there appears to have been no argument based directly and expressly on *Hadley v Baxendale*. Delivering what was in effect the judgment of the House, Lord Hoffmann indicated[11] that, before damages could be calculated, it was necessary

[8] In particular, *Victoria Laundry (Windsor) Ltd v Newman Industries Ltd* [1949] 2 KB 528 and *The Heron II* [1969] 1 AC 350.

[9] As in the contrast between the approaches of the majority arbitrators and the courts below on the one hand, and the judgments of Lord Hoffmann and Lord Hope on the other.

[10] (1848) 1 Exch 850; 154 ER 363.

[11] [1997] AC 191, 211.

for the plaintiff to show that the defendant was in breach of a duty owed to him in respect of the kind of loss suffered. The scope of the duty, in the sense of the consequences for which the valuer was responsible was, he said,[12]

> that which the law regards as best giving effect to the express obligations assumed by the valuer [and] not extending them so as to impose on the valuer a liability greater than he could reasonably have thought he was undertaking.

Subsequently in his judgment in *The Achilleas*, his Lordship summarised the effect of *Eagle Star* as being[13]

> to exclude from liability the damages attributable to a fall in the property market notwithstanding that those losses were foreseeable in the sense of being 'not unlikely' (property values go down as well as up) and had been caused by the negligent valuation in the sense that, but for the valuation, the bank would not have lent at all and there was no evidence to show that it would have lost its money in some other way. It was excluded on the ground that it was outside the scope of the liability which the parties would reasonably have considered that the valuer was undertaking.

In *The Achilleas* itself, the owners of a vessel, in anticipation of its redelivery on the due date, had arranged a follow-on time charter with another company under the terms of which the new charterer had the right to cancel if redelivery were delayed. When it became clear that the redelivery would be late, the owners negotiated a later commencement date for the follow-on charter but, because market rates had fallen, had to accept a reduced rate of hire. Here again, at the time the original charter was entered into, it was readily foreseeable, both that a follow-on charter would have been entered into and that, because charter rates fluctuated, the result of a delayed redelivery could have been a drop in the rate payable with consequent loss to the owners. Below, by a majority and in reliance on *Hadley v Baxendale*, arbitrators found the original charterers liable for the reduction in hire payable in respect of the whole 191-day term of the follow-on charter.[14] That conclusion was upheld both at first instance[15] and by the Court of Appeal.[16] The arbitrator who had dissented did so on two grounds, one of which was that there was a general understanding in the shipping industry that in such cases the original charter's liability would be restricted to the period of the late delivery, although there had been no previous binding decision on the point. The other ground was that, in his view, a reasonable man in the position of the charterers would not have understood that he was assuming liability for a completely unquantifiable risk. To hold otherwise would be to create undesirable commercial uncertainty.

In the House of Lords, their Lordships were all agreed that the appeal should be allowed, albeit on differing grounds. But for present purposes, what makes the case important is the reasoning of Lord Hoffmann, supported by Lord Hope, for

[12] Ibid at 212.
[13] [2009] 1 AC 61, 69.
[14] Ibid at 63, 66.
[15] [2007] 1 All ER (Comm) 379 (Clarke J).
[16] [2008] 1 All ER (Comm) 685.

both of whom the result hinged on the extent to which the defendant could be said to have assumed responsibility for the owner's loss. For Lord Hoffmann,[17] the case raised 'a fundamental point of principle in the law of contractual damages'. The question he posed was,

> is the rule that a party may recover losses which were foreseeable ('not unlikely') an external rule of law, imposed upon the parties to every contract in default of express provision to the contrary, or is it a prima facie assumption about what the parties may be taken to have intended, no doubt applicable in the great majority of cases but capable of rebuttal in cases in which the context, surrounding circumstances or general understanding in the relevant market show that a party would not reasonably have been regarded as assuming responsibility for such losses?

For him it seemed 'logical to found liability for damages upon the intention of the parties (objectively ascertained) because all contractual liability is voluntarily undertaken'.[18]

In the course of his judgment, his Lordship referred to the responsibility thus assumed as being of liability, variously, for the 'kind',[19] 'type',[20] or 'form'[21] of loss in question. He spoke, too, of the assumption as being of the 'risk' of such loss[22] which, in the context, seems to have been an alternative way of saying what an assumption of liability or responsibility entailed. For him, whether and what liability had been assumed depended ultimately, in effect, on the interpretation of the contract, read as a whole, in the light of the surrounding circumstances.[23] Lord Hope, too, spoke of the assumption as being of responsibility for the 'type'[24] or the 'risk'[25] of loss and for the 'consequences' of breach.[26] For him, the relevance of the ordinary rules as to remoteness was that they raised a rebuttable presumption as to what responsibility had been assumed.[27]

Assumed or Imposed?

As was entirely predictable, this concept of liability for damages (let alone the rules as to remoteness) as something intended and assumed by the parties when they enter into a contract, has been strongly resisted. After all, it runs counter to that very widely held perception that, as in tort, liability in contract is something

17 [2009] 1 AC 61, 67.
18 Ibid at 68.
19 Ibid at 68, 70, 71.
20 Ibid at 70, 71.
21 Ibid at 70.
22 Ibid at 68, 70.
23 Ibid at 71.
24 Ibid at 72.
25 Ibid.
26 Ibid at 73.
27 Ibid at 74.

imposed by law *ab extra* on parties who, in the case of contract, have fulfilled the technical requirements for formation. It is a perception which may owe something to the fact that the writ of assumpsit was in form an action on the case. (Although, on the other hand, the very word 'assumpsit' could be taken to imply the contrary.) Manifestations have included some of the classic reasons given for the institution of contract. Among them are a supposed need to recognise the sanctity of and give effect to the human will; to protect the institution of promising and its moral basis; to safeguard the reasonable expectations generated by promises; and to prevent detriment to those who have relied on them. Each of these examples appears to require or at least postulate an intervention by the law *ab extra*. Then, too, there is the also widely held view, espoused most famously by Lord Denning,[28] that when faced with an agreement containing an exemption clause it is 'necessary to look at the contract apart from the exempting clauses to see what are the terms expressed or implied which impose an obligation on the party'. Those clauses then operate if at all as defences, at the point of adjudication, to accrued rights of action. It was this sort of approach that was used to justify the decision of the Court of Appeal in *Harbutt's 'Plasticine' Ltd v Wayne Tank and Pump Co Ltd*[29] and, more generally, to support the doctrine of fundamental breach as something which, as a matter of law, could override the express terms of a contract. Another example, referred to by Sir Frederick Pollock as 'the secret paradox' of consideration,[30] was the view that the parties' contractual obligations to each other could not be consideration because they could not (as consideration requires) be exchanged at formation, being imposed on the parties by law as the *result* of formation. The answer to the secret paradox is that, as already suggested, it is not the obligations created by the contract which constitute the consideration but, rather, the mutual assumption of those obligations. But it does not necessarily follow from that that the content of the secondary obligations thus assumed would not be as prescribed by law. It would be quite consistent for the rules of remoteness laid down in *Hadley v Baxendale* and its successors to apply because the law had determined what they should be.

However, assuming *pace* Lord Hoffmann and Lord Hope, that this latter view were the correct one, it would certainly not be without its difficulties. Notoriously, even under *Hadley v Baxendale* and its successors, it is not for every contemplated or reasonably foreseeable loss that defendants are held liable. It is a reluctance of the courts to impose liability where it would seem unjust or unfair to do so which has led to the adoption of such devices as the concept of the 'kind' or 'type' of loss which can be used, as required, either to expand or to limit the extent of liability in a particular case. Another is to categorise a loss as highly unlikely although, here again, there could be cases where the defendant ought in justice to be held liable, even for such a loss, because at least one of the purposes of the particular contract

[28] *Karsales (Harrow) Ltd v Wallis* [1956] 1 WLR 936, 940.

[29] [1970] 1 QB 447.

[30] In an anonymous review in (1914) 30 *LQR* 128, 129.

was, expressly or impliedly, the avoidance of a loss of that sort. These self-same exceptions could, of course, on the approach by Lord Hoffmann and Lord Hope, be used, not as final determinants of liability, but as indications of what the parties must have intended by their contract.

The First Question

To revert now to the two questions raised earlier. It is clear from the judgments of Lord Hoffmann and Lord Hope that, in their view, just as the incidents of the ordinary rules governing remoteness of damage can be modified expressly, so too can they be modified impliedly or implicitly. That was true in respect of both the loss that was caused in *Eagle Star* by a fall in the market price of properties and, in *The Achilleas*, by the loss of hire incurred beyond the period of overlap. Since the position in relation to express modifications is too clearly established to be disputed, it would be somewhat arbitrary if the courts were to deny the parties, as between themselves, any similar right or opportunity to agree to modify their secondary obligations implicitly or by implication. The situation of common carriers provides a possible illustration. From the fact that goods have been consigned without a special acceptance, it can be implied that the liability assumed has been merely that of an ordinary carrier. As a matter of interest, in *Photo Production Ltd v Securicor Transport Ltd*[31] Lord Diplock at one point appeared to confine the modification of secondary obligations to those made by express words, but elsewhere in the same case he referred to modifications as being by words and conduct.

The Second Question

The greater problem, doctrinally, is the one posed by the second question, namely whether the ordinary rules of remoteness apply as a requirement of the law or merely as, admittedly very strong, indications of intention. Since *Hadley v Baxendale*, there have been relatively few judicial statements that obligations of the secondary kind need to be assumed by agreement in cases which fall within the second rule. A notable early example was a dictum by Willes J who, in *British Columbia and Vancouver's Island Spar and Saw-Mill Co v Nettleship*,[32] said in relation to the second rule:

> The knowledge must be brought home to the party sought to be charged under such circumstances that he must know that the person he contracts with reasonably believes that he accepts the contract with the special condition attached to it.

[31] [1980] AC 827, 848–49.
[32] (1868) LR 3 CP 499, 509.

That was a case concerning a carrier and the learned judge's approach was to some extent, therefore, reminiscent of the already mentioned reference, by counsel in *Hadley v Baxendale* (of whom he was one), to the need for a special acceptance where the potential loss was unusual. In more modern times, what was said by Willes J was echoed by Diplock LJ, as he then was, when *The Heron II* came before the Court of Appeal. Speaking generally, he had this to say:[33]

> When a party enters into a contract with another party the obligations towards the other party which he thereby undertakes to fulfil and the rights against the other party to which he is entitled are those and only those which by his words and conduct at the time of the contract he has reasonably induced the other party to believe that he is accepting a legal obligation to fulfil or asserting a legal right to claim. This is so, not only in respect of what may for convenience be called the primary obligations and rights created by the contract, that is, those which are discharged by performance of the contract, but also in respect of the secondary obligations and rights which arise upon non-performance of his primary obligations by one of the parties to the contract. Of these the most important is the obligation of the non-performer to make to the other party, and the corresponding right of the other party to claim from the non-performer, reparation in money for any loss sustained by the other party which results from the failure of the non-performer to perform his primary obligation.

Addressing specifically the position under the second rule, he said:[34]

> The second rule, which was regarded as an exception to the first, entitled an injured party who owing to circumstances peculiar to himself had sustained as a result of the breach a greater loss than would arise naturally according to the usual course of things from the breach, to recover such loss, but only if the contract-breaker at the time at which he entered into the contract knew that a breach on his part would lead to an exceptional loss of the kind in fact sustained and entered into the contract in such circumstances as would induce the other party to believe that in the event of breach he would accept liability for such exceptional loss. The latter part of the second rule, which requires, in addition to knowledge, an acceptance of contractual liability for exceptional loss, was laid down in *British Columbia Saw-Mill Co v Nettleship*; but except in the case of a person, like a common carrier, who has no right to decline to enter into a contract, it has little application in practice, for it requires no more than that the nature of the exceptional loss should be communicated by the party who will sustain it to the other party in the course of the negotiations for the contract. If the other party then enters into the contract without disclaiming his responsibility for the exceptional loss, he will be liable for such loss if it occurs as a result of his breach.

(In an article written since *The Achilleas*, Lord Hoffmann cited the earlier of those passages and drew support for his position from it.)[35] However, Lord Diplock, as he had by then become, seems subsequently to have modified his earlier view. In the course of his judgment in *Photo Production Ltd v Securicor Transport Ltd*,[36]

[33] [1966] 2 QB 695, 730–31.

[34] Ibid at 728.

[35] Lord Hoffmann, '*The Achilleas*: Custom and Practice or Foreseeability?' (2010) 14 *Edinburgh LR* 47.

[36] [1980] AC 827, 848–49.

while observing that a contract was just as much the source of secondary obligations as it was of primary obligations, he went on to say:

> Every failure to perform a primary obligation is a breach of contract. The secondary obligation on the part of the contract breaker to which it gives rise *by implication of the common law* is to pay monetary compensation to the other party for the loss sustained by him in consequence of the breach (italics supplied).

This more recent view is not inconsistent with the proposition that, when primary obligations are assumed, so too are the secondary obligations that go with them. But the passage tends to suggest that, for Lord Diplock, their actual content had come to be seen as imposed by law although he did, of course, allow that that content could be modified, as by the use of exception clauses. This, then, would be consistent with the view that where special circumstances are present but no special arrangements have been made, the second limb of Alderson B's formula applies.

If it is accepted in answer to the first question that modification of secondary obligations can, as consistency seems to require, be made by implicit or implied agreement, the second question has still to be finally answered. In suggesting that, as regards residual secondary obligation, the rules of remoteness take effect merely as indications or rebuttable presumptions, Lord Hoffmann and Lord Hope may seem to have gone beyond the previous law. But if, as already stated, any such alteration to the law would be unlikely, except as a matter of bias, to effect a significant change in the result of any particular case, one might well ask why the prospect should have prompted so much comment and concern. Ultimately what makes any development of the law in this direction seem so problematic, it is submitted, is once again that long-standing and widely held perception that contractual obligations are imposed by law *ab extra*: a perception, it is also submitted, that is at the very least vulnerable to analysis. On the other hand, if it were once accepted that, as the writer has argued for so long, contractual obligations are assumed by the parties in their act of entering into the contract rather than being imposed upon them *ab extra*, it could more easily be recognised to be of relatively less practical importance whether the contents and incidents of the secondary obligations remaining *after* express or implied modification by the parties should be as prescribed by law or whether, on the other hand, the traditional rules were to give rise to, at most, strong, albeit rebuttable, inferences, indications, or presumptions.

Conclusion

Whichever of these two views prevails, it can be claimed that the judgments of Lord Hoffmann and Lord Hope provide clear prima facie support for the writer's premise that both primary and secondary contractual obligations are assumed rather than imposed *ab extra*, whether or not the law to some extent dictates the content of the obligations thus assumed. The fact that their Lordships saw assumption as determining the actual content of even residual secondary obligations makes their support for the premise even stronger, certainly in the context of remoteness, and potentially much more widely.

Predictably, their Lordships' view has been met with scepticism, not least from members of the judiciary.[37] And it is to some extent arguable that, in *The Achilleas*, theirs was a minority view. On the other hand, in *Supershield Ltd v Siemens Building Technologies FE Ltd*[38] the English Court of Appeal (Mummery, Richards, and Toulson LJJ), in a judgment delivered by Toulson LJ, has since stated:

> The law on remoteness of damage in relation to claims for breach of contract is grounded on the policy that the loss recoverable by the victim should be limited to loss from which the party in breach may reasonably be taken to have assumed a responsibility to protect the victim. It follows that the question of remoteness cannot be isolated from consideration of the purpose of the contract and the scope of the contractual obligation. The underlying policy is implicit in Lord Reid's speech in *C Czarnikow Ltd v Koufos*, where he referred to what the parties may be supposed to have contemplated as grounds for the recovery of damages and linked this to the question whether the loss was sufficiently likely to result from the breach to make it proper to hold that loss of that kind should have been in the contract breaker's contemplation. It has been made more explicit in the decisions of the House of Lords in *South Australia Asset Management Corp v York Montague Ltd (sub nom Banque Bruxelles Lambert SA v Eagle Star Insurance Co Ltd)* and *Transfield Shipping Inc v Mercator Shipping Inc.*

For anyone inclined to subscribe to the present writer's thesis, that is at least encouraging. But the real test will be whether this approach, that both primary and secondary contractual obligations are assumed, will be extended, as consistency would require, to other areas of contract.

[37] *ASM Shipping Ltd of India v TTMi Ltd of England (The Amer Energy)* [2009] 1 Lloyd's Rep 293, 294–95 per Flaux J; *Classic Maritime Inv v Lion Diversified Holdings* [2010] 1 Lloyd's Rep 59, 71 per Cooke J.

[38] [2010] 1 Lloyd's Rep 349, 355. See also *The Kos* [2010] 1 Lloyd's Rep 87, 95 per Andrew Smith J. (*The Achilleas* was not referred to in either of the subsequent appeals [2010] 2 Lloyd's Rep 409 (CA); [2012] 2 AC 164 (HL).)

13

Contract: An Underview*

Introduction

Professor Taggart, your Honours, ladies and gentlemen.

I think it rather pleasant that a colleague and former student, whose inaugural lecture I introduced, should now have introduced my own valedictory. I hope I shan't upset anyone if I say that of all the students I've had in the last 34 years, MB Taggart was the most—I think 'memorable' is the word. I mean that as a compliment! He didn't take Contract with me in Law I. Had he done so, who knows to what heights he might by now have attained!

Another pleasing conjunction comes from the presence on the platform of Donald Dugdale. He was a speaker at the dinner former students gave AG Davis on his retirement 30 years ago. Donald has remained a firm friend of the Law School. And I greatly valued the 20 years we served together on the Contracts and Commercial Law Reform Committee.

May I also say how honoured I am that a number of you have come from a distance. I'd never myself have presumed to suggest any one should do that. But the Dean had no such inhibition, so, very many thanks for coming.

And to all of you, thank you for being here.

Finally, my very best thanks to Bernard Brown who, by reading part of the lecture, will put all of us in his debt, particularly because he'll be reading the most difficult bits![1]

Choice of a Topic

I hesitated a long time before agreeing to give a valedictory lecture. It's all very well for someone like Jock Brookfield who is expert on an interesting, important, and topical subject like the Treaty of Waitangi.[2] But a contract lawyer has much greater problems. Who is interested in my kind of contract anyway? I can imagine what

* Text of a valedictory lecture delivered at the University of Auckland on 21 November 1994.

[1] I was suffering from a throat infection on the evening of the lecture.

[2] Professor Brookfield's valedictory was delivered at Auckland on 21 November 1993.

most of my current students would say—at least judging by examination scripts I've been marking lately! If I were to talk about the future of contract or, for that matter, about the future of legal education,[3] I might well appear to be a prophet of doom. On the other hand, a retrospective, drawing together the themes on which I've written over the years, could make me seem to be the only person left in step. And since there are quite a few of those themes, the subject matter would make the lecture too dense. At the end of the day I've decided not to even try to hide it. I *am* the only one in step! And there's the consolation that it will be the content, not the audience, which is too dense.

I Am a 'Formalist'

But why, you may ask, an 'underview' rather than an 'overview' of contract? The answer is that I belong to a declining academic underclass, what you might call an endangered species. Both in New Zealand and overseas, I'm classified as a 'formalist'. In fact, according to a book published in England in 1987,[4] I'm a quintessential formalist, in the same extreme category, it seems, as Lord Diplock![5] Well, in the words of Lord Justice Asquith, that is a consequence I must face with such fortitude as I can command.[6]

The word 'formalist', you'll appreciate, is an academic swear word, a currently fashionable put down. As I apply it to myself, it comprehends those who believe that the answers to most legal questions can be found within the law; that the common law is a more or less coherent body of rules, doctrines, principles, and concepts which for that reason, and because of the doctrine of precedent, is reasonably predictable; that ideally, at least, it endeavours to treat like cases alike; and that it ought to develop incrementally rather than by arbitrary fiat or from the merely personal predilections of the judiciary.

But I'm Not the Only One

At one time, of course, it was a perfectly respectable position to hold. In fact, it constituted the mainstream of contract scholarship in this country. And I think it can be claimed that New Zealand contract scholarship has not been negligible. In addition to a considerable number of articles and notes in international journals over the years, there have been monographs published in England by CB Morison

[3] My inaugural lecture was 'A Law Teacher Looks at his Trade' (1968) 3 *NZULR* 38.

[4] Adams & Brownsword, *Understanding Contract Law*, 121, 153. My review of this book appeared at (1988) 104 *LQR* 308.

[5] See the same authors, 'Understanding Contracts as a Social Phenomenon' (1987) *Legal Studies* 205, 218.

[6] *Candler v Crane, Christmas & Co* [1951] 2 KB 164 (CA) 195.

on Rescission, Sir John Salmond on Contract, James Williams on the Statute of Frauds, RG McElroy on Frustration, AG Davis on Commercial Letters of Credit, Martyn Finlay on Privity, and myself on Exception Clauses. To those should be added Sir Alexander Turner's rewrites of the three Spencer Bower books. I would also add Professor McLauchlan's book on the Parol Evidence rule and Dawson & McLauchlan on the Contractual Remedies Act, both published locally but of clear international quality and significance.

That record is creditable for a country with so small a population and so far as books published overseas are concerned, may well be particularly so. What made this last feature possible, of course, was the unifying effect of appeal to the Privy Council.

I mention this tradition of New Zealand contract scholarship because all these books published overseas were formalist in the sense in which I have used that word. And though I wouldn't presume to categorise Professor McLauchlan and Mr Dawson themselves, I think the same can be said of their two books also.

The irony is that though formalists like me have become the Fred Flintstones of the academic world both here and overseas, there are still quite a few judges and other members of the profession who in practice operate within the same 'outmoded' tradition. To mention a recent example, at the admission ceremony in Hamilton earlier this year,[7] the Chief Justice spoke of the need to maintain the rule of law, and saw nothing wrong with the law being a conservative institution not given to rapid transformation. At the same function, the titular leader of the New Zealand Bar asserted that the most critical element of the law was its consistency. And some of you will have noticed an extract from a book review by Judge Posner reproduced a few weeks ago in the *New Zealand Law Journal*.[8] In it, that one-time typically realist US law professor defended the place in law of rules and principles. He is not the only American academic to have found his or her views on formalism being modified by experience on the bench.[9]

Why, then, is this long-standing tradition nowadays so much in the academic descendant? I think there are two basic reasons. One is the influence of United States' legal scholarship. The other is that some degree of uncertainty is unavoidable, at least in the short term, in any system of judge-made law.

United States' Legal Scholarship

At one time, the approach to legal scholarship in the United States was not so different from that on the other side of the Atlantic. What started the eventual

[7] Reported at [1994] *NZLJ* 254.

[8] [1994] *NZLJ* 356.

[9] Compare, Edwards, 'The Growing Disjunction between Legal Education and the Legal Profession' (1992) 91 *Mich L Rev* 34.

divergence, I believe, was the plight of teachers in the national law schools of the United States, which is a federation where every state has a different common law. And for a number of reasons, which included an elected judiciary and an expanding geographical frontier, the differences between the various common laws could be significant. Since one could not hope to teach one's students the separate common law of every state, how did one cope with a subject like contract?

One possibility was to return to the fountainhead. That was the solution adopted at the Harvard Law School by Dean Langdell, who is widely regarded as the inventor of the case method, a means of instruction as much concerned with technique as with content. In 1871, he produced a case book on Contract, followed later by what was in effect a textbook,[10] both of which were based principally on English cases. Understandably, that solution held little appeal for teachers of a more nationalist persuasion. For them the solution had to be an indigenous one. But the diversity of the case law of the various states was such that, in the words of the great Professor Corbin, authority could be found 'for both sides of almost any question'.[11] Inevitably, this diversity led to scepticism. If common law reasoning could lead to differing results in different states, the inference to be drawn was that the real reasons for legal decisions could not be those which the judges articulated. And if the reasons given could not be believed, it followed that the law, as such, was largely indeterminate. The reasons of policy which provided the real answers to legal problems were to be found outside the law. Hence the recourse, over the years, to such disciplines as sociology, political science, psychology, economics, literature and more recently Marxism, feminism, structuralism, and other aspects of modernist and post-modernist thought.[12]

These realist insights have led to, or been reinforced by, several other notions. One is the theory that all law is purposive, from which there's been a tendency to conclude that if a particular law has a particular result, that must also be its purpose. That purpose should dictate the incidents of the law and anything inconsistent with it ought to be discarded. A well-known application of this approach is the reasonable expectations theory of the nature of contract. Contracts arouse expectations. Enforcement protects them. It follows that the purpose of the law of contract must be to protect expectations, at least to the extent that they are reasonable. That purpose in turn ought to determine what the incidents of the law of contract should be. Professor Waddams' well-known text book on the *Law of Contract* in Canada is a sustained illustration of this sort of reasoning.

Another realist insight is that the reasons judges give for distinguishing between cases are merely technical or conceptual and, having therefore no substance, can be disregarded. This greatly raises the level of generality of legal decisions and, by thus multiplying apparent inconsistencies of result, reinforces the perception of

[10] It formed part of the second edition of the case book.

[11] 'The Law and the Judges' (1914) 3 *Yale Review* 236, 246, cited in La Piana, *Logic & Experience* (1994) 147.

[12] See, eg, Tushnet, 'Legal Scholarship in the United States; An Overview' (1987) 50 *MLR* 804.

indeterminacy. Let me give just one illustration, taken from that book published in England in 1987 to which I referred earlier.[13] Many of you will remember *Hopkins v Tanqueray*[14] which concerned the sale of a racehorse by auction at Tattersalls. The day before the auction the seller told a potential buyer that the horse was perfectly sound in every respect. That same potential buyer was the successful bidder the following day. The horse proved to be unsound but it was held that the seller's statement had not been intended to be a warranty. There were several reasons. Horses were customarily sold at Tattersalls without warranty. A separate arrangement for a warranty not notified to the other bidders would probably have been illegal. It would certainly have been contrary to the code of honour of the racing fraternity. The conclusion had to be that the contractual intention necessary for a warranty had been lacking.

The authors of this book contrast *Hopkins v Tanqueray* with the subsequent Irish case of *Schawel v Reade*,[15] where an assurance about the soundness of a horse had been made three weeks before its sale by negotiation. It was held that there was a warranty. A formalist like me would say that the two cases are clearly distinguishable, and that the circumstances surrounding the sale by auction in the earlier case negatived the sort of inference of contractual intention which could quite properly be drawn in *Schawel v Reade*. In the book, though, the two cases, because they both involve pre-contractual statements, are treated as inconsistent and as being explicable only on the basis 'that realist Judges had manipulated the criteria in order to achieve a desired result'.[16]

Another aspect of realism is the idea that, in contract matters, the function of the court is to resolve disputes by balancing competing policies and interests rather than to adjudicate according to law. That perception was reinforced in America by an emphasis in administrative law on balancing the competing interests of individuals and the state.[17] I don't doubt that recourse to the courts is one means of determining disputes. But except where they are exercising a completely unfettered discretion, the determination they make is required by law to be an adjudication according to law. If different kinds of resolution are sought, there are alternative agencies in my view much better suited to provide them.

Yet another realist notion is that, until reversed, the law is whatever the most recent case decided it to be, irrespective of the position occupied by the court in the hierarchy. On this view, the weight of a decision will depend on the degree to which it stands in a continuum rather than on the authority of the court that made it.

[13] Above, note 4.
[14] (1854) 23 LJCP 162.
[15] [1913] 2 IR 64.
[16] At 129.
[17] Tushnet, above note 12.

All of this goes back to the realist rejection of what Justice Holmes referred to as the 'theological' view of law;[18] a rejection, that is, of the idea that the common law is based on doctrines, principles, rules and concepts. In 1960, Grant Gilmore, the *Death of Contract* man, ascribed the emergence of realism in the United States to the overwhelming proliferation there of reported cases.[19] That proliferation, he suggested, was overwhelming because of the way in which the doctrine of precedent is understood in America. According to Gilmore, a case in the United States stands only for its particular facts so that to find an answer to a legal problem one must search for a case on all fours with one's own. I take that to be the sort of approach under which, if one's client has a broken arm, one looks out all the cases on broken arms. In England by contrast, where the doctrine of precedent accepts the reasons given by the judges for their decisions, one would merely have to look out the odd leading case on negligence. It is this different view of precedent which according to Gilmore has made it possible for the English to continue to live with an old-time case law system.

Dean Langdell's answer to the problem of proliferation was, in effect, the English one. The common law, he believed, was based on principles which could be established by recourse to a relatively limited number of cases. That particular solution was, of course, unacceptable to the realists.

I am not suggesting all realists hold all the views I've mentioned. Not all of them are fully consistent. Nor am I saying that it is wrong to hold them. After all, lawyers much more distinguished than I have subscribed to them. I may also to some extent have overstated or misstated the realist position though, if so, I am doing no more to realists than they do to formalists.

What is one to make, for example, of the ascription to formalists of such bold propositions as:

1. 'It is no consideration to do what you are already legally bound to do'.
   Or
2. 'There can be no relief for mistake in contract unless the mistake is that of each of the parties and unless it makes the subject matter "a different thing" from what the contractual subject matter was supposed to be'.[20]

Where the Canadian writers, who ascribed those statements to formalists got them from, I find hard to imagine. They cannot represent the views of those formalists who have any command of the common law of contract.

[18] He described Langdell as 'perhaps, the greatest living legal theologian' in (1880) 14 *Am L Sch Rev* 233.

[19] 'Legal Realism: Its Cause and Cure' (1961) 70 *Yale LJ* 1037.

[20] Reiter & Swan, *Studies in Contract Law* (1980) 3. My review appeared in (1981) 19 *UWOLR* 357.

Realism Outside the United States

I believe the realist views I've been describing have to be seen against the background from which they came: that of a federation where every state has a different common law. It is understandable that these views may also have some appeal in Canada and Australia, both being federations, even though in one respect their situations differ significantly from that of the United States. As an inheritance from the days of Privy Council appeals, both those countries have a single common law. That is, the Supreme Court and High Court respectively settle the law for the whole country. On the other hand, it *is* possible for the courts in the different states or provinces at any one time to reach different conclusions on particular questions of law. When that happens, realists are doubtless tempted to conclude that there are therefore as many common laws as there are states or provinces, whatever the constitutional position might be.

When we come to unitary systems, however, such as those of England and New Zealand, it seems to me that the principal justification for realism no longer exists. No one suggests that, because judges of the High Court sitting in different parts of the country may disagree, there is for that reason one common law (say) for Auckland and another for the rest of New Zealand. (Though I seem to recollect a well-known commentator on the judiciary suggesting years ago that, thanks to the activities of a certain stipendiary magistrate, there did exist a separate law for Auckland's North Shore.)

I hope no one thinks I believe the common law of contract is a perfect code or that the common law system has no problems or failings. After all, I was involved in statutory law reform for 20 years. As I said at the beginning, the uncertainties inherent in the common law system have certainly contributed to the scepticism with which my type of formalism is nowadays regarded.

The Problems of Judge-Made Law

The problem is of course that the common law derives from adjudications in particular cases by judges who have to work under considerable constraints and who have largely to depend on arguments adduced by advocates who are similarly constrained. Academic lawyers can spend months or years thinking about and researching a legal problem. Barristers and judges usually enjoy no such luxury. Inevitably there will be times when either or both get it wrong. What really matters in the long term, I believe, is the capacity of the system to rectify mistakes where they occur.

I think much could be done to dispel the myth of indeterminacy in contract if first, we could get the basics right, and second, could avoid a few traps into which common lawyers can easily fall. In what follows, I shall try to illustrate what I mean. (It is at this stage that the content becomes really dense!)

Getting the Basics Right

Thanks to the pressures under which lawyers work it is never very easy to persuade them of the importance of basic principles. Well-known judges like Lord Denning[21] and Lord Goff[22] deny the value of legal theory—which in their case is rather hard to take seriously since they both clearly work or have worked from basic premises, whether they articulate them or not. More surprising was to come across, as I did a couple of months ago, an academic lawyer writing that basic concepts might be important in the Law of Restitution but didn't really matter in Contract and Tort.[23] That is simply not true. The development of the Law of Contract has been significantly affected by the application of basic concepts, starting with theories of the nature of contract and of the reasons why the law recognises and enforces them.[24]

There is, of course, no time tonight to go into these foundation questions in detail, but at least it is possible to look briefly at some of the difficulties.

Contract Definitions

Contracts are commonly defined as either promises or agreements which the law will enforce. Neither definition is more than partly true. Some promises the law enforces are not contracts and not all contracts are agreements. Likewise, the classic contract theories can, also, all be shown to be similarly incomplete.

Contract Theories

The famous will theory, that contracts should be enforced because they are expressions of the human will, has been tremendously influential but besides being rather too metaphysical to be acceptable nowadays, it is inconsistent with the observable facts. By and large Contract is concerned with the will and intention of the parties only insofar as these can be deduced objectively from their words and actions. There is certainly no guarantee that what will be enforced is their actually held will or intention.

[21] In his book, *The Family Story* (1981) 240.

[22] According, that is, to a lecture given by him on a visit to the University of Auckland Law School.

[23] Unhappily, I failed to keep a note of the citation!

[24] I dealt with these matters at much greater length in 'The Essence of Contract' (1988) 1 *JCL* 91, 94 *et seq* reprinted as Chapter 2 of *Assumption*.

Then there is the theory that all contracts are bargains. That is not only untrue of systems which have no doctrine of consideration. It takes no account of our own contracts by deed which also require no consideration. The theory that promises ought to be kept and should be enforced for that very reason also has its drawbacks, and not only because the law doesn't in fact enforce all promises. (Human nature being what it is, that is just as well.) But there is also the widely held notion that promises are merely statements of intention to do something in the future. From that, it has been deduced that it is not possible to promise the impossible, or to promise the existence of a past or present fact. Both these conclusions are demonstrably inconsistent with the common law. It is perfectly possible to contract to sell a non-existent tanker on a non-existent reef[25] or to give a warranty of existing quality on a sale of goods.

I've already mentioned the reasonable expectations theory of contract. Reasonable expectations may be aroused by a contract but they are certainly not necessary to its existence. Much the same can be said about the alternative theory that contracts arise or derive from actions performed in reasonable reliance. If that were true, contracts to be performed in the future could not exist until performance began.

All these theories still have their adherents. All are flawed because each seizes on a feature of some contracts and makes that feature the basis of what purports to be a comprehensive theory. But all is not lost. There *is* a theory of contract which I like to think is general enough to cover all contracts of every kind, in every legal system, and in every age.[26]

Contracts as Assumptions of Contractual Obligation

The theory starts by agreeing with the common law that a promise is more than a mere statement of intention; rather, it is an assumption or, taking upon oneself, of obligation. Ordinarily, of course, the obligation a promisor assumes is a moral or a social one. But, as we know, moral or social obligations are not always kept. There are times when it will be in the interests of a promisor to take upon herself a more obviously binding commitment, usually because she wishes to secure something in return. One way, historically, of undertaking a higher level of commitment was to swear an oath and, by so doing, to assume a religious obligation. What the institution of contract does is to provide a facility by which it is made possible for a promisor to undertake yet another form of obligation, a specifically legal contractual one.

[25] *McRae v Commonwealth Disposals Commission* (1951) 84 CLR 377.

[26] This theory was expounded in 'The Essence of Contract', above note 24 at 190 *et seq*.

On this reasoning, a contract is a promise or undertaking in respect of which legal contractual obligation has been assumed by a means which the law recognises as effective for that purpose. To make a contract, therefore, one has to take contractual obligation upon oneself, by the use of a legally recognised means.

The means which the law recognises for denoting contracts have varied widely from time to time and from one legal system to another. The list includes shaking hands and having a drink (traces of which remain in our own society). But it also includes such things as reciting a formula, mingling blood, exchanging hostages or tokens (which the Anglo-Saxons called weds—whence our word 'wedding'), and bending down to touch the ground. One means I rather like was encountered by Burton on his search for the source of the Nile. It required the parties to blow a white liquid in each other's faces. In the most recent to have come to my notice, the parties blow an hallucinogenic powder into each other noses. In that jurisdiction, I gather, making contracts has tended to become something of a habit.

All these are means by which an intention to assume contractual obligation could be manifested, and a contract made, by the use of concrete signs or symbols. Our own equivalent is the execution of a deed. For simple contracts by agreement, though, the means we have developed is rather more abstract, consisting as it does of exchanging considerations with an intention to contract, the presence of the intention being determined objectively.

The notion that contracts involve an assumption of some kind of obligation is not new. The word 'assumption' appears often enough in contract cases and for centuries the main common law remedy for breach of contract was the writ of assumpsit, which expresses the same idea. If it is once accepted that the obligation assumed by making a contractual promise is in fact a contractual obligation, a significant number of conceptual problems disappear from our law, as I shall shortly try to demonstrate. What I find odd, though, is how widespread is the view that the obligations assumed under a contract are not contractual but merely moral or social.

Associated with that widespread perception is the equally common view that in contract the law *imposes* legal obligation on those who make promises and fail to keep them; that the function of the law of contract is not to provide a facility but to punish non-conforming behaviour. That in turn supports the idea that contract is a species of tort and as such is part of a single law of obligations. It follows, of course, that if the law imposes contractual obligations anyway, there can be no room for the promisor to take them upon herself.

It is true that the law prescribes and limits the extent to which it will, by lending enforcement to contracts, enable obligations to be assumed. It can also impose particular obligations on those who have contracted. But the parties become subject to that law because in the first instance they have taken it upon themselves to do so by a means which the law recognises as effective for the purpose. The sanctions applied on breach are there, not for the sake of controlling behaviour, but because without legal sanctions no legal obligations could be assumed. In other words, contract is a facility by which, within certain constraints, the apparatus of a state is made available to its citizens to empower them legally to regulate their own affairs. The constraints, of course, can be considerable, which is why I never myself use the expression 'freedom of contract'. It is nevertheless still a remarkable privilege.

One consequence of the contrary view, that contract obligation is imposed rather than assumed, is that it is the law rather than the parties which has to determine whether a promise is a contract. The search for an answer to that problem is what lies behind the classical contract theories, with all their inadequacies. If it were once recognised that it is the parties who choose which of their promises are contractual, the problems would disappear. It would also be more apparent that the real reasons the law lends it enforcement are not metaphysics, economics, morality, or a concern to protect expectations or reliance, but simply the classic concerns of peace, order, and good government. The notion of contract as assumption also sheds light on several other basic problems of the common law system.

The Doctrine of Consideration

One of these is the doctrine of consideration, which many have found confusing. The idea that consideration is essential to the very notion of a contract is a typical common law conceit, but it is quite untrue. If it were true, common law countries would be the only ones which knew what a contract was. Then there is the bargain theory, that consideration is concerned with equality of exchange and that the functions of contract are purely economic—again, quite untrue as a general proposition. There is also the idea that consideration is merely a fictional device to enable the courts to pick and choose, on other grounds, which agreements they will enforce. A particular misconception which has become increasingly common has been confusion between the consideration for a contract on the one hand, and the performance of the contract on the other. One example is the so-called joint promisee principle devised by the High Court of Australia in *Coulls v Bagot's Executor and Trustee Co Ltd.*[27] Their idea was that if, say, a husband and wife were each to order a meal in a restaurant and when they left the husband paid, it was the husband who provided the consideration. If that were really true, and since consideration is necessary for the *formation* of a contract, there would be no contract in existence while the couple ate their meal, unless it had been paid for in advance. Clearly, in an executory bilateral contract of that kind, the contract arises when the meal is ordered and the consideration is to be found not in payment, which is matter of performance, but within the promises, express or implied, which are exchanged at that point. In the case I'm referring to,[28] it was

[27] (1967) 119 CLR 460; 'Consideration and the Joint Promisee' [1978] *CLJ* 301 reprinted as Chapter 5 of *Assumption.*

[28] *Lockett v Charles* [1938] 4 All ER 170.

because the wife impliedly promised to pay that the court was able to hold that she was a party to the contract. For myself, I would be even more specific and say that the consideration the parties offer each other is not their promises as such but the reciprocal assumptions of legal contractual obligation expressed in those promises.

A precisely similar confusion between consideration and performance occurred in the recent English Court of Appeal case of *Williams v Roffey Bros & Nicholls (Contractors) Ltd*[29] where it was held that consideration lay in the benefits to the promisee of the actual performance of a contractual promise that had previously been made to that same promisee. That is something which a differently constituted Court of Appeal[30] has found impossible to reconcile with the decision of the House of Lords in *Foakes v Beer*.[31]

Then there is the wider question whether it can be good consideration to promise something already promised, not to the same promisee but to a third party, as the Privy Council has twice held to be the case in recent years.[32] The answer is 'yes' because the same obligation can be assumed separately to more than one person. On the other hand, a purported second assumption of an obligation already (and still) owed to the *same* party is a mere tautology, a vain repetition, and cannot constitute consideration, as indeed the law maintained consistently until *Williams v Roffey Bros*.[33]

The only time when actual performance can be consideration is where a promise is made to reward the performance of an act which is not itself promised—the classic unilateral contract. If I promise to pay a reward to whoever finds and returns my dog, no one is bound to look for it but, if someone does return the dog, consideration has been provided by performance and I become obliged to pay. In the case of a bilateral contract by contrast, consideration always lies in the assumption of obligation. Where such a contract fails for want of consideration, it will not be because of economic disparity (after all, the promise of a peppercorn is enough) but because the promise itself is void for uncertainty, or is otherwise an ineffective assumption of contractual obligation.[34]

[29] [1991] QB1; 'Consideration and Benefit in Fact and in Law' (1990) 3 *JCL* 23 reprinted as Chapter 3 of *Assumption*.

[30] *In re Selectmove Ltd* [1995] 1 WLR 474.

[31] (1884) 9 App Cas 605.

[32] *New Zealand Shipping Co Ltd v A M Satterthwaite & Co Ltd* [1975] AC 154; *Salmond and Spraggon (Australia) Pty Ltd v Port Jackson Stevedoring Pty Ltd* [1981] 1 WLR 138; 'Pity the Poor Stevedore!' [1981] *CLJ* 13.

[33] 'The Essence of Contract', above note 24 at 198.

[34] See further 'The Essence of Contract', above note 24 at 192–193, 198.

Intention

Another basic concept which has been found confusing is intention.[35] Intention is of course central to contract and it crops up in several contexts. There is intention to contract, intention to offer and to accept, and intention in relation to interpretation and the implication of terms.

There have been two main sources of confusion. One I've already mentioned is confusion between subjective and objective intention. Subjective intention is rightly a concern of the criminal law, so much of which is directed to deterring naughty behaviour and punishing guilt. But the concerns of contract are quite different. I've already suggested that contractual sanctions are not punishments. Sanctions are there to help define and determine the character of the obligations undertaken. Without the sanctions, there could be no contractual obligation to assume. The concern of contract then is not with punishment, but with the needs of the parties to communicate to each other, and to third persons, just what it is they are binding themselves to. The concern of contract is also with the need of each party to be able to rely on the inferences to be drawn from the respective words and actions of the other. Accordingly, the common law has regard primarily to objective intention, the main exceptions being where one party actually knows the subjective intention of the other.

The other source of confusion in relation to intention has been what Professor Lon Fuller called 'nominalism', by which he meant the belief that one can intend only those things which are present in the mind at the relevant time.[36] An example would be the belief that one cannot intend to be bound by the contents of a document if one does not know what they are. Another is the belief that implied terms are sheer fictions if they apply to matters the parties did not consciously have in mind at the time they made their contract. The problem lies partly in thinking we cannot intend something in the abstract, and partly in ignoring the fact that statements of intention are very commonly hedged by qualifications which are none the less real because we do not state them or have not consciously adverted to them. If I tell my tenant she can bring a pet on to the premises and she brings home an elephant or a crocodile, I would be entitled to say I didn't intend that sort of pet, even though at the time I'd given no thought to such animals.

Damages

If we can get the basics right and, in particular, if contracts are seen as assumptions of obligation, light is also thrown on several problems of damages. If contracts

[35] An article on intention in contract is still 'in preparation' (subsequently published as 'Reflections on Intention in the Law of Contract' [2006] *NZLR* 183 and reprinted as Chapter 2 of this volume).

[36] 'American Legal Realism' (1934) 8 *U Pa L Rev* 429, 444–46. See also *Basic Contract Law* by Fuller & Eisenberg (5th edn, 1990) 699 *et seq.*

are assumptions, the primary enquiry ought always to be 'what obligations did the promisor assume?' Prima facie, the sanction ought where practicable to be either specific performance, or the cost of getting someone else to perform. If, as I've suggested, sanctions are the other side of obligation, anything which limits the sanction also limits the extent to which obligation can be assumed. This can come about through agreement, by the use of exception or limitation clauses, which is why I have argued for so long that the real function of such clauses is to help delimit obligations.[37] It can also come about because of the way sanctions are applied by the courts. An excellent illustration of the latter is provided by *Tito v Waddell No 2*[38] where the three governments of Britain, Australia, and New Zealand promised the inhabitants of Ocean Island that once they had extracted the phosphate they would replant the island. This they failed to do. The island became uninhabitable and the islanders were transported 1600 miles south to an island in the Fiji group. When they eventually sued for the cost of replanting their homeland, it was held that, since they were no longer in a position to carry out a replanting, they were entitled only to the diminution in value of their land. What that means, on the facts of that case, is that it was not possible in law for the governments to accept an unqualified obligation to replant. Having moved the Islanders elsewhere, they had bound themselves only to compensate for the value of the land destroyed. I don't doubt that in some situations compensation for diminution in value is what parties contract about. But I do doubt whether that is what was really intended under the Ocean Island contracts or was the obligation the parties thought was being assumed. The counter argument, that to give the Islanders the cost of what they had both bargained and paid for would be to give them a windfall, seems to me an abuse of language. Over the last few months, the English Court of Appeal has been strongly moving back to acceptance of the cost of performance as the normal measure of damages and has been saying that it is no business of defendants what plaintiffs do with their damages.[39] To some extent, our own Court of Appeal has also been having second thoughts.[40] It is ironic, therefore, that the New Zealand legislature should at present be considering a Bill to prevent the application of that same approach to covenants to render up premises in good repair, at the end of a lease.[41]

Another problem is whether contract damages should be based, like tort damages, on the foreseeable consequences of the wrongful act, or whether they should depend on the obligations undertaken. For example, should damages in contract for loss of enjoyment, anxiety, and emotional hurt be confined, as they are in England and Australia, to situations where a particular state of mind has itself

[37] Beginning with *Exception Clauses*, especially Ch 1, reprinted as Chapter 6 of *Assumption*.

[38] [1977] Ch 106.

[39] *Ruxley Electronics Ltd v Forsyth* [1994] 1 WLR 650; *Darlington Borough Council v Wiltshier Northern Ltd* [1995] 1 WLR 356; *Samuel Moore Foods Ltd v Gaiger Bros Ltd* (unreported, 1 July 1994).

[40] *Maori Trustee v Rogross Farms Ltd* [1994] 3 NZLR 410.

[41] That proposal has since been withdrawn.

been contracted for,[42] or should they be an automatic constituent of damages in virtually all but commercial cases, as in New Zealand?[43] Similarly, should liability for the loss of pre-contractual expenditure be confined to cases where that liability was accepted under the contract, or should it be an automatic constituent of damages for breach of the subsequent contract as in *Anglia TV v Reed*?[44] In the spoiled holiday[45] and *Anglia TV* cases, and in the New Zealand cases on mental states,[46] what has happened is that the rules governing remoteness of damages have been used, not to restrict the damages recoverable as they were originally designed to do, but, in effect, to add to and extend the obligations undertaken in the same way as foreseeability goes to both liability and remoteness in tort.[47] A final point concerns damages for breach of a contract to confer a benefit on a third party. The traditional view has been that if the promisor fails to perform, the promise can recover nothing, since the loss is suffered not by the promisee but by the third-party beneficiary. In *Woodar Investment Development Ltd v Wimpey Construction UK Ltd*,[48] Lord Scarman suggested an answer could be found to that problem. I agree. In my view, the promise ought to be able to recover the cost of securing someone else to perform the promisor's obligations.[49]

So much for the basics. I want now to turn briefly to five traps which are very easy to fall into and which make for unnecessary uncertainty in the law. I've elected to reveal there are *five* traps, despite Bernard Brown's sage advice that to do so would be likely to make your hearts sink even further!

Five Traps

Unjustified Generalisations

The first of these concerns unjustified generalisations. One type I mentioned earlier is the generalisation which takes no account of the actual reasoning in cases which involve very roughly similar facts. The example I gave was the difference between *Hopkins v Tanqueray* and *Schawel v Reade*. Another type is the generalisation from the existence of defences like mistake, duress, and misrepresentation to a positive requirement that consent to contract be full, free, and true—a conclusion which is completely inconsistent with common law notions

[42] *Hayes v James & Chas Dodd* [1990] 2 All ER 815 (CA); *Baltic Shipping Co v Dillon* (1993) 176 CLR 344.

[43] *Mouat v Clark Boyce* [1992] 2 NZLR 599 (CA).

[44] [1972] 1 QB 60 (CA).

[45] Eg, *Jackson v Horizon Holidays* [1974] 1 WLR 1468 (CA).

[46] As, eg, *Mouat v Clarke Boyce* [1992] 2 NZLR 599 (CA).

[47] A point made rather obliquely at (1974) 6 *NZULR* 92.

[48] [1980] 1 WLR 277 (HL).

[49] 'The Essence of Contract', above note 24 at 200.

of objectivity. A not dissimilar case is the generalisation from the defences of fraud and unconscionability to a positive requirement of good faith, particularly in negotiation, which some academics maintain despite denial by the courts.[50] A fourth example is the generalisation from quite discrete lines of authority to the existence of a new doctrine, fundamental breach being one example. As Justice Holmes once wrote: 'We do not get a new and single principle by simply giving a single name to all the cases to be accounted for'.[51]

Characterisation

A second pitfall is the inaccurate characterisation of a legal problem. A classic example of this was *Midland Silicones Ltd v Scruttons Ltd*,[52] a claim in tort against a stevedoring company which had dropped and damaged some cargo. The company relied on a limitation clause contained in the bill of lading to which, of course, the stevedore was not a party. The House of Lords characterised the problem as one of contract and held in consequence that, there being no privity of contract, the stevedore was unprotected. Had they characterised the problem as one of tort rather than contract, it ought to have been clear that being party to a contract was not necessary for the exclusion of liability. Another well-known example is *Raffles v Wichelhaus*[53] which concerned those two ships named 'Peerless', from Bombay. What was actually a case which failed for uncertainty has since been characterised as one dealing with mistake, leading eventually, by a rather convoluted route, to our own rather controversial *Conlon v Ozolins*.[54] A further example occurred when the use of the words 'without prejudice' was characterised as purely evidential in a case where they were clearly intended to show an absence of intention to contract.[55] Deviation was wrongly characterised by the House of Lords in *Hain v Tate & Lyle*[56] as being an ordinary breach of condition. One could go on.

Ambiguity

A third pitfall can arise from the use of one word to cover more than one concept. The classic illustration here is the use of the word 'rescission' to cover both discharge for breach at common law and rescission *ab inito* in Equity.

[50] Eg, Brownsword, 'Two Concepts of Good Faith' (1994) 7 *JCL* 197.

[51] *The Common Law* (1882) 204.

[52] [1962] AC 446; *Exception Clauses*, Ch 9.

[53] (1864) 2 H & C 906; 159 ER 375.

[54] [1984] 1 NZLR 489; 'The Contracts and Commercial Law Reform Committee and the Contract Statutes' (1988) 13 *NZULR* 160, 173 *et seq*.

[55] *Tomlin v Standard Telephones & Cables* [1969] 3 All ER 201 (CA). See 'Without Prejudice Communications' [1979] *NZLJ* 87.

[56] [1936] 2 All ER 597. See 'The Effect of Discharge for Breach on Exception Clauses' [1970] *CLJ* 221 reprinted as Chapter 8 Part I in this volume.

Confusion between the two in England had the result that for many years damages could not be recovered on the discharge for breach of a contract for the sale and purchase of land.[57] Another well-known example is the use of the words 'fundamental breach' to cover both discharge for breach and also those extreme types of breach which, according to the doctrine of fundamental breach, no exception clause could exclude. One result of this confusion was the decision of the House of Lords in *Ashington Piggeries Ltd v Christopher Hill Ltd*,[58] that there is no failure to comply with the description by which goods are sold if the goods delivered are of the same *genus* as those contracted for; peas rather than beans for example. One wonders whether those who drafted our Consumer Guarantees Act appreciated that. Another example is the confusion between promissory conditions and conditions precedent to obligation. That sort of confusion led some judges to believe that employers must pay workers for work not done while they were on strike, unless the employer had actually dismissed them.[59] A further example which has been of particular concern to me has been the use of the word 'relief' to cover both relief proper, and remedies for enforcement.[60] The contract statutes for which the Contracts and Commercial Law Reform Committee were responsible characteristically set out, not so much to change the substantive law, as to expand the powers of the courts to grant relief from particular aspects of contracts, or from the effects of the law where the common law had become rather inflexible. In the event, though, intended relief provisions have been perceived as creating new remedies for enforcement, the strongest example being the Contractual Remedies Act. There, section 9 has been treated as creating an independent claim for damages notwithstanding that it is expressly stated in three consecutive sections of the Act that rights to damages are not to be effected. As Mr Dugdale has pointed out, if the legislature really did intend a radical reform of the law of damages, why should it have restricted the reform to contracts which had been cancelled, and have left damages for all other breaches unchanged?[61] Another disquieting illustration has been the use of the Contractual Mistakes Act to turn the defence of mistake into a cause of action.[62]

Lastly, a continuing potential source for confusion is the treatment of the word 'unconscionable' as a synonym for 'unconscientious'. Historically, the former has

[57] The so-called 'heresy' of Cyprian Williams identified by Albery QC at (1975) 91 *LQR* 337. I had earlier made the same point in 'Recovery of Unpaid Deposits' (1973) 5 *NZULR* 293.

[58] [1972] AC 441. See 'Correspondence with Description in the Law of Sale of Goods' (1976) 50 *ALJ* 17 reprinted as Chapter 6 in this volume.

[59] Eg, *McClenaghan v Bank of New Zealand* [1978] 2 NZLR 528 about which I wrote in 'Wages for Workers on Strike' (1982) 10 *NZULR* 177.

[60] This is something to which I drew attention in 'The Contracts and Commercial Law Reform Committee and the Contract Statutes', above note 54 at 180 *et seq* and subsequently in 'Remedy and Relief under the Contractual Remedies Act 1979 (NZ)' (1993) 6 *JCL* 141 and 'Allocation of Risk under the Contractual Remedies Act 1977' [1993] *NZ Recent Law Review* 434.

[61] See Dugdale & Walker, 'Harmonisation of the Sale of Goods Act 1908 and the Contractual Remedies Act 1979' *Contract Statutes Review*, NZ Law Commission Report No 25 (1993) 122.

[62] 'Allocation of Risk under the Contractual Mistakes Act 1977', above note 60.

required reprehensible conduct of a particular kind. The latter refers to a general precondition of equitable remedies and relief, and can involve something no more reprehensible than an innocent misrepresentation.

Either/Or

The fourth pitfall is the propensity of common lawyers to think in extremes of either/or. A well-known example in New Zealand concerns concurrent liability in contract and tort. At one time it seems to have been supposed that either the parties to a contract could never be liable to each other in tort or, alternatively, that they always could. The correct answer is, of course, that in some cases claims can be brought concurrently and in others they cannot.[63] Then there is the classic common law perception that contractual promises are absolute rather than qualified. This has made the implication of terms qualifying such promises extremely difficult. There is also the difficulty many common lawyers have experienced with a case like *Bowmakers v Barnet Instruments*[64] which establishes that one can recover goods of which possession, but not title, has passed under an illegal hire-purchase agreement, once the hirer commits a discharging breach of the hire-purchase contract, as for example by failing to pay the instalments due under the agreement. This is supposed to amount to an enforcement of the illegal contract. In fact it is not. The owner sues on the basis of her ownership. The relevance of the illegal agreement is only as evidence of how far the owner's rights of possession were transferred away. A further criticism made of the *Bowmaker* rule is that it would enable, say, an accomplice to recover a murder weapon. But this is another example of the either/or approach. In fact, the courts have an inherent jurisdiction to refuse to hear scandalous and impertinent actions, as was demonstrated in the famous highwaymen's case[65] where one highwayman sued the other for a share of the spoils. Both plaintiff and defendant ended up on the gallows. I should add that their solicitors were both fined and one of them was in due course transported to Australia!

'Sauce for the Goose'

The fifth and last type of trap I want to mention might be called 'sauce for the goose' by which I mean a failure to accept the implications of one finding for another. To give just one example, the profession quite properly protested when

[63] 'Contract, Tort and Contributory Negligence' [1982] *NZLJ* 294.

[64] [1945] KB 64 (CA); 'Another look at *Bowmakers v Barnet Instruments* (1972) 35 *MLR* 38 reprinted as Chapter 9 in this volume.

[65] *Everet v Williams* (1725) reported (1893) 9 LQR 106.

a Member of Parliament recently threatened to use parliamentary privilege to reverse the effect of a High Court order. On at least two counts, that was clearly contrary to the separation of powers. On the other hand, the use by the courts of the Illegal Contracts Act to reverse the substantive effect of Acts of Parliament, a similar breach of the separation of powers, has been accepted with equanimity.[66]

Does it Matter?

If one takes the view that the law is indeterminate, one might well question whether it really matters if the courts should get things conceptually wrong. In practice, though, it is not at all difficult to find examples of cases where a conceptual wrong turning did lead to subsequent practical problems.

Midland Silicones is a good example. Its finding that the stevedore (and, by implication, other third parties) could not be protected by the limitation clause was so commercially inconvenient that it led to statutory reforms[67] and to the Privy Council twice inventing a contractual link between goods owners and stevedores, by recourse to unilateral contract.[68] More recently, the Court of Appeal in England has held third parties protected by exception clauses in contracts to which they were not parties, by the device of using those clauses to help justify a refusal to find the existence of a tort.[69]

A Canadian example of a wrong turning is *Turney v Zhilka*[70] where what most of us would characterise as a condition precedent to an obligation was held by the Supreme Court of Canada to be a condition precedent to the existence of the contract itself. That has led to a long list of cases where attempts have been made to avoid the effect of that characterisation.

Then there was the decision of the House of Lords in *Gourley*,[71] that damages for loss of earnings should be reduced by the tax which would otherwise have been payable. Until that case, the question of tax in relation to such damages had been seen as a matter exclusively between the taxpayer and the Commissioner of Inland Revenue. What brought about the change was the PAYE system, which for the first time led wage and salary earners to think in terms of their net income. The Supreme Court of Canada[72] has refused to follow *Gourley* and in this country

66 'Validation under the Illegal Contracts Act' [1992] *NZULR* 80.

67 Eg, s 16 Carriage of Goods Act 1979; Art 25A, Warsaw Convention as amended by the Hague Protocol; Art IV bis, Hague Rules as amended by the Brussel Protocol. See, too, the Contracts (Privity) Act 1982.

68 See cases listed above at note 32.

69 *Norwich CC v Harvey* [1989] 1 WLR 828, cf *The Gudermes* [1993] 1 Lloyd's Rep 311.

70 (1959) 18 DLR (2d) 447; 'When Can a Condition be Waived?' [1962] *NZLJ* 104.

71 *British Transport Commissioners v Gourley* [1956] AC 185.

72 *R v Jennings* (1966) 57 DLR (2d) 644.

the Court of Appeal has refused to apply it in breach of contract cases.[73] The High Court of Australia initially rejected it and then later changed its mind.[74]

A New Zealand case which many would think falls into a similar category was *Conlon v Ozolins*[75] in which section 6(1)(a)(iii) of the Contractual Mistakes Act was applied in a way which threatened the existence of the objective principle. A felt need to distinguish that case has led later courts to a potentially unsatisfactory extension of the concept of 'interpretation' under section 6(2)(a).[76]

Righting the Wrongs

I said early on that what really matters in the long term is the capacity of the system to right mistakes, where they have occurred, even where at one stage that may have seemed most unlikely to happen.

One example was the rejection of fundamental breach in *Photo Production Ltd v Securicor Transport Ltd*,[77] after a 16-year period during which that doctrine was strongly supported by most (though note *quite* all) of the academic community. That case also re-established that there is a distinction between discharge for breach on the one hand, and deviation on the other and that a discharge for breach is not a literal termination of the contract. In another case about the same time, *Johnson v Agnew*,[78] the House of Lords also distinguished between rescission *ab inito* and discharge for breach and held that damages were, after all, recoverable on the termination for breach of contracts for the sale and purchase of land. In the *Sudbrook Trading Estate* case,[79] the House of Lords put a stop to the extraordinary notion that a party could unilaterally defeat a contract by simply failing to appoint an arbitrator. And in *Miles v Wakefield Metropolitan District Council*,[80] the House distinguished between promissory conditions and conditions precedent and on that basis was able to hold that at common law workers did not have to be paid while on strike, even though they had not been dismissed.

Of course that leaves a lot of other matters waiting to be revisited. One case which I prophesy is almost certain to be reversed before long, despite what the academic commentators say, is *Williams v Roffey Bros*. Indeed, if that decision is ever affirmed by the House of Lords, the case for any brand of formalism will have

[73] *North Island Wholesale Groceries Ltd v Hewin* [1982] 2 NZLR 176.

[74] The later case was *Cullen v Trappell* (1980) 146 CLR 1.

[75] Above, note 54.

[76] McLauchlan, 'The Demise of *Conlon v Ozolins*' (1990) 14 *NZULR* 229.

[77] [1980] AC 827. A summary of my earlier pieces on fundamental breach is contained in 'The Second Rise and Fall of Fundamental Breach' (1981) 55 *ALJ* 788 reprinted as Chapter 7 of *Assumption*.

[78] [1980] AC 367.

[79] *Sudbrook Trading Estate Ltd v Eggleton* [1983] 1 AC 444.

[80] [1987] AC 539.

been pretty well fatally compromised. I should feel compelled to consider early retirement!

Potential Criticisms

I know that arguments for consistency in the law risk a number of criticisms, one being that too great an emphasis is being placed on the force and appropriateness of rational argument. After all, Justice Holmes' best known aphorism was that 'the life of the law is not logic; it has been experience'.[81] And a few years later, Lord Halsbury said: 'I entirely deny that [any case] can be quoted for a proposition that may seem to flow logically from it'.[82] On the other hand, another Lord Chancellor, Viscount Simon, declared a further 40 years on, that if a view which had hitherto prevailed were found to be based on a misapprehension of legal principles, it was of great importance that those principles should be correctly defined for, if not, there was a danger that the error might spread in other directions and a portion of our law be created on a false foundation.[83] One pays one's money and one takes one's choice.

Then there is the question of how far an internally consistent system of law could adapt to new situations and correct injustice where it occurs. When the common law works injustice, I believe, it is usually because it has been misunderstood or misapplied, or because inappropriate analogies have been followed, or because there has been some failure of imagination in the use of the resources of the common law. As history shows, the common law has in fact been able to change and adapt, even in the hands of formalists. But it is one thing to develop the law by the application to new situations of basic legal principles. I am not at all sure, though, that it is either constitutionally or practically appropriate for the courts to take over the functions of a legislature. For example, while one can sympathise with attempts by courts in federations like Canada and Australia to recast the doctrine of privity, I think our own experience shows that that sort of change involves so many issues that it is better achieved through statutory law reform.[84]

Finally, there is the criticism that it is unrealistic to hope for consistency in any system of judge-made law. But that is like saying that it is unrealistic to have a code of morality because those subject to it will not always observe all its tenets. In both

[81] *The Common Law* (1888) 1.
[82] *Quinn v Leathem* [1901] AC 495, 506.
[83] *Fibrosa Spolka Akcyina v Fairbairn Lawson Combe Barbour, Ltd* [1943] AC 32, 44–45.
[84] 'The Contracts (Privity) Act 1982' [1984] *NZ Recent Law Review 108*.

cases, what is involved are matters of aspiration. And it would be sad if one could no longer aspirate!

Conclusion

That, you'll be glad to hear, is all I propose to say about contract.

To finish on a more personal note. I'm about to go on what I like to think of as a rather extended study leave. If I were to say 'retirement', I'd only confuse my contemporaries, most of whom thought I'd retired in 1961 when I became an academic! The Law School provides a small room for the use of the four emeritus professors. The table in it is also small, but it is round, so at least there should be no problems over precedence! I hope to keep on writing until I can no longer find a publisher, or until I secure a seat in that 'Great Law Library in the Sky'—whichever is the sooner. Certainly, the Law of Contract is an inexhaustible subject. To keep on writing, though, I may have to learn how to use a word processor. If nothing should appear during the next three or four years, you'll know I'm still trying to get the thing to work for me.

I don't think I shall miss teaching, as such, very much. It's become increasingly stressful over the years. What I *shall* miss is what I imagine most former teachers miss. Each year's class seems to contain at least some delightful young people whom it's been a joy to know. Naturally, that description can be taken to apply to all of my former students who are here tonight.

One thing I emphatically deny is that during my 'extended study leave' I shall 'return' to professional wrestling. If you wonder why I mention that, it's because in the preface to a recently published *Student's Companion to Contract*, one of my former pupils writes: 'Few people know that apart from being a distinguished academic, Professor Coote was formerly a professional wrestler, making several appearances in "On the Mat" as "The Contract Killer" (his motto—"no consideration given or received")'.

Finally, if you should have any 'questions, comments, or suggestions', I'm afraid they'll just have to await another time.

INDEX